MEMOIRS OF
BERTHA VON SUTTNER

THE RECORDS OF AN
EVENTFUL LIFE

AUTHORIZED TRANSLATION

VOLUME II

PUBLISHED FOR THE INTERNATIONAL SCHOOL OF PEACE
GINN AND COMPANY, BOSTON AND LONDON
1910

CONTENTS OF VOLUME II

RECORDS OF AN EVENTFUL LIFE

trade. Audience with King Leopold. Invitation to the Interparliamentary Conference. Reception the evening before. Pithy sentences from Rahusen's address. Opening. " No other cause in the whole world...." Second day of deliberation. Stanhope. Gladstone's proposal. Debate over the tribunal plan. Dr. Hirsch puts on the brake. Rejoinder by Frédéric Passy and Houzeau. Randal Cremer. Concluding festivities in Scheveningen.

CONTENTS

vii

RECORDS OF AN EVENTFUL LIFE

CONTENTS

SUPPLEMENTARY CHAPTER, 1904

PART SEVEN
[CONTINUED]

XL

FROM HARMANNSDORF AND FROM CHICAGO

Slow increase · Far-reaching endeavors from our quiet corner · Childlessness · With Aunt Lotti · My brother ·The World's Fair at Chicago, and
the Peace Congress · Olga Wisinger-Florian · I am represented by Olga
Wisinger · Congress of Religions · Petition of the various ecclesiastical
bodies to the governments in favor of a court of arbitration

SO now there existed in the capital of Germany a
Peace Society, about which as a center branch societies would presumably group themselves in all the
larger German cities. The proposed task of forming a
widespread public opinion was, therefore, well under way.
I saw with delight, in my imagination, an undeviating
development of the movement. I clearly recognized,
however, that the beginnings were comparatively insignificant. What were our two or three thousand organized members compared to the thousand five hundred
millions that populate the earth? And how puny, not
only in numbers but also in power and reputation,
compared to the representatives and supporters of the
old system! But what is the significance of the first
violet-dotted patch of grass compared to the fields,
stretching miles and miles, still covered with the snows
of March? It signifies that the spring is at hand.
What signifies the first gleam of dawn penetrating the
mantle of night? It signifies that the sunrise is coming.

Thus I accepted the modest results achieved up to that time by the peace idea, and harbored no doubt that the element of spring, the element of light that abides in it, must come to fulfillment in gradual but uninterrupted and ever swifter progression.

I have no doubt of it either, even at the present day; but I have learned from experience that such movements do not take place in so straight a line and in such a regular tempo as I then supposed. It is a zig-zag line, now attaining great height and speed, then sinking down again; it apparently vanishes, and then with a new start reaches quite unexpected points. And all direct, methodical (*zielbewusste*) work — to use the tiresome, hackneyed word — is on the one hand hampered, on the other helped, by unanticipated, invisible secondary influences; more often helped than hampered, for, where any innovation is to be introduced, its forces converge from all directions.

Our life was now richly filled. We enjoyed two special blessings which one can hardly think of in combination, — impetuous reaching out into the wide world, and peace in our quiet corner. Full of hopes, expectations, struggles, in flaming enthusiasm or in overwhelming indignation, we set sail into the future; and a sheltered, safe little nest, beautifully pillowed with love and gayety, was ours at that time.

Many expressed their pity for us because we were childless. The blessing of children is, indeed, regarded as the highest happiness; but I have never expressed

4

in these memoirs one single word of regret for this lack, nor have we, either of us, ever complained of it. Possibly, if we had known that good fortune, we should not have been able to comprehend how such a deprivation can be borne without pain; but it is a fact, our childlessness never cost us a sigh. I explain this in this way: not only did we find perfect satisfaction in each other, but that need of living for the future which lies at the basis of the desire to have offspring and to work and provide for them was satisfied in our case by our vocation, which also was striving for the future, and which delighted in something still in its infancy, but growing and flourishing. Besides, we had our literary activity, and it is well known and recognized in popular language that authorship is a kind of paternity (*Autorschaft ist eine Art Vaterschaft*).

And yet how absolutely different my life had shaped itself from what had been anticipated in my childhood and youth! I often had at this time occasion to turn my thoughts back to those days of youth and childhood, and to refresh my recollections of them. My old Aunt Lotti, Elvira's mother, who was now quite alone in the world and had nothing to love except me, had moved into our neighborhood. She lived about an hour's walk from Harmannsdorf, and I used to drive over to see her at least once a week, and chat with her for an hour or two, on old reminiscences for the most part. She took the liveliest interest in my domestic happiness and my labors, and yet we liked best to talk together of times gone by, of the days when Elvira and I played " puff " together.

Aunt Lotti was really the only link that connected me with my early life. My brother was still alive, to be sure, but, except for an exchange of letters once in a great while, we were quite out of touch with each other. So in these recollections I have had nothing to say of him. He was an odd fish, living perfectly aloof from mankind and isolated in a small Dalmatian city, occupying himself with floriculture and chess. His company consisted of a number of cats. Solitary walks along the seashore, the reading of botanical and mineralogical works, were his only passions. I had not seen him since 1872, and up to the time of his death, which occurred a few years ago, we never met again.

In the year of 1893 we did not attend any Peace Congress. Ever since I was carried away by this movement, I have counted the stations of my recollections for the most part by journeys to Peace Congresses, for these always brought visible tokens of the progress of the cause that was so dear to my heart and the possibility of taking an active part in helping it along. They brought me into touch, too, with the old friends, and led to the formation of new friendships; finally, they took us to new places in environments hitherto unknown, and they procured for us that enjoyment which My Own drank in with the greatest avidity, — travel itself. To get into a carriage together, and then to be off and away — it was an indescribable joy!

The Congress this year was held at Chicago, in connection with the exposition which was called the " World's Fair." Our means were not sufficient for such a long journey and we gave it up. I intrusted the duty of representing me at this Congress to my friend Malaria, the celebrated painter Frau Olga Wisinger. She had been with us in the Austrian delegation at Rome, and was an enthusiastic adherent of the cause; so the mission was in good hands. The name " Malaria " is only a nickname and does not refer in any way to the great artist's feverish propensities. This was its origin: at Rome all the participants had to register their names and occupations, that a list of those present might be printed and distributed; so in the Austrian group we read, " Signora Olga Wisinger, Malaria," for that was the way the Italians had deciphered the word *malerin*, "painter."

During the World's Fair, countless congresses were held in Chicago, and one of them was the Congress of Religions. All the great sects of the world had sent their dignitaries to represent them. This was certainly the first time that the promulgators of different creeds had come together, not to proselyte or to battle with one another, but to bring out the principles that are common to them all. And Christian bishops, Mosaic rabbis, Buddhist and Mohammedan priests, found themselves at one in the principle: God is the father of all; therefore all are brethren. So there was also a peace principle resulting from this Congress of Religions.

The actual Peace Congress which met August 14–19, in the Art Institute, under the Administrative Department of the Columbian Exposition, was presided over by Josiah Quincy, Assistant Secretary of State. Among the participants and speakers was William Jennings Bryan, who in the year 1904 ran as Roosevelt's opponent for the presidency of the United States, and who may perhaps at some future election win the victory.

In this Congress delegates from Africa and China participated. Europeans were only slimly represented. The journey across the great pond, which means for Americans only "a trip," still frightens the inhabitants of our continent. Dr. Adolf Richter went from Germany, Dr. Darby from England, Moneta from Italy, and from Austria — "Malaria." The Americans of course were well represented and by distinguished men, — scholars, judges, statesmen. A soldier even, General Charles H. Howard, gave an address on the International Tribunal. A special church convention joined the movement by referring to the projected petition of the various Christian bodies of the world to the governments in behalf of the Court of Arbitration. This plan was carried out, and the petition, which was signed by about a hundred ecclesiastical dignitaries of all countries, was subsequently laid before all the heads of governments. I was intrusted with the duty of presenting the copy destined for the Emperor of Austria.

8

XLI

VASÍLI VERESHCHÁGIN

NOW I will tell about Vasíli Vereshchágin. When I learned that the great Russian painter, who was battling with his brush against the same foe that I was fighting with my pen, was staying in Vienna, where he was exhibiting a number of his pictures, I hastened to the city to see those celebrated paintings, — "All Quiet before Plevna," the "Apotheosis of War," and all those other variously named indictments of war. Even in the titles that he gave his pictures the artist expressed the bitterness which, next to the pain, animated his brush. The sentinel forgotten in the wilderness of snow, standing there until the drift reaches half to his breast, — that was what Vereshchágin's genius saw back of the generals' well-known dispatch, "All quiet before Plevna"; and a pyramid of skulls surrounded by a flock of flapping ravens, — thus he depicted the "Apotheosis of War."

Even before I had managed to get to the exhibition,

I received a note from the painter inviting me to come to the studio on a certain day at ten o'clock in the morning; he would be there and would himself do the honors. We were on hand punctually, My Own and I. Vereshchágin received us at the door. He was of medium height, and wore a long gray beard; full of animation and fluent in speech (he spoke in French), he had a passionate nature subdued by irony.

"We are colleagues and comrades, gracious lady"; such was his greeting. And then he led us from picture to picture, and related how each came to be painted and what idea was in his mind as he worked. At many of the paintings we could not suppress a cry of horror.

"Perhaps you believe that is exaggerated? No, the reality is much more terrible. I have often been reproached for representing war in its evil, repulsive aspect; as if war had two aspects,— a pleasing, attractive side, and another ugly, repulsive. There is only one kind of war, with only one end and aim: the enemy must suffer as much as possible; must lose as many as possible in killed, wounded, and prisoners; must receive one blow after another until he asks for quarter."

As we stopped in front of the "Apotheosis of War," he called our attention to an inscription in small Russian letters near the border of the picture.

"You can't read that; it is Russian and means, 'Dedicated to the Conquerors of the Past: the Present and the Future.' When the picture was on exhibition in Berlin, Moltke stood in front of it. I was by his side, and I translated the words for him; the dedication was a dig at him too."

Another painting represented a road buried in a thick covering of snow, with here and there hands or feet sticking out of it.

" What in heaven's name is that?" we cried.

" No work of the imagination. It is actual fact that in winter, both in the last Turko-Russian war and during other campaigns, the road along which the regiments were passing was covered with corpses; one who had not seen it would find it hard to believe. The wheels of the cannons, the tumbrels and other wagons, would crush the wretched men, still living, down into the ruts, where the dead bodies were deliberately left that the road might not be injured; and they were pressed way down under the snow, only the protruding legs and arms showing here and there that the road was a thickly populated graveyard. . . ."

" I understand," said I, " that you were blamed for depicting the most horrible things that you saw."

" The most horrible? No. I found much dramatic material from which I absolutely recoiled, because I was utterly unable to put it on the canvas. For instance, I had the following experience: my brother,[1]

[1] Sergyeĭ Vasílgevitch Vereshchágin. Still another brother, Alexander Vasílgevitch Vereshchágin, was wounded in the same campaign, and gives vivid pictures of the horrors of the march in his volume, "At Home and in War."

who was an aide to General Skobelef, was killed during the third assault on Plevna. The spot where he fell was held by the enemy, so I could not rescue his body. Three months later, when Plevna was in our hands, I went to the place and found it covered with bodies, — more correctly, with skeletons; wherever I looked I found skulls grinning at me, and here and there skeletons still wearing shirts and tattered clothes. They seemed to be pointing with their hands somewhere into the distance. Which of these was my brother? I carefully examined the tatters, the configuration of the skulls, the eye sockets, and I couldn't stand it; the tears streamed from my eyes, and for a long time I could not control my loud sobbing. Nevertheless, I sat down and made a sketch of this place, which reminded me of Dante's pictures of hell. I wanted to produce such a picture, with my own figure searching among all those skeletons — impossible! Again, a year later, two years later, when I began on the canvas, the same tears choked me and prevented me from proceeding; and so I have never been able to finish that picture."

I am warranted in saying that I am repeating Vereshchágin's own words, for I urged him then and there to incorporate in an article what he had just told me, and send it to me for my monthly periodical. He granted my wish, and in the seventh and eighth issues of *Die Waffen nieder* for 1893 Vereshchágin published these reminiscences and many others besides.

VASÍLI VERESHCHÁGIN

"In order to get a clearer idea of what war is," continued Vereshchágin, "I made up my mind to be an eyewitness of the whole thing. I participated in an infantry charge on the enemy, and, as it happened, I led the attack. I have been in a cavalry skirmish and victory, and I have been with the marines on board of a torpedo boat in an attack on great ships. On this last occasion I was punished for my curiosity by a severe wound, which almost sent me to kingdom come, to continue my observations there."

Well, we know to-day that it was indeed his fate to be dispatched into the next world by a Japanese mine. Almost the first news that startled the world at the time of the Russo-Japanese War was that of the sinking of the ironclad *Petropavlovsk*, which ran on a mine. Vereshchágin, pencil in hand, was on board, sketching. A shock, a cry of anguish from eight hundred throats, and down into the depths sank ship and crew! Vereshchágin's intention was to observe and depict the events of the most modern of wars—what would those pictures have turned out to be? Perhaps it would have been as impossible to finish them as it was to reproduce the scene at Plevna. There are horrors which incapacitate the artist's hand or darken the observer's mind. The Russo-Japanese War brought the general madness to a head. Vereshchágin's vibrant artist spirit would perhaps have been the first to become mad if he had ever tried to paint the scenes which have been enacted on barbed wire and in wolf-pits (*trous-de-loup*).

A few years later — let me here complete my personal recollections of Vereshchágin — I met him a second time. He was giving in Vienna an exhibition of his series of Napoleon pictures. It is said that Emperor William II, on seeing one of these paintings, remarked to him: "With these, dear master, you are battling against war more effectually than all the Peace Congresses in the world."

Nevertheless, I believe that the artist's intention was not in the least to engage in that sort of battle. He wanted to be true. He did not hate war at all; he found in it the excitements of the chase.

" I have many times killed men in battle," — these are his own words, — " and I can say from experience that the excitement, as well as the feeling of satisfaction and contentment, that comes after killing a man is precisely like the sensation which comes when one has brought down uncommonly large game."

XLII

THE COMMITTEE MEETING AT BRUSSELS
AND ITS RESULTS

Committee meeting of the Interparliamentary Union at Brussels · Letter from Senator Trarieux · Address to Gladstone · Address to the French and Italian deputies · Warning as to the duties of the Union · The "inevitable war" between France and Italy · The case of Aigues-Mortes · Settlement through the friends of peace in both countries

IT was decided at the Interparliamentary Conference which was held at Bern in the year 1892, that the next one should meet at Christiania; but this intention was frustrated by circumstances. The conflict between Sweden and Norway, which led, twelve years later, to the separation of the two countries, had even then taken such form as to make it clearly inadvisable to select the Norwegian capital as the seat of an international conference.

So the Conference itself fell through. As a substitute for it the members of the bureau, or managing board, of the Interparliamentary Union met at Brussels for a committee meeting. This board had been organized the preceding year at Bern, and consisted of the following members: Dr. Baumbach, member of the Prussian Upper House (represented by Dr. Max Hirsch); Baron von Pirquet, member of the Imperial Parliament (Austria); Don Arturo de Marçoartu, senator

15

(Spain); Trarieux, senator (France); Right Honorable Philip Stanhope, member of the House of Commons (England); Marquis Pandolfi, deputy (Italy); Ullman, president of the Storthing (Norway), represented by Frédéric Bajer, deputy (Denmark); Rahusen, deputy (Netherlands); Urechia, senator (Roumania); Gobat, national councilor, head of the Interparliamentary Bureau (Switzerland).

I got very little information from the newspapers regarding the sessions of this committee. I only knew that Pandolfi wanted to propose the institution of a permanent diplomatic council for the adjustment of national quarrels, and Stanhope the establishment of an international tribunal. So, in order to get more definite information, I wrote to Senator Trarieux and received the following reply:

Senate, Paris, November 3, 1903
Dear Madam:

I was glad to learn from your letter that our Brussels Conference made a good impression in your country, and I thank you sincerely for the personal sympathy that you manifest toward us.

I believe, just as you do, that, although we must regret that we did not meet in a full conference at Christiania, in accordance with the vote at Bern, nevertheless we succeeded in counteracting this disappointment by the important transactions of our bureau.

Although each regular group of the Interparliamentary Union was represented by only one delegate at Brussels, yet we felt strong because of the assurances of confidence which were transmitted to us from thousands of colleagues; and our resolves, if approved, have scarcely less authority than if they had been the result of the votes of our mandators themselves.

Our chief labor was the final determination of the order of business which in the future is to obtain in the deliberations of the Union. I trust they will be accepted by the next Conference.

Above all we endeavored not to step out of the sphere within which we have from the start confined our undertaking. We cherish the conviction that in order to reach our goal we must not dream of being an academy in which all questions can be treated.

We do not desire to be confounded with revolutionary cosmopolitanism; we therefore exclude from our programme everything that might cause the governments to look on us with suspicion. We do not talk of changes in the map of Europe, nor of rectification of boundaries, nor of any attack on the principle of nationality, nor of a solution of those problems of external politics on account of which nations hold themselves ready for war; we take up only the study of those proposals which aim directly at doing away with war and substituting for it the solution of difficulties through a regularly constituted jurisdiction, — that is a ground on which the broad-minded patriots of all countries may meet.

We have not limited ourselves to the preparation of our programme, but have also passed several resolutions, the importance of which you must have recognized if they came to your knowledge.

Thus we voted to send to Mr. Gladstone a congratulatory address regarding the words which he uttered in the English House of Commons on the proposed court of arbitration; moreover, we have sent a petition to our colleagues of the regular groups in the French and Italian parliaments, urging them most strongly to work with all their energies for a *rapprochement* of their two great countries, which now are unfortunately kept apart through imaginary antagonism.

I am sending you, gracious lady, both of these documents, which, on account of the ideas expressed in them, deserved to be made publicly known throughout the whole world. They are only words, to be sure, but words which exert an influence, because they correspond to the highest endeavors of mankind and contain nothing that arouses criticism even from the most timid of the practical-minded. He who contemns them makes a mistake; contempt and skepticism are out of place when it is a question of penetrating into the secret thoughts of nations, of finding the way to their hearts, and of bringing new truths before the minds of rulers.

Kindly remember me to Baron Suttner, and accept, gracious lady, my most respectful homage.

L. Trarieux, Senator

Inclosed were copies of the addresses sent by the Bureau of the Interparliamentary Union to Gladstone and the French and Italian deputies. I here print the text of these documents, long since buried in the archives and forgotten, because I believe that they afford valuable information for those of my readers who are seeking from my memoirs to acquaint themselves with the history of the peace movement. In the letter to Gladstone can be seen the development of the principle of the court of arbitration, which a few years later found expression in the Hague Tribunal and numerous arbitration treaties. The actual origin goes still further back, to be sure; but the phase here elucidated gave the impulse to its speedy accomplishment, as is shown still more clearly in the report of the Interparliamentary Conference of the following year (1894) at The Hague.

To the Prime Minister, William E. Gladstone

Your Excellency:

We have just read the debates that have been held in the English House of Commons[1] concerning the motion of Mr. William Randal Cremer and Sir John Lubbock relative to a permanent treaty of arbitration between Great Britain and the United States, and we

[1] Session of June 10, 1893. — B. S.

take the greatest possible satisfaction in the following passage from your speech[1]:

" I will only say in conclusion these few words; and although these declarations in favor of arbitration and in the general interests of peace, as well as against vast military establishments, are of great value, there is another method of proceeding which, I think, in our limited sphere, we upon this bench have endeavored to promote, and to which I have attached very considerable value, and that is the promotion of what I may call a Central Tribunal in Europe, a Council of the Great Powers, in which it may be anticipated, or at all events may be favorably conjectured, that the rival selfishnesses, if I may use so barbarous an expression, may neutralize one another, and something like impartial authority may be attained for the settlement of disputes. I am quite convinced that if selfishness were to be sunk and each state were to attain to some tolerable capacity of forming a moderate estimate of its own claims, in such a case the action of a central authority in Europe would be of inestimable value."

These declarations and resolutions, sir, have interested us greatly, and while we thank you from the bottom of our hearts for the powerful support they give to the ideas of which we have constituted ourselves the official representatives in the eyes of Europe, we take it upon ourselves to emphasize their political importance.

Thanks to you, it is now a certainty that the great states will accept the idea of breaking with the barbaric rule of war and, by means of a systematic organization of international law, of preparing the way for the peaceful solution of conflicts such as might arise between the different nations. It seems to us that your wise and noble words cannot have too wide a publicity, and we shall endeavor to circulate them as far as possible in the states which we have the honor to represent.

But we do not confine ourselves to offering this public homage to you; we are also bold enough to append a respectful request.

Words are forgotten and signify nothing without deeds. It is far more possible for you than for us to give them an effectual sanction

[1] In the course of this speech Gladstone made the statement, "Militarism is indeed a most terrible curse for civilization." — B. S.

by taking the initiative for positive resolutions, — of course, as far as is permitted by diplomatic considerations.

It seems to us that England is in a position to set a great example by making a proposal like that made by the United States of America, and it would delight us if you regarded it as possible, now that the official negotiations with that great power have been begun, to go a step further and offer to negotiate arbitration treaties with such other powers as should be favorably disposed, since you have so openly declared yourself in their favor. In our opinion these would be the best means of assuring peace among the nations.

We believe that no voice would have greater authority than yours in bringing these new ideas to the attention of the governments, and that the result of such a work would be the noblest crown of a glorious career, which perhaps appears more splendid by reason of the services which you have performed in behalf of humanitarian ideas than of those which you have rendered to your own country.

The second address shows very distinctly what views were held during the first year of its existence by the Interparliamentary Board regarding the tasks and duties of the members of the Union. Our contemporaries who follow parliamentary proceedings will, alas, be able to attest that these tasks were not accomplished.

LETTER TO THE FRENCH AND ITALIAN DEPUTIES

Your Board of the Interparliamentary Conference has just completed its labors, and you will receive its report; but it has thought it expedient, before separating, to call your most earnest attention to the obligation which is incumbent upon you, of working with all your might to dissipate the clouds which of late have been rolling up between your two great countries.

The strained relations between France and Italy could not fail to awaken the apprehensions of the Interparliamentary Board, and, while it does not wish to criticise diplomatic actions, the modification of which is not within its province, it desires, nevertheless, to express the opinion that there exist no grounds for insoluble disagreement, and that cordial relations, which are of such weighty importance for the peace of the world, can be resumed.

If existing alliances — as the contracting parties are continually asserting — are intended only to guarantee the European balance of power, then there can be no reason for nations which are united by the holy bond of common origin to live on a footing of such enmity as might at any moment degenerate into menace. Exaggerated sensitiveness or regrettable misunderstandings are alone responsible for a state of affairs which at all costs must be cleared up. The French and the Italian people are fundamentally inspired by an eager desire for peace. The idea of an armed conflict is repugnant to them both. A fratricidal strife which should bring them face to face on the battlefield would be a real crime and would mean a backward step in civilization. Public opinion, it would seem, might be easily roused against such a misfortune. To enlighten public opinion, to remind it of its real interests, — this it is for which you should exert your influence. Endeavor above all things to make your colleagues in the parliaments to which you belong, share in your anxieties, which doubtless are equal to those borne by us. Conjure the journals of both your countries to be serviceable to you by avoiding in their discussions everything that might embitter the controversies; or, better still, let them use their efforts to calm excited feelings. Make it plain to your fellow countrymen that such insignificant motives should not be allowed to end in the most horrible of all disasters.

Your board has no doubt, honored colleagues, that this act of intervention would be worthy of you and that it would redound to the glory of the Interparliamentary Conference, and it begs you most earnestly not to let our appeal remain unheard.

The ill feeling between Italy and France referred to in this letter has long since given way to a friendly relationship. But at that time it had reached the point that seemed to give occasion for the certain "inevitable war" always seen by the military circles as everywhere threatening; that is to say, beckoning. Then there is incitement in this direction on the part of the press, there are irritations among the people, and it comes to brawls and fights which keep adding to the bitterness.

In the summer of 1893 a fight had taken place in a workshop in a village of southern France, — Aigues-Mortes, — where Italians were employed. What first gave rise to it was the fact that an Italian workman washed some dirty trousers in a French spring. I find the following observation regarding this circumstance jotted down in my diary:

September 8. The international affairs of Europe rest on such sound and reasonable foundations that such an occasion is all that is required to bring so-called "high politics" into action, and to make historians resigned to the necessity of entering in their annals beside the War of the White and Red Roses the War of the Dirty Trousers.

The incident gave rise to many articles in the papers — the Aigues-Mortes story was headed "Franco-Italian Friction " — and to national demonstrations.

But fortunately there was already a peace movement. The Italian Chamber on the one side, with four hundred members belonging to the Interparliamentary Union; on the other the action of the Frenchmen, Frédéric Passy, Trarieux, and others, managed to dispel the danger. Of course the "war-in-sight-loving" circles were not contented. The following dispatch from Rome was sent to the *Figaro* on the twenty-second of August:

> The Conservatives have agreed to send an address to the King; they blame the Ministry for showing too great weakness in hindering the national demonstrations and putting up with the demonstrations favorable to the French.

So only hostile demonstrations are to be encouraged!

XLIII

FROM DIARY AND PORTFOLIO

Extracts from diary · Caprivi in support of the military bill · Bebel's inter-
pellation · Invention of a bullet-proof cloth · Settlement of the Bering question · King Alexander to his Servians · Dynamite tragedies in Spain · Visit
of the Russian fleet at Toulon · Marcoartu's letter to me · His letter to Jules
Simon · General inquiry of the Paris *Figaro* as to a gift for the Tsaritsa ·
My answer to it · Exchange of letters with Émile Zola

WHEN I look back for further recollections of
the year 1893, and turn the leaves of my diary
to refresh my memory, I discover that I was not interested in incidents of my own life, but rather in the
events of contemporary history, and especially in such
political phenomena as appertained to questions of
peace and war. Among the complicated doings of
the world, the features which I followed — and still
continue to follow — with passionate interest were the
phases of a battle, — the battle which a new idea,
a young movement, had begun to wage with deep-
rooted existing phenomena. After the manifestations
and impressions produced by the powerful "Old," I
listened toward the future and followed with the keenest attention and hopefulness the growth of the as
yet invisible and feeble "New," whereof the great
mass of people still had no knowledge. I saw clearly
that the tiny plant had started to grow, but I was

also well aware how stony the soil was, how harsh were the winds that opposed the development of its life.

How different are the contents of my diary and the pictures in my memory now from those of my youth! Then the center was my own person and all that concerned it, — plans for an artistic career and for marriage, worldly pleasures, domestic cares, and such a lack of understanding and of interest in the events of the day that I scarcely knew what was going on; and a contemporaneous war was noted only after it had broken out, and was disposed of with a line in my day's records. But since I had become engrossed in the peace question my soul had become a kind of seismograph, which was affected by the slightest political shocks.

Here are a few extracts from my diary of the year 1893:

January 18. Caprivi's speech in support of the military bill was pure *fanfare*. It almost signalized the advance of the hostile troops through the Brandenburg Gate, and once more brought into circulation the word " offensive," which had in a large measure gone out of fashion; for in the last twenty years pleas for armaments have been made only in the name of defense. The Danish Peace Society entered a protest against the insinuation in the Chancellor's speech in regard to the probable attitude in the next war. As if, indeed, the next war were thus to be announced! We talk about the horrors of *a* possible war of the future in Europe, but the definite article we do not like to use, — we do not speak of "the next *auto-da-fé.*"

March 1. The question of peace and arbitration came up yesterday for open debate in the German Reichstag. Bebel inquires whether the authorities are going to join with England and the United States in their endeavors to bring about a solution of international differences by a court of arbitration. Secretary of State von Marschall replies that the United States had, in their brief communication, made no tender in this direction. Nature makes no leaps; still less does official politics. The question came to debate without result, but it was not pushed aside with a smile.

March 20. A man named Dowe is said to have invented a bullet-proof cloth. If the contest between resistance and penetration, as it is carried on between torpedo and armor plate at sea, is to involve the land forces also, there will probably ensue the accelerated ruin of the nations and a *reductio ad absurdum* of all warfare. Just imagine! a new military bill for providing the millions of the army with bullet-proof wadding, — this voted and furnished at the same time in all countries; and this, if war should break out at this stage of the game, would afford a lovely campaign of unwoundable opponents! Then there would have to be a hasty majority demand for new offensive weapons with bullet-proof-wadding-pierceable bombshells (fired, wherever possible, from mines and balloons, from the frog's- and bird's-eye view), then the introduction of armored umbrellas and mine-proof overshoes, — and all this for " the maintenance of Peace." . . .

April 4. To-day the arbitrators meet in the building of the Ministry of Foreign Affairs in Paris, to settle the Bering question. Such an event ought to give the editorial writers of the whole world subject matter for extended observations, and ought to be accompanied by magnificent pageantry.

April 10. Our papers have published the news of the Bering arbitration without comment. On the other hand, the *Westminster Gazette* writes: " If the intrinsic importance of events and the outward demonstrations were in proportion, the report of the Bering arbitration would ring throughout the world to-day." And the *Daily Telegraph*: "The Bering arbitration, as well as that on the *Alabama* question, affords mankind to-day a majestic spectacle." An estimate of the importance of the event — typical of the daily press — is afforded by the Paris *Figaro*, which adds the observation that the seal question, if it is decided by the arbitration commission in a humanitarian manner, will involve a rise in the price of sealskins and persuade our fine ladies to have economical recourse to rabbit skins !

September 8. King Alexander addressed his Servians on his *seventeenth* birthday; "Heroes! For ten
years I have belonged to the army, and as your general in chief (*oberster Kriegsherr*) I will live for the
glory of the Servian arms!" Ah, how delightful to be
still a child. . . .

This entry of my diary makes me especially medita-
tive when I compare it with later events, — the slaughter of the king in the year 1903 by Servian "heroes"
with Servian weapons.

Beginning of November. Terrible dynamite tragedies have taken place in Spain. Bombs hurled in the
auditorium of the Barcelona theater, spreading death
and terror (the coming revolution, if righteous social
reforms do not obviate it, will be unthinkably terrible
through its explosive weapons); and the catastrophe
of Santander, — a harbor, a whole harbor, in bright
flames; ships blown up, thousands of human beings
on the ground, heaps of corpses, a whole railway train
shattered, houses transformed into piles of rubbish;
the air rendered pestilential by the smell of burning
powder and petroleum mills; chimneys flying through
space; anchors flung from the bottom of the sea, three
hundred meters into the air; the sea beaten and roaring, not by a storm but by the explosion of twenty-
five cases of dynamite, — all this gives a foretaste of
the deliberate, not accidental, episodes of future naval

battles, in which the explosion of mines and the like is already provided for. With the era of explosives and electricity an annihilating power is put into men's hands which demands that henceforth humanity come to the truth. The beast and the devil, the savage and the child, — all these must be overcome in the human race, if, with such means at hand, they are not to turn the earth into a hell, a madhouse, or a desert waste.

An event of the year 1893 which aroused my liveliest interest was the visit of the Russian fleet to Toulon and the fraternal festivities that were associated with it. I followed with close attention the twofold effect produced by this incident. It gave rise to chauvinistic passions and at the same time to "pacifistic" sentiments. Demonstrations in the one or the other direction took place alternately or broke out simultaneously. On the one hand the *Dreibund*, or Triple Alliance, on the other the *Zweibund*, or Double Alliance, were celebrated as guaranties of peace or as organizations for offensive enterprises; between the two lay the conception that they signified the established equipoise.

The official Russian utterances were unwearied in declaring that the visit of the fleet to Toulon was a peaceful demonstration, and in reiterating that absolutely nothing of an aggressive or provocative character could be related to the festivities in France. The French journals were constrained to print these assurances and the *Figaro* hastened to add: "Of course! *Une manifestation essentiellement et exclusivement pacifique*"; besides, the French press, and especially the *Figaro*, would never in the world have upheld any other manifestation! But a few days later the same *Figaro* proposed that during the Russian festivities "Les Danicheffs" should be performed in the Odéon Theater, "in which piece one passage would be certain to elicit storms of applause,—'As long as there are Russians and Frenchmen and wild beasts, the Russians and French will stand in alliance against those wild beasts'"!

The whole tone of a large part of the Parisian press during the period preceding the festivities was calculated to exacerbate hatred of Germany. After a time, however, the festivities took the form of peace assurances, and the gala performances in honor of the Russian guests ended with an apotheosis representing peace.

At that time I received the following letter from Senator Marcoartu:

Madrid (Senate), November 13, 1893

Dear Madam:

While in Paris I witnessed the Franco-Russian demonstrations in favor of peace. This once more awoke in me the idea which I promulgated in 1876 in my English work, "Internationalism" (or the ten years' truce of God). Herewith I send you the letter that I wrote to Jules Simon. It seems to me that the friends of peace, instead of falling asleep under the tent of arbitration, should now start an agitation in behalf of a ten years' truce. The thing would be feasible and salutary.

Another question of present moment to which I should like to call public attention is the neutralization of straits, isthmuses, and

FROM DIARY AND PORTFOLIO

the like. On this point read the bulletin of the *Société d' Économie politique*, Paris, 1892, p. 88, and in *Le Matin* of October 29, 1893, the interview which an editor of that paper had with me during the Franco-Russian festivities.

In cordial friendship, your very devoted

Marcoartu

Here is the letter to Jules Simon:

Paris, October 29, 1893

Dear Sir:

The congratulatory telegram from his Majesty the Emperor of Russia to the President of the French Republic, in which he declares his desire to coöperate in the confirmation of universal peace, has made such a vivid impression on me that I am addressing you with the following question:

Do you not believe that, in view of Gladstone's speech in the English House of Commons, on the 16th of June, in which he urges the establishment of a permanent international court of arbitration, and in view of the Emperor's telegram from Gatchina, the moment has now arrived for a sincere and honorable peace agreement for the whole civilized world? Since a very strong compact between the great empire of the North and the great French Republic for the establishment of universal peace exists; since, further, as you told me, the Emperor of powerful Germany has been outspoken in favor of peace; since the sovereigns and public opinion of Austria and Italy favor peace; since England has no thought of other than commercial conquests; since the whole world is sensible of the necessity of stable peace in order to diminish the colossal burdens which the present war footing, even in time of peace, entails upon the nations; would it not be possible to bring about a sort of truce of God, to last until after the World's Exposition at Paris in 1900, which is going to demonstrate by its splendor the progress in civilization made by the nineteenth century?

An international agreement would have to bind nations to refrain from every hostile action during those ten years. Every question of war would be postponed; an Areopagus would have to settle all differences not determined diplomatically.

31

During this new peace era governments would be occupied in developing the resources of their countries, improving the condition of public health, furthering education and works of general utility, settling economic, social, and financial questions, or at least studying how finally to civilize countries still backward, so that by the year 1900 all nations would have the opportunity to show how far they had progressed intellectually and materially, and by how much human prosperity had been increased.

We have lived through twenty years of peace in constant dread of war; now let an attempt be made for once to bring about a ten years' peace, free from the care and cost of war.[1] Many years ago I wrote:

"In the first third of the century Steam said to the earth, 'There are no mountains any more'; and the rails have made smooth the surface of the planet.

"In the second third of the century Electricity spoke to the waters: 'There is no ocean any more'; and the thought-bearing wires encircle the globe.

"To-day I hope and beseech God that in the last third of the century Reason may say to men, 'There is no war any more.'"[2]

Accept, dear sir, my, etc.

Arturo de Marcoartu

Apropos of the Franco-Russian festivities the Paris *Figaro* published an inquiry as to what gift should be sent to the Empress of Russia as a memento of the Toulon days. I sent in an answer to the question. Together with many other suggestions, the paper (under date of October 7) printed mine, introducing it with the following words:

---

[1] The justified hope of the proposer was that a definitive peace (*definitivum*) would develop from this provisional one (*provisorium*.)

[2] Even to-day reason is not yet heeded, because the all-powerful megaphone of the political press is closed to it. — B. S.

FROM DIARY AND PORTFOLIO

We award the prize to the jewel proposed by Baroness Berthe de Suttner, — an olive branch in diamonds, the significance of which she thus explains:

" Pacific demonstration, — such is the character which the Russian government has declared its wish to give to the visit of its squadron to France; therefore the jewel offered to the Tsaritsa to commemorate this event should be an emblem of peace.

"And precisely because the ultra patriots (*les chauvins*) of all countries will take advantage of the Franco-Russian festivities to attribute to them or see in them a defiant and threatening character, the partisans of peace must take this occasion to emphasize the opposite tendency.

"At the bar of history a peculiar situation will be presented by this year 1893: two groups of allied powers, believing themselves reciprocally threatened, having exhausted all their forces of sacrifice and devotion in preparing an efficacious defense, declare loudly, in the face of Europe, that their dearest desire, their most sacred mission, is to spare our continent the unimaginable horror of a future conflagration. Both of them, while making this solemn proclamation of pacific intentions, are at the same time exhibiting their formidable military forces, their keen swords, their invincible armor. Both sides have demonstrated that their alliances and their friendships are assured, that they are ready to fulfill all their obligations and kindle with every enthusiasm. Thus they find themselves face to face, equal in power, equal in dignity, and — with the exception of a few divergent secondary interests — desirous of the same thing, — peace.

" Unless one or both lie — and what right would one have to make such an accusation? — this situation can have logically no other end than a definitive pacification; consequently overtures might be made from one side or the other, or simultaneously, without the slightest imputation of weakness or of fear.

" Peace offered by the stronger may be humiliating for the weaker; and hitherto, in fact, treaties of peace have been signed only after a war and under the dictation of the conqueror. But in the present conditions, the element of the ' weaker party ' having disappeared, a new element might make its advent into the history of social

33

evolution, namely, the treaty of peace before — that is to say, in place of — war; in other words, the end of the barbarous age.

"If the days which are in preparation are called to facilitate the greatest triumph which the genius of humanity will have ever won, the jewel which shall commemorate them will be the most beautiful adornment which ever a queen wore. The olive branch inaugurated by the Tsaritsa might in future fêtes be adopted by the wives of all monarchs or presidents who were gathered together; and as the emblem need not invariably be in diamonds, the women of the people might likewise adorn themselves with it, for only the festivals of peace can be at the same time festivals of liberty."

Here also let one bit of French correspondence be added from the year 1893. In connection with the annual meeting of my Union I desired to get from Émile Zola an expression of his sympathy, and I asked him for it. Here is his reply:

Madame: Paris, December 1, 1893

Alas! I dream, as do all of you, of disarmament, of universal peace. But, I confess, I fear that it is simply a dream; for I see in all directions threats of war arising, and, unfortunately, I do not believe that the effort of reason and of pity, which humanity ought to make toward exchanging the great fraternal embrace within a brief time (*pour échanger à bref délai le grand baiser fraternel*), is within the range of possibility.

What I can promise you is to work in my little corner (*mon petit coin*), with all my powers and with all my heart for the reconciliation of the nations.   Accept, madame, etc.,   Émile Zola

I did not want to leave this letter unanswered. I wrote back:

Master: Château de Harmannsdorf, December 13, 1893

Accept my sincerest thanks; your letter, containing the precious promise that you will work with all your heart for the reconciliation of the nations, has aroused the enthusiasm of our general assembly.

34

FROM DIARY AND PORTFOLIO

The fraternal embrace? Universal love?... You are right; humanity has not as yet got to that point. But it does not require mutual love (*tendresse mutuelle*) to give up killing one another. What exists to-day, and what the peace leagues are combating, is the system of a destructive, organized, legitimized hatred, such as does not in the last analysis exist any longer in human hearts.

There has been talk of late of an international conference, having in view a coalition against the danger of anarchy. Never will the foolishness of the present situation have been more glaring than when these representatives of states which are living together in absolute anarchy — since they acknowledge no superior power — shall deliberate around the same table on methods of protecting themselves against five or six criminal bombs, while at the same time they will go on threatening one another with a hundred thousand legal bombs!

Perhaps the idea might occur to them of saying: To unite in face of a common enemy, we must be reconciled; to defend civilization against barbarism, let us begin by being civilized ourselves; if we desire to protect society from the danger which the action of a madman may inflict upon it, let us, first of all, do away with the thousandfold more terrible danger which the frown of one of the mighty of the earth would be sufficient to let loose upon it; if we wish to punish the lawless, let us recognize a law above ourselves; if we wish to parry the blows of the desperate, let us cease to spend billions in fomenting despair.

But in order that the official delegates may use this reasonable language, they must have back of them the universal acclaim (*la clameur universelle*) to encourage them, or, better still, to compel them to do so.

The evolution of humanity is not a dream, it is a fact scientifically proved. Its end cannot be the premature destruction toward which it is being precipitated by the present system; its end must be the reign of law in control of force. Arms and ferocity develop in inverse ratio, — the tooth, the big stick, the sword, the musket, the explosive bomb, the electric war engine; and, on the other side, the wild beast, the savage, the warrior, the old soldier, the fighter of to-day (so-called safeguard of peace), the humane man of the future, who,

35

in possession of a power of boundless destructiveness, will refuse to use it.

Whether this future be near or far depends on the work done in *les petits coins*. Allow me, then, monsieur, not to share in your *hélas !* but to congratulate myself in the name of all the peace workers to whom you have promised your powerful aid, — a promise which I note with a feeling of deep gratitude.

Accept my, etc.,

Berthe de Suttner

XLIV

VARIOUS INTERESTING LETTERS

Increase of correspondence · Countess Hedwig Pötting · Gift from Duke
von Oldenburg · Schloss Erlaa · The duke's consort · Peace efforts of
Prince Peter von Oldenburg thirty years ago · Letter from this prince to
Bismarck · Letter from Björnstjerne Björnson

MY public activity brought numberless voices from
all parts of the world into my house. Signed or
anonymous letters; letters from my own country;
letters from other parts of Europe and from beyond
the sea; letters with explosions of admiration or of
coarseness; letters requesting information or making
all sorts of propositions for the surest and speediest
attainment of our object, — a farmer proposed a special
manure system, which, through the creation of good
harvests and the consequent enrichment of the people,
would unquestionably lead to national peace; manuscripts of from ten to a hundred pages, containing
treatises on the problem of war; offers of lifelong zeal
in the service of the cause, if only the person might be
assured a satisfactory sum in compensation for giving
up his profession, — all this sort of thing came to me
by mail in ever-increasing proportions.

Of course it was not possible for me to answer them
all, and this the more because I had not ceased to

carry on my literary labors; at that time I was writing my novel *Die Tiefinnersten,* and My Own, who assisted me as much as he could in my correspondence and in editing the review, was working at a second sequel to his *Kinder des Kaukasus.*

Many of the letters were really so interesting that they could not be left unanswered. One day, after the evening meeting of the Peace Society, which had been held under my chairmanship, I got such a beautiful letter, glowing with such genuine enthusiasm, that the desire awoke in me to become acquainted with the writer. The signature was that of one of my own rank, also a canoness, and this very circumstance astonished me. It is not consonant with the nature of the aristocratic women of Austria, particularly of the elder canonesses (*Chorschwestern*) of the nunneries, to be enthusiastic in behalf of politically revolutionary ideas, and to give spontaneous and frank utterance to such enthusiasm. So I answered the letter by going myself to the writer's residence, and, as I did not find her at home, I left my card with a few hearty words on it.

The following day she hastened to me, and as a result we formed a cordial friendship. To-day I have no dearer friend than the Countess Hedwig Pötting, and Hedwig has no truer friend than I. We absolutely understood each other. And an equally profound mutual understanding arose between her and my husband. Her views so absolutely coincided with his, that they came to the conclusion they must have been brother and sister in some previous incarnation, and they called each other *Siriusbruder* and *Siriusschwester*.

Intimate friendship rarely exists without nicknames, and so I used to be called, not only by Hedwig but also by My Own, not Bertha but *Löwos*, and I used to call Hedwig *die Hex* (the witch). That does not sound very friendly, but as it was the pet name which her own idolized mother — a splendid old lady of clear and open mind — called her by, I also adopted it. Die Hex helped me faithfully in my life work; she became one of the officers of the Union; she adapted my novel, *Die Waffen nieder*, for young people under the title *Marthas Tagebuch* (" Martha's Diary "); she gave me much useful counsel; and in many trying hours was a support and comfort to me.

" Yesterday at Erlaa received a very valuable gift "; this entry I find in my diary of May, 1894. Erlaa is the name of a castle in the vicinity of Vienna, occupied by Duke Elimar von Oldenburg and his family. There we were often invited to dinner. The castle is surrounded by a splendid park, and I remember how, during that May time, the intoxicating perfume of elder blossoms poured in at the open terrace doors, and what a sweet tumult thousands of songsters made in the shrubbery. The duke's consort — she was called duchess from courtesy, but, inasmuch as she was morganatically married, she had only the baronial title — was a striking personage of tall, overslender, willowy

39

figure. Being very musical, she delighted in attracting artists into her house, and she herself, as well as the duke, used to spend many evenings at the piano and melodeon, or with the violin and cello. The duchess — since every one gave her that title, I will call her so too — was not particularly well disposed to me. I discovered that afterwards. Coming from a sternly puritanic family, she found my free religious views rather repugnant to her. I have letters from her in which she attempted to convert me to stricter articles of faith; but I learned through remarks that she made to others that she accused me of "materialism," that my novel *Die Tiefinnersten* had particularly displeased her, because in it — according to her idea — I ridiculed everything ideal, profound, or sacred. Now the novel ridicules only the stilted and mystical style of those who are always making use of the words "profound" and "inmost," when they cannot find anything clear to say.

The circumstances connected with the gift mentioned in my diary were these: in the course of a conversation at table, when the subject of peace was mooted, the duke said to me: "I am not the first one of my family, baroness, to be interested in your cause. My father's brother, Prince Peter von Oldenburg, worked in his day for the abolition of war. Although on his mother's side he was grandson of the Emperor Paul, and although he held the rank of a general in the Russian infantry and was at the head of the Stavodub regiment of dragoons, he was a militant friend of peace. He did not regard the matter simply as an ideal and as a dream to be realized in centuries to come, but worked strenuously to bring it about; he traveled from court to court, laid his ideas before the Queen of England and the King of Prussia; yet at that time, thirty years ago, his efforts remained fruitless. . . ."

"What!" I exclaimed; "and nobody heard anything about it!"

"My uncle kept on resolutely with his efforts," continued the duke. "I possess the draft of a letter addressed to Bismarck in 1873, in which he set forth his ideas, — also without result."

"Oh, if I might see that letter!"

"It has never been published, but you shall have a copy of it."

With the heartiest thanks I accepted the gift. Here is the letter written to the aged Chancellor:

Your Serene Highness:

Fearing that I may have no opportunity for a serious conversation with you during your busy sojourn in St. Petersburg, I am bold enough to present in writing what, by word of mouth, would probably be less explicit and evident.

My letters to your gracious sovereign, as well as my application to M. Thiers and the steps that I have taken in trying to induce my imperial master to assure the peace of Europe forever, are well known to your Highness. With the same object in view I applied to the ex-Emperor Napoleon in the year 1863, and I have reason to believe that during and after Sedan he must have regretted having acted in opposition to my views and those of so many other right-thinking men.

41

RECORDS OF AN EVENTFUL LIFE

Who knows better than your Serene Highness the situation of Europe and Germany? Is it satisfactory or not? The answer to this question I leave to the great statesman whose name will be immortal in the history of the world.

Surely every right-thinking person was rejoiced at the meeting of the three emperors in Berlin. The visit of your Emperor at St. Petersburg strengthens the opinion that a guaranty for peace is to be found in the friendship of two powerful imperial states existing side by side. But how contradictory to the peace idea are the enormous military establishments of all states! Even Russia is now introducing the Prussian system of universal conscription, and, although the Prussians regard this as a guaranty of peace, yet that increase of the army and of the military budget is a heavy burden for Russia, diminishing its resources for prosperity.

During my visit with M. Thiers in Versailles last year he said to me:

"Que voulez-vous que nous fassions? Nous sommes les faibles, les vaincus, mais du moment qu'il y aura des propositions de désarmement de la part des vainqueurs, nous sommes prêts à entrer en négociations."[1]

I reported this conversation to my emperor and wrote as follows to yours:

"A solemnly serious, fateful moment has come. In the scales of Destiny the mighty word of the German Emperor is of heavy weight. The history of the world is the tribunal of the world (*Die Weltgeschichte ist das Weltgericht*). William the Victorious is chosen by the God of battles to bear the immortal name of the Blessed, as founder of peace."

This historical mission he shall and must fulfill: God has aided him to make the volcanic center of revolutions harmless for a long time to come, and, we hope, forever. Now it must be his task to extirpate *en principe* the root of evil, the highest potency of sin, — war; for never will a permanent prosperity obtain on earth as long as governments (1) act contrary to Christianity; (2) stand in the way of true civilization.

---

[1] "What would you have us do? We are the weak, the vanquished; but as soon as there are propositions of disarmament coming from the victors we are ready to enter into negotiations."

VARIOUS INTERESTING LETTERS

What, according to the notions of the law, is the essential character-istic of the *civis?* Obedience to the laws. But war is a disorganization of legal conditions; therefore it is the renunciation of civilization. In the present circumstances civilization is only an illusion, consisting purely of intelligence for material objects, such as railways, telegraphs, and the invention of instruments of annihilation.

After the tremendous successes of the German arms in the last war the question arises, With whom and for what object shall any other war be waged? Prussia's position in Germany and vis-à-vis to Austria and Denmark is clear; Italy united; France harmless and on good terms with Russia, — all this is a guaranty of peace.

What problem, then, is before us now? That of combating revo-lutionary, communistic, democratic ideas, that are opposed to religion, the monarchical principle, and the social foundation of the State.[1] Sub-versive ideas, however, are not overcome by bayonets, but by means of wise ideas and regulations, which must proceed only from those who reign by the grace of God and are chosen by Providence to establish the happiness of nations.

The peace idea would be the very best means of meeting the French idea of revenge. Although the French are not to be relied on as a nation, I am persuaded that the notion of a perpetual peace would nevertheless appear plausible to the propertied and intelligent mass of the population, even if the government conducted by M. Thiers should be supplanted by another; for the motto of the French is *gagner pour jouir*, and I believe that the mass of the population would pre-fer *jouissance* rather than *gloire*.

Even in Prussia the multitudinous lawsuits against persons who try to get rid of compulsory service show how many feel that it is a burden; and God forbid that the alleviation should ever proceed from below instead of from above.

The latest history of Russia is an edifying example of what the will of a noble, humane, and magnanimous monarch can do to bene-fit his people. So when two monarchs, related by race and friendship,

---

[1] At the present time one would say "in combating social misery, in en-nobling and elevating the masses, in ethicalizing all classes" (*Ethisierung aller Stände*). — B. S.

43

clasp hands, may God aid them to make their union a blessing for their countries and for suffering mankind.

In my memorial to your emperor I said, "Only a fool or a knave can think of a state without an armed force"; and in my letter to M. Thiers I wrote, *abolir la force armée serait une idée criminelle et insensée.*

One cannot express one's self more energetically on this point. In Prussia, to abolish a system to which it owes its historical position would be as imbecile as for Russia to think of holding the Poles in control and of protecting the tremendous frontier from the Black Sea to the Pacific Ocean against savage tribes, without an army. The question, therefore, is simply this: What numerical extension should one give to the principle of universal compulsory service, and in what proportion should the military budget stand to the other expenditures of the State?

In my humble opinion it should be thus regulated:

1. *En principe* abolish war between civilized nations and let the governments guarantee to each other the possession of their respective territories.

2. Settle questions at issue by an international commission of arbitration, after the example of England and America.

3. Determine the strength of armaments (*die Stärke der bewaffneten Macht*) by an international convention.

Even should the abolition of war be relegated by many to the domain of fairy tales, I nevertheless have the courage to believe that therein lies the only means of saving the Church, the monarchical principle, and society, and of curing the State of the cancerous evil which at the present time is preventing its perfection; and, on the other hand, through the reduction of the war budget, of procuring for the State the following means for its internal development and prosperity: (1) reduction of taxes; (2) improvement in education and promotion of science and art; (3) increase in salaries, especially of teachers and the clergy; (4) improvement in the condition of the laboring classes; (5) provision for beneficent objects.

The accomplishment of such lofty, purely Christian, and humane ideas, proceeding directly from two such mighty monarchs, would be

44

the most glorious victory over the principle of evil; a new era of blessing would begin; one cry of jubilation would ring through the universe and find a response among the angels of heaven. If God is on my side, who can be against me, and what worldly power could resist those who would act in the name of the Lord?

This is the humble opinion of a man growing old, heavily tried by fate, one who, not fearing the opinions of the world or its criticism, looking to God and eternity, merely following the voice of his conscience, seeks nothing else on this earth than a quiet grave beside his dear ones who have gone before.

Dixi et salvavi animam meam.

With the highest consideration, I have the honor of being

Your Serene Highness's most devoted servant

Peter, Prinz von Oldenburg

St. Petersburg, April 15 (27), 1873

What answer Bismarck gave, or whether he replied at all, Duke Elimar did not know.

There is surely nothing more interesting than such old authentic letters. They show how ideas later become facts, and how events which afterwards develop were, long before, thoughts in men's minds. Here I find also among my correspondence the following letter from Björnson. In view of the disunion of the Scandinavian countries, which eventuated ten years later, it assumes a quite especial significance:

Schwaz, Tirol, July 20, 1894

My dear Comrade:

— But be consoled; when Norway becomes mistress of her external affairs (this is the object of the struggle) we shall go immediately to Russia and demand a permanent court of arbitration for all disagreements. If that succeeds, — and why should it not? — we will proceed to all other matters. As soon as our relationship to Sweden permits of it, we shall transform our army into an internal police force.

RECORDS OF AN EVENTFUL LIFE

One example is stronger than a thousand apostles! The great majority of the Norwegians have wholly lost belief in the beneficence of armaments and are ready to set the example.

At the same time Sweden is arming on a scale quite extraordinary for a people not rich. The general feeling in Sweden — so I am told — threatens Norway with war, merely because Norway desires to have charge of its own affairs.

Sweden might educate us by means of war to be good comrades in arms! It would be the first time in history that the two great opposites had stood in such blunt opposition, — on the one side a permanent court of arbitration for all eventual quarrels, and no army any more; on the other side, war to compel us to keep a larger army and to enter a firmer military alliance.

But I trust that the struggle will end peaceably; I trust that the general feeling in Norway in favor of the principle of "arbitration instead of war" is also making progress in Sweden. In fact, already the spirit of freedom in Norway — to the great annoyance of the highly conservative court of the Swedish nobility and other great lords who are powerful there — has spread widely in Sweden.

Accept my heartiest congratulations and gratitude, my dear Baroness; were it not so far, I would come and make you a visit!

Your most devoted

Björnstjerne Björnson

XLV

PEACE CONGRESS IN ANTWERP AND INTERPAR-
LIAMENTARY CONFERENCE AT THE HAGUE

Preparation for the Congress by the Belgian government · Houzeau de
Lehaye · A reminiscence of the battlefield of Sedan · Concerning free
trade · Audience with King Leopold · Invitation to the Interparliamentary
Conference · Reception the evening before · Pithy sentences from Rahusen's address · Opening · "No other cause in the whole world. . . . " · Second
day of deliberation · Stanhope · Gladstone's proposal · Debate over the tribunal plan · Dr. Hirsch puts on the brake · Rejoinder by Frédéric Passy
and Houzeau · Randal Cremer · Concluding festivities in Scheveningen

MY memory retains as the most important events
of the year 1894 our participation in the Sixth
Peace Congress at Antwerp and in the Interparliamentary Conference which followed immediately at
The Hague. Another festal journey into unfamiliar
countries, and another stage of progress in the triumphant march of an Idea!

Before the assembling of the Congress the Belgian
Minister of State, Le Bruyn, laid before King Leopold
a report setting forth the remarkable growth of the
movement and adducing as a proof of it the fact that
in countries like Austria and Germany, which hitherto
had held aloof from the cause, great peace societies
had sprung into existence and found fruitful soil. The
king's reply to this report was the establishment of
a committee whose duty it should be to forward the

labors of the Peace Congress that was to meet at Antwerp. The committee, composed of thirty members, included the most distinguished names in Belgium, in large part officials connected with the government.

The opening session took place on the twentieth of August, in the great hall of the Athenæum. We had arrived the day before, and had looked about a little in the commercial metropolis of Belgium, and had spent the evening in pleasant intercourse with several of our friends who had journeyed thither from all parts of the world.

Our new president, Houzeau de Lehaye, was in the number, — a lively little man, full of wit and possessing the gift of fascinating eloquence. As chairman he conducted the proceedings with tact and firmness, and whenever in succeeding Congresses he took part in the debates, as he was particularly apt to do if any obstacles had to be avoided, one could always depend on his tact.

" Twenty-four years ago," Houzeau told us that first day, " I visited the battlefield of Sedan. I have the impression of it still before me, — those corpses, those temporary graves, those flocks of ravens, the troops of maddened horses tearing over the plain, the wounded and dying lying in their gore, the teeth clinched in the agony of tetanus, the columns of prisoners of war, the heaps of discarded weapons, and in the midst of a grass plat the brass instruments of a military band surprised by the enemy in the climax of the saber song from 'The Grand Duchess of Gerolstein.' And I saw white sheets of letter paper, covered with the simple messages of love of mothers and sweethearts, flying round in the autumn wind until they fell into lakes of blood; and the horrible vision of countless bones and bleeding flesh all trodden down into the mire. ... The peasants had fled from their villages across the neighboring boundary, and were then returning slowly to find misery and ruin, to which they would later have to succumb; and this," he added, as he concluded his reminiscences with restrained passion, "is this to be the sum of civilization?"

Houzeau de Lehaye is a decided advocate of free trade. In his opening address, in which he depicted the errors and prejudices lying at the foundation of any defense of the institution of war, he said:

There is still another error which does not indeed involve a brutal battle of saber and cannon, but nevertheless is not much less calamitous. In spite of all the counter-evidence of the political economists, in spite of repeated results based on experience, yet how widespread is the prejudice that a nation becomes poor when the prosperity of neighboring peoples makes too rapid advances. And in order to preserve an imaginary equilibrium they hasten to have recourse to a protective tariff. And this war of the tariffs is not less destructive than the other. By a righteous retribution this weapon chiefly wounds those that wield it. And all these errors have their foundation in the false notion of the source of wealth and prosperity. It is worth while to note that there is only one source, — labor!

One would think that such simple truths would not require to be stated at this late day, for it is clear enough that wealth can be increased only from the creation of material things and not through mere change of place, — from Peter's pocket into Paul's; a transaction which, in addition, often means the destruction of the values shuffled this way and that. But the simpler, the more self-evident a truth is, the more it is wrapped up in the veils and fogs of old prejudices and current phraseology, and therefore it does much good to hear it once again spoken out so frankly and clearly.

This time there was a Portuguese at the Congress, — Magelhaes Lima, the publisher of the radical-liberal newspaper *O Seculo*. From America came Dr. Trueblood, who has never missed any of the European Peace Congresses.

I remember a lovely trip on the Schelde in a steamship put at our service by the government. Then a trip was made to Brussels between two sessions. A deputation of five members of the Congress, conducted by Houzeau, was received in audience by King Leopold. Frédéric Passy, Count Bothmer from Wiesbaden, my husband, and I made up the deputation. We drove from the railway station to the palace. In the audience chamber the king came to meet us, — recognizable instantly even at a distance by his long, square white beard, — and Houzeau presented the rest of us. I no longer recollect anything that was said; probably it was of small consequence. I only know that the king seemed to be on very jovial terms with Houzeau de Lehaye, for he slapped him several times

laughingly on the shoulder. I remember one sentence
that King Leopold said to us:

"The sovereign of a perpetually neutral state, like
Belgium, must naturally feel interested in the question
of international pacification. But of course," he added,
— and thereby all that he had said before was "of
course" taken back, — "to protect this neutrality we
must be armed."

"What we are working for in our circles, your
Majesty," one of us replied, "is that the security of
treaties should rest on law and honor and not on
the power of arms."

Houzeau did not wait to be dismissed, but himself
gave the signal for departure. "The train does not
wait — it knows no etiquette," said he. There was
another little *tape d'amitié* on our president's shoulder:
"You care mighty little for etiquette yourself, my dear
Houzeau. . . ."

Immediately after the Antwerp Congress the Interparliamentary Conference was opened. This year,
having been invited by the Netherlands government,
it met at The Hague. As we were not Parliamentarians we had no title to be present, but Minister
van Houzeau had sent me the following letter under
date of May 23:

Dear Baroness:
    On account of my appointment as Minister I have left the commit-
tee on organization of the Interparliamentary Conference; yet I hope,
as representative of the government, to give to the Conference the

address of welcome in September. The limited space in the hall where the meetings are to be held will permit only a small number of guests and representatives of the press to be present; nevertheless the committee will doubtless assure so prominent an advocate of the peace cause a place among the very first. It will delight me to greet you as well as your husband here in September, and also our friend Pirquet and, if possible, others from your country.

Our hospitable city, with its splendid beach, will permit visitors to combine the useful with the agreeable; and the assured visit of many prominent men will, it is to be hoped, permit the Conference, in which the presidents of both our chambers will take part, to accomplish something beneficial in regard to the practical promotion of international arbitration.

With friendly greeting, your devoted

S. van Houzeau

Thus the opportunity was afforded us of being present during the notable debates of that national representative Conference which was the precursor — and, one may say the cause — of the later Conference of nations at The Hague.

On the day of the opening session, the third of September, there was a reception in the rotunda of the Zoölogical Garden. Here the participants and the guests met together. The president of the Conference, Rahusen, made an address to the foreign Parliamentarians, from which I took down in my notebook the following sentences:

If we pass beyond the boundaries of our country, do we imagine ourselves in a hostile land? Have you had any such experience in coming here? I believe that I am justified in saying No.

... It is a phenomenon of our time that we find a solidarity among the nations such as did not formerly exist.

52

PEACE CONGRESS IN ANTWERP

... I know well that there are still men who ridicule such ideas; meantime let us rejoice that no one condemns them.

... The morning glow of international righteousness indicates the setting of the old war sun. If the last rays of this sun — which, decrepit with age, has already lost its blaze and its warmth — shall once be wholly extinguished,[1] then we, or those who come after us, shall be filled with jubilant joy, and shall be astonished that the civilized world could ever have called in brute force as an arbiter between nations no longer inimical to each other but bound together by so many common interests.

After this official part of the evening the company sauntered out into the open air, where the friends, some promenading, some taking places at tables about the rotunda, met and remained chatting till midnight.

At ten o'clock the next morning the formal opening took place in the assembly hall of the First Chamber of the States-General, a hall not very large but as high as a house and having its ceiling decorated with splendid paintings. I had a place in the gallery and enjoyed the magnificent spectacle, as the representatives of fourteen different parliaments took their seats one after another at the green-covered tables, while the members of the government who were to greet the Conference took places on the president's dais. Minister van Houten, of the Interior Department, made the first address:

" No other cause in the whole world," said he, " equals in magnitude that which is to be advocated here."

I must delay a moment over this statement. It

[1] Yet how singeing hot these rays are still burning in the Transvaal and in Manchuria! (Observation of 1908.) — B. S.

expresses what at that time formed (and forms equally to-day) the substratum of my feelings, thoughts, and endeavors, and likewise explains why in this second portion of my memoirs the phases of the peace movement take up so much space.

"No other cause in the whole world equals this in magnitude," — I am not expressing a personal opinion, I am quoting; this is a conviction so deeply and religiously instilled into my mind (this is usually called a vocation!) that I cannot confess it often and loudly enough. Even if I knew that nine tenths of the cultured world still disregarded and ignored the movement, and one of these nine tenths went so far as to be hostile to it, — that is of no consequence; I appeal to the future. The twentieth century will not end without having seen human society shake off, as a legal institution, the greatest of all scourges, — war.

In writing my diary I am accustomed, when I am making note of situations which are threatening or promising, to mark them with an asterisk, then to turn over twenty or thirty blank pages and write, "Well, how has it resulted? See p. —." Then when, in the course of my entries, I come quite unexpectedly on this question, I can answer it. And so here I ask some much, much later reader, who perchance has fished this book out from some second-hand dealer's dust-covered bookshelf, "Well, how has it resulted? Was I right?" Then he may write on the margin the answer, — I see the gloss already before me, — "Yes, thank God!" (19??)

And now, back to The Hague, 1894. The proceedings of the first day resulted in nothing noteworthy.
The second made up for it! Whoever reads the report
of that day's proceedings from a critically historical
point of view can detect in it the embryo of the later
Hague Tribunal, which, in turn, is at present only the
embryo of what is yet to be.

Goals attained? The believer in evolution does not
require them for his assurance; the line which shows
the direction taken is enough.

I took my seat in the gallery in the greatest excitement, as at the theater when an interesting star performance is promised by the programme. The order
of the day ran: "Preliminary Plan for the Organization
of an International Tribunal of Arbitration," presented
by Stanhope.

A new man, — the Right Honorable Philip James
Stanhope, Lord Chesterfield's younger brother and intimate friend of the "grand old man," Gladstone. At
Gladstone's direct instance Stanhope had come to the
Conference in order to put before it the outcome of
June 16, 1893, when in the English House of Commons Cremer's motion was carried, and the Premier,
in supporting it, appended the dictum that arbitration
treaties were not the last word in assuring the peace
of the world; a permanent central tribunal, a higher
council of the powers, must be established.

Stanhope began his speech amid the breathless
attention of the assembly. He speaks in the purest

French, almost without accent. And in spite of all his unruffled clarity he speaks with such fire that he is frequently interrupted with shouts of applause. After he had explained Gladstone's proposal he proceeded:

It is our duty now to bring this demand courageously before the governments.

Everything which up to the present time appertains to so-called international law has been established without precise principles, and rests on accidents, on precedents, on the arbitrary decisions of princes. Consequently, international law has made the least progress of all sciences, and presents a contradictory mass of ambiguous waste paper (*de paperasses vagues*).

Two great needs stand before the civilized nations, — an international tribunal, and a code corresponding to the modern spirit and elastic enough to fit new progress. This would insure the triumph of culture and do away with the criminal recourse to deadly encounters.

As things are to-day, fresh military loans are demanded in every parliament, and we are lashed by the press until we give our consent.[1] It would be otherwise if we could reply: "The dangers against which the armaments demanded are to protect us would be obviated by the tribunal which we desire." Therefore a project ought to be elaborated which we might lay before the governments.

Here Stanhope developed a few points which were to be established as the basis of the organization, and he concluded with these words:

If next year we approach the governments with such a plan, and if our action were in unison, the future would give us the victory; at all events, the moral victory would be assured to us in having done our whole duty.

Then came a debate. The German deputy, Dr. Hirsch, — from the beginning the Germans have

[1] This is the case even to-day (1908). — B. S.

performed the function of the brake in the Peace Conferences, — speaks against Stanhope's proposition,
nevertheless recognizing the noble ideas so eloquently
presented:

It is essential that the members of the Conference should pass
only such resolutions as are comprehensible and practicable, and as
may be presented to the parliaments with some probability of their
being accepted; now Herr von Caprivi would certainly *never* take
into consideration the project of an international tribunal. We ought
to avoid also inviting the curse of absurdity through plans of that
kind; for opponents are only too much inclined to ridicule the members of the Conference as dreamers.

Houzeau de Lehaye springs from his seat like a
jack-in-the-box:

In view of such great ideas [he shouts] as those that have just
been developed, in view of the establishment of a cause by such men
as Stanhope and Gladstone, the word "absurd" should never be
uttered again! [*Applause.*] I second the motion.

Now the revered Passy arises:

I should like to enter my protest against a second word which
my honored friend, Dr. Hirsch, has used, — the word "never." No
great advancement, no innovation, has ever been carried through,
but that the prediction has been made at the beginning that it could
never be done. For example, that parliamentarians from all nations
should meet to discuss the peace of the world, that they should do
this in the assembly hall of the Upper House of a monarchical state,
— if the question had been propounded five years ago, When will
all this happen? who would not have answered, "Never!"

And, in fact, — Passy accidentally hit upon the very
figure, — five years later, on the 29th of July, 1899, the
International Tribunal was established in the very city

where the plan for such a tribunal, proposed by Gladstone, was laid on the table. Dr. Hirsch's "never" did not last very long! To be sure, this tribunal does not as yet possess a mandatory character; the protesters who were active in objecting to the establishment of the tribunal at all saw to it that it should not have this character. And all who cling to the institution of war are also persuaded that this shall *never* be.

Many other speakers supported the motion, and at last it was adopted with acclamation.

I felt deeply moved; so did My Own, who sat beside me; we exchanged a silent pressure of the hand.

The members were then chosen who should formulate the plan which was to be laid before the next year's Conference.

This plan, — I anticipate events in order to show that that session was really historical, — this plan was presented to the Conference of 1895, at Brussels, was accepted and sent to all the governments, and assuredly contributed to the calling of the Hague Conference in 1898, and served as a basis for the establishment of the Permanent Court of Arbitration and its regulations.

That session brought one other sensation. After Stanhope's motion was adopted, Randal Cremer mounted the platform. He was greeted with loud applause. He, together with Frédéric Passy, had been the inaugurator of the Interparliamentary Conferences. He had secured the signatures for the Anglo-American arbitration treaty, first in his own country and then, after crossing the ocean, in the United States; and it was due to him that the motion on that famous sixteenth of June, 1893, was adopted with Gladstone's aid. His mode of speaking is simple and unadorned; he betrays clearly the former laboring man.

After the session he came up to us in the corridor and informed us that before leaving home he talked with Lord Rosebery; that he had not been permitted to repeat at the Conference what the Premier had said to him, but it had been of the most encouraging character. His feeling of confidence communicated itself to us.

The concluding banquet took place in the assembly room at Scheveningen. The orchestra played all the national hymns in succession. I sat between Rahusen and Houzeau. Stanhope delivered an extraordinarily keen and witty speech, the venerable Passy one full of eloquence and fire. I also had to speak. Fireworks were set off on the esplanade. The final apotheosis formed the words *Vive la Paix*, glowing in fiery letters, over which beamed a genius with a branch of palms.

What thoughts were in the minds of the guests of the watering-place as they promenaded by and stared at us? Probably none, and they were not so very far wrong; for what is left after the words have ceased, the toasts have been pledged, and the fireworks have been sent off? Nothing! From far down in the depths must the energies come through which epochs are changed. . . .

XLVI

VARIOUS RECOLLECTIONS

AFTER our return from Holland to our beloved
Harmannsdorf we resumed our quiet, happy,
laborious life. My Own began writing his two-volume
novel entitled *Sie wollen nicht*, which was to be his
ripest work. Max Nordau wrote to him regarding it:

> Forgive me for delaying until to-day to thank you for your highly
> interesting novel *Sie wollen nicht*. It takes a long time for me to find
> opportunity, in my over-busy life, to read 730 pages of prose, no
> matter how very easy and agreeable may be its style, unless it
> happens to fit in directly with my line of work.
>
> What I think of your character I should not be permitted to tell
> you. I know that men of real character find any praise of their char-
> acteristics disagreeable. At any rate I may say in brief that I admire
> the German writer who has the courage to-day to create the figures
> of a Gutfeld, Zinzler, and Kölble. Artistically your novel stands high.
> Perhaps there are too many threads interwoven, and the web is,
> perhaps, not drawn tight enough. That the main drama is not in-
> troduced until the last chapters, with the appearance of Palkowski,
> is no advantage from the standpoint of composition; but all that
> is a trifle compared to the great advantage of its wealth of motives
> and the vital energy of the complicated multitude of personages.

Old Jörgen alone would suffice to make your novel ever fresh in the reader's memory.

At that time I was writing *Vor dem Gewitter*. The editorial work on my monthly periodical likewise gave me abundant occupation, and my correspondence even more. I wrote regularly to Alfred Nobel in order to keep him informed as to the development of the peace cause. I constantly had long, stimulating letters from Carneri as well as from Rudolf Hoyos, Friedrich Bodenstedt, Spielhagen, Karl von Scherzer, M. G. Conrad, and others. I found a new, and to me personally unknown, correspondent in an old French naval officer, Rear Admiral Réveillère. I cannot now remember whether he wrote to me first or I to him. Whether or no, our correspondence was based on similarity of ideas and a mutual knowledge of each other's writings. The first time I ever heard of Réveillère was at the banquet of the Interparliamentary Conference of 1894, at Scheveningen, when Frédéric Passy, in proposing a toast to the sea which was roaring beyond the doors of the hall, said he was quoting the words of his friend Réveillère.

Born in 1828, in Brittany, he had long followed the sea, and now was living in retirement in Brest, his native city, known to fame as a savant and a writer. He occupied his leisure time in writing books and articles. He had participated in many naval battles and many battles of ideas. The list of the titles of his books shows to how many countries he had traveled in the performance of his duties, and also how manifold were the regions which he had explored as a poet and thinker: "Gaul and the Gauls," "The Enigma of Nature," "Across the Unknown," "The Voices of the Rocks," "Journey Around the World," "Seeds and Embryos," "Against Storm and Flood," "The Three Promontories," "Letters of a Mariner," "Tales and Stories," "The Indian Seas," "The Chinese Seas," "The Conquest of the Ocean," "The Search for the Ideal"; still later came "United Europe" (Paris, Berger Levraut, 1896), "Guardianship and Anarchy" (Ibid., 1896), "Extension, Expansion" (Ibid., 1898).

He wrote me once how it happened that he, the son of conservative Brittany, grown gray in the naval service, had joined the pacifists:

Often we are inspired by two ideas which have no apparent connection, and it sometimes takes years before the bond that connects them is discovered. It has cost me much time and thought to explain the connection between the two ruling passions which possess me and which had seemed to me to have no relationship with each other, — a deep-seated enthusiasm for the federation of Europe, and an instinctive cult for dolmens and menhirs.

From my earliest childhood I have been fascinated by the riddle that is presented in stone on all sides in my Breton homeland; and ever since my childhood I have been in love with the beautiful dream of a European federation, — a dream which is bound to come true in spite of the prejudices of statesmen and the prepossessions of crowned heads. The great work of the European alliance must begin with the *rapprochement* of those nations whose customs and ideas have the closest analogy. The nations living along the Atlantic coast have been the only ones to assimilate the principles of the French Revolution: I mean the following countries: Scandinavia, Holland, Belgium,

VARIOUS RECOLLECTIONS

France, Portugal, and ancient Helvetia, the oldest of the European republics. England had, long since, already passed through her revolution. Later my archæological studies taught me that this was the very region of the dolmens. All these nations had common ancestors, — the Megalithians; from the North Cape as far as Tangiers the same race occupied the coast; there were the same burial rites, always based on the same articles of faith; and the result was that to me the dolmens and menhirs came to stand as the symbols of a Western federation.

And another time:

The accident of birth made me first of all a Breton patriot. When I emerged from the narrow egoism of childhood, my first love was directed to Brittany. When the development of my intellect permitted me to realize the solidarity of my little homeland with the French fatherland, I became a French patriot. Later I learned from history that all the nations on this side of the Rhine once formed a glorious Federation; then I became a Gallic patriot. Still later study of the Megalithic monuments revealed to me a new connection, — that with the Megalithic race. As logic continued its work, I became a European patriot; finally, a patriot of humanity. In our day national love is an imbecile love unless it is illuminated by the love for mankind.

I have read only the three last-named works of the admiral; but he regularly sent me the articles that he published in the journal *La Dépêche*, in which he always took a consistent attitude — that of "illuminating" love for mankind — toward all the questions of the day; not, however, in the least in a visionary way, nor with any smack of mysticism, which so constantly stirs the spiritual lives of poetically inclined seafarers. He based his political ideals on actual and positive considerations, drawn particularly from the domain of national economy. Thus he wrote:

In order to meet the industrial rivalry of the United States of America and the yellow races, it would be desirable — in the interest of France and Germany — to see a customs union formed, embracing Germany, Belgium, Holland, and France, and including, at the same time, the colonies of these countries. It really seems almost impossible at the present time to swim against the stream of protective tariffs, and yet every nation is conscious of the necessity of extending its market. If there is opposition to this extension on European soil, why is not an effort made to gain it through a colonial union, — a union by means of which the federated countries might insure to their citizens, their vessels, and their products the same rights and privileges in all the colonies?

With regard to the lot of the masses, which so greatly needs to be improved, Réveillère says that this amelioration depends on the general production of useful articles. As long as the masses are wasting their energies in unproductive labors there is no alleviation possible for them, . . . and at the present time the nations are wearing themselves out in unproductive and destructive labor. There is no halfway measure; either international anarchy (that is to say, the lack of a code of laws regulating the intercourse of nations), with poverty, or federation, with wealth.

My Breton friend was inclined not to mince words in speaking of the politicians: "Steam has changed everything in this world except the routine of our statesmen!" And in the following letter:

Engineers and scholars are all the time at work filling up the graves which the professionals in statecraft are digging; the engineers are expending all their energies in increasing the productivity of labor, the politicians are doing everything they possibly can to make it sterile.

Many persons are of the opinion that the end sought is too broad and distant, and the initiation of it is beset with too great difficulties, to be willing to attempt the regulation of a pacific mutual relationship among the European states; especially at the present time, when almost every state has to endure so much trouble and disturbance arising from the violent national and social battles which are raging within its own borders. An answer to this objection is afforded by the following passage from one of Réveillère's books (" Extension, Expansion," p. 23):

When a physician has to treat a case of consumption, his first care is to prevent his patient from breathing poisoned air.. If he has to perform an operation, he sees to it that the room in which the operation is to take place is purified of every contagious germ. Exactly the same principle holds with regard to national diseases. No state can think of curing its internal ills before the European room is disinfected. Certainly it is the duty of every nation to do everything possible to modify the ills of its own people; but to claim that serious internal reforms can be carried out without having first secured European federation is just like caring for wounded men in a hall filled with microbes.

I kept up a correspondence with Admiral Réveillère for a long time. Of late years our letters fell off in frequency. A short time ago — in March, 1908 — he died. Ah, when we have grown old, how often we have to report of our friends that they are no more! In childhood life is like a nursery; in youth, like a garden; in old age, like a cemetery.

Tidings of a death which affected us painfully — I am now telling of what happened in the year 1895 —

came to us suddenly from the Caucasus, — Prince Achille Murat had shot himself. Was it suicide or an accident? I never learned the exact truth. It happened in Zugdidi, in the villa which My Own had built for the Murats. Princess Salomé, who was sitting in the next room, heard the report of a shot in her husband's room. She hastened in and found the unfortunate man fallen back in an easy-chair, with a pistol between his legs, the barrel pointing up in the air. Had he been cleaning the weapon carelessly, or was it weariness of life? As I said, I do not know.

And still another loss: On the 17th of October, 1895, Duke Elimar von Oldenburg departed this life, in his fifty-second year, at his castle of Erlaa. A short time before, he had given me a second article by his uncle, Prince Peter, entitled "Thoughts of a Russian Patriot," which ends with these ringing words:

Let me be permitted to express the dearest wish of my heart, as I face God and Eternity, — an agreement of all governments in the interest of peace and humanity! May that happy day dawn when men can say, War between civilized nations is at an end.

Duke Elimar's widow was completely overwhelmed by this sudden and premature bereavement. To my letter of condolence she wrote me the following answer, which throws a brilliant light on the noble characteristics of the departed and his consort:

Dear Baroness: Brogan, October 29, 1895

Most hearty thanks for your warm, sympathetic words, and also for the splendid wreath sent by the Society of the Friends of Peace, which, with so many other gifts of love and tokens of respect, adorns the last resting-place of the deceased. There is *no* consolation for such hours. What I have lost no one can truly realize who does not know how the inner bond that united us, joining every fiber of our two lives together, had been interwoven in the nineteen years of undivided, untroubled wedlock, so that with the uprooting of one life the thousands and thousands of roots of the other were torn from the ground. The profound loneliness which has come upon me through this loss is often scarcely to be endured, and at the present time I can hardly imagine how in this life, on this earth, I can ever again take root. One who has lived for nineteen years in such intimate relationship with a man like my husband cannot easily become accustomed to other persons.

The pure, lofty idealism which — I may say — formed the very quintessence of his being and made him so extremely lovable, so winning, and so attractive to all who came into contact with him, I shall never again find anywhere so embodied as in him, and since he has gone from me I miss him always everywhere to such a degree that it is often simply unendurable for me to be with others. And yet the proofs of *unofficial*, genuine, heartfelt sympathy from so many good and noble people in these days has done me unspeakable good. To you also, my dear Baroness, my best and heartiest thanks once again for all your sympathy.

Your sincerely devoted

Natalie von Oldenburg

A few years later she sent me a volume of poems dedicated to the memory of the departed and breathing a pathetic grief.

And yet a third loss: On the 31st of October, 1895, Ruggero Bonghi, so beloved in our circle, died in Torre del Greco at the age of sixty-eight. Italy mourned in him the reformer of public education, the professor of philosophy, the editor of the *Nuova Antologia*, the founder and director of the orphan asylum at Anagni;

67

we mourned the active apostle of our common cause, the man who from a lofty tribune had spoken these beautiful words: " We promoters of peace, who work for it with glowing zeal, have in the last analysis no other object than this, — that man shall become *wholly human*." Our Austrian Union telegraphed the following words to Rome for the funeral: *Sincero dolore e riconoscenza eterna.* "Sincere grief and eternal gratitude."

XLVII

FURTHER VARIED RECOLLECTIONS

The Union for Resistance to Anti-Semitism once more · Article by A. G.
von Suttner · In the house of Christian Kinsky · Recollection of a home
dinner with the Empress · War between Japan and China · Appeal of the
Peace Congress to the Powers for intervention · Answer of the Russian
Minister of War, Giers · The fruits of German military instruction in
Japan · The Peace of Shimonoseki · Interparliamentary Conference in
Brussels · Sending out the formulated and accepted plan for an arbitration
tribunal · First appearance of the Hungarian Group, with Maurus Jókai
and Count Apponyi at its head · Hopeful and distressful signs of the
times · From the Congress of the Association Littéraire in Dresden · Trip
to Prague · At Professor Jodl's · Lecture in "The German House" ·
Banquet · La Busca · Visit at Vrchlicky's · Trip to Budapest · Founding
of the Hungarian Peace Society · War in sight between England and
the United States · Removal of the danger

THIS year — I am still speaking of 1895, as I turn
the leaves of the volume containing my diary for
that period — we did not make any journey to a Peace
Congress, for the simple reason that no Congress was
held. But we did not on that account spend the whole
year at Harmannsdorf. Trips were made to Prague,
to Budapest (with lectures), to Lussinpiccolo, which I
will describe later on; and we visited Vienna a number of times, whither we were called by duty and
pleasure.

The business of his Union caused My Own much
labor and much anxiety. Anti-Semitism, against which

he was waging battle, had increased rather than diminished in violence. Dr. Karl Lueger, a leader in the Anti-Semitic party, had been nominated and elected by that party as mayor; but the Emperor did not confirm the election, to the indignation of a large part of the bourgeoisie and to the consternation of those higher circles who, under the influence of their spiritual advisers, supported the candidature of Karl Lueger.

An Austrian aristocrat holding an important position told me of finding himself in a company at court when the news of Lueger's nonconfirmation was brought. " Oh, the poor Emperor!" cried the Duchess of Württemberg, daughter of Archduke Albrecht, "the poor Emperor — in the hands of the Freemasons!" And a year later, in the same circle, where my informant happened to be again when the news of Lueger's confirmation came, the same princess raised her eyes and her clasped hands to heaven with the words, " God be praised! Light has dawned on the Emperor at last!"

That was the time when a Jew-baiting chaplain — Deckert was his name — preached from the pulpit and in pamphlets in the most vehement terms against the Jews — with success. This induced the "anti"-union to enter the field and to appear with a protest before the president of the House of Deputies. But I will let my husband himself have the floor. He published in the *Neue Freie Presse* the following article, the contents of which will best show what was going on in

FURTHER VARIED RECOLLECTIONS

the camp of the Anti-Semites, and what thoughts and
purposes were awakened thereby in the camp of their
opponents:

THE PRESENT SITUATION

> Now the wily old magician
> Once again his leave has taken !
> Spirits that owed him submission
> Now shall at my call awaken.
> I his cell invaded ;
> I have learned the spell !
> I 'll do — spirit-aided —
> Miracles as well !
>
> Goethe : *Der Zauberlehrling*

For twenty years now the " Magician's apprentice " (*Zauberlehrling*)
has been trying his experiments in Austria. The old master who
knew how to exercise and to exorcise the spirits has gone; constitution, parliamentarianism, the fundamental law of the state, have
become mere documents, and the unbridled spirits are up to their
mad tricks. And now, since it has resulted as all who were not
hiding their heads in the sand saw that it would result, the cry of
dismay echoes through the land:

> Lord, the need's immense !
> Those I called — the spirits —
> Will not vanish hence !

Or perhaps it will still be claimed that they were never summoned ?
Would any one wish to deny that we looked on with remarkable
patience, endured them, — yea, verily, absolutely defended them, —
instead of calling on the master who would have driven away the
demons while there was still time ?

Yes, if with us a system had not grown into a standard separating
so-called " serious " politicians from dilettanti ! The system, which is
called in plain English "I dare not " (*Ich trau' mich nicht*), has been
wrapped up by the " serious " in a distinguished-appearing vesture,

and elevated under the title of "Opportunism" to the concept of political wisdom.

What this Opportunism has on its conscience is fearful! It is the brake, the slave chain holding back every energetic activity, hindering everything, making every transaction impossible; it is the cause of the broken-winged condition that obtains to-day, of the distrust, of the fatalistic *après nous le déluge;* it is the cause of the universal discontent and apathy on the one side, of the loud shouts of triumph, the renewed efforts on that side yonder, which is now only one step away from its appointed goal.

Here I can add a word from experience, for I have been standing in the very midst of the stormy waves, and I shall still stand there as long as the office is intrusted to me of representing that portion of my fellow-citizens which has undertaken to oppose the assaults of the preachers of hatred and the apostles of persecution. By virtue of this office I feel myself called upon, indeed in duty bound, to put in my word and to speak of the experiences which the Union for Resistance to Anti-Semitism has had since it was founded.

I need only to point out the Rescue Society as an example of what opposition humanitarian associations meet with from the influential classes. Our Union was meant to be a rescue society in a certain sense, namely, for the purpose of rescuing the good old Austrian spirit, the spirit of patience, of justice, of brotherly love, the spirit that used to prevail at that time when, in the struggle for freedom and human dignity, Christians and Jews stood together in the very van, united in purpose and in genuine brotherhood, to conquer or to die. This spirit we desired to help rise to its old honorable condition; this was the reason for our emerging from our peaceful calm in order to take up the battle against poisoned arrows and every kind of disgusting weapon.

What was more natural and more justifiable than for us to yield to the expectation that every one who had any claim to culture and morality should joyfully join with us and thus raise a millionfold protest against the mad actions of the thoughtlessly unbridled spirits? What was more reasonable than to hope that in the influential circles in whose hands the reins are placed we should be greeted with joy as the breakwater against the onrush of the destroying billows, as the dam which is to be carefully repaired and made secure at a time when a freshet is expected? . . .

Yes, we believed and expected that, but we had forgotten just one thing, — Opportunism. Only gradually did we come to realize that warm feelings, honorable enthusiasm, fresh, fiery zeal, are ideal concepts which have found no place in the lexicon of higher politics; we learned that everything must be diplomatically weighed, accurately, even to milligrams, so that if possible, even in the most heterogeneous conditions, a transaction may be satisfactory to A and B and C; in short, that all things and everything must first be placed on the scales of the Opportune before there can be any departure from reserve.

We have, indeed, attempted to emancipate ourselves at times from this terrible thing, and to undertake several little *coups d'état* on our own responsibility, but even then the capital O had to appear on the door before it would open for us; and when we were admitted we heard nothing more comforting than that "in case of exigency," that is to say, in case it should ever become opportune, our desires would be taken into consideration.

We have seen how these pledges were kept in the affair of the Rescue Society; in short, we were obliged to recognize that no support was to be found in the quarter where it should have been freely offered us.

And yonder in the camp of our opponents they were not blind. This buttoned-upness (*Zugeknöpftheit*) which we met with was a direct encouragement to them to continue in the direction marked out, and they have made the most of it in order to make capital out of it, in order to win new support. Was that not to have been foreseen? Ought we to wonder that in view of such official toleration the defection among officials and teachers over to that side should grow ever more and more serious? . . .

A frank, a decided word from above, spoken at the right time, in place of evasive circumlocutions which, like the answers of the ancient oracles, may be stretched and twisted to suit any interpretation, would have prevented what had to come to-day — nay, not had, but was allowed, to come. And this definite, frank utterance, open to no misinterpretation, is the right of that portion of our fellow-citizens who, contrary to all civil order, are exposed to the wildest insults and threats, without protection and practically declared to be outlawed. This frank utterance is: *Anti-Semitism, in print, in word, and in deed, is a movement dangerous to society, deeply injurious to the existence of the state and the fundamental laws of the state. No government can permit it any more than anarchy or other endeavors which, through exercise of force, tend to disturb internal peace and to bring about civil war.*

We have labored to have this or a similar judgment pronounced, and in so doing we have done our duty. Come what will, we will not desert the breach; for we have in our hearts the consciousness of occupying a standpoint which every right-feeling and right-thinking man must take. This consciousness is sufficient to keep up our courage. In our ranks there is not one who is striving for any personal advantage from the realization of these principles; on the contrary, we know that to-day we stand just as unprotected, just as much exposed to all insults, as are those whose rights we desire to see secured.

But, in conclusion, an old proverb says, "God helps those that help themselves," and it must come to self-protection if this particular form of anarchy, which is already making the doors of Austria ring with its blows, shall succeed in breaking them down. Let us rally if it must come to that !

A. Gundaccar von Suttner

I said above that duty and pleasure took us to Vienna. Our pleasure consisted chiefly in going to the theater. Oh, it was indeed a delight to attend plays with My Own, who was so keen to enjoy, so thoroughly one of "the thankful public"! Especially in jolly plays he could laugh as no one else did! And next to the theater came social intercourse with sympathetic friends. We had long chats on literary and

74

pacifistic topics with Carneri and Hoyos, with Groller, Herzl, and various other men of the pen.

Great pleasure was afforded us also in visiting at the house of my cousin, Christian Kinsky. Every time we came to Vienna we were invited to dine with him and his thoroughly sensible wife, Therese. Christian was then provincial marshal of Austria. The burden and dignity of his office took nothing from his coruscating humor, from his inexhaustible wit. And at the same time such free, clear-cut views of things! Therese also was very liberal-minded in all matters. Quite the contrary was Christian's sister, Countess Ernestine Crenneville, who often came up of an afternoon with her handiwork for a little gossiping (*Plausch*). She occupied a lower floor in the Kinsky house in the Laudongasse, and, like the generality of the Austrian aristocracy, was very religious and ecclesiastically inclined. She had many times tried to convert her brother, but he always evaded the issue with laughter and bantering; and they got along together very well. It would indeed have been hard not to get along well with Ernestine, for her piety was tolerant, and she was goodness and gentleness itself. I had known her in her blooming, youthful beauty; now she was old, but still a pretty little lady, and had much that was interesting to tell of her life.

Once I jotted down in my diary a reminiscence of hers. The conversation had turned upon our Empress and her mania for traveling about the world so restlessly.

" I remember," related Ernestine, "how one day
we were sitting together after a little dinner at the
Empress's — a very small party, the Archduchess
Valerie, the Duke of Cumberland, and I. A few ladies
of the court were near. The Empress was very silent
and sad. Suddenly she cries out, 'Oh, let us go outside,
out on the green grass and far away!' Archduchess
Valerie springs up: 'For mercy's sake, mamma . . .'
The Duke of Cumberland exclaims soothingly, 'You
are right, your Majesty,' and whispers to her daughter,
'Only never let her go alone, never alone.' "

War had broken out between Japan and China.
Such events no longer left me so indifferent as they
did when I was young. Even though this tragedy was
being enacted far away, in another quarter of the
globe, the fact that the fiend against whom our party
was fighting had broken loose again indicated a setback for our movement; for who could tell what
future wars, in which Europe might also be involved,
this war would bring in its train?

Even during the Peace Congress at Antwerp, in the
autumn of 1894, the Sino-Japanese conflict was rising
threateningly above the horizon, and I remember that
among the resolutions at that time one contained an
exhortation to the two empires, and also to the other
powers, to avoid the outbreak or the continuance of
the war by means of arbitration or intervention; but
we were not heard. The only government which paid

any attention to this action was the Russian. From that came the following answer:

Ministry of Foreign Affairs, St. Petersburg, October 15, 1894
M. A. Houzeau, President of the World's Peace Congress
Dear Sir:

I received in due time the letter which you addressed to the Imperial Government, urging the great Powers in common to take steps to put an end to the bloody war between Japan and China. The success of such intervention would, above all, depend on unanimity of views and endeavors, which latter his Majesty's government will always be ready to support for the possible avoidance, diminution, and prevention of the horrors of war.

In giving you this assurance I beg you, my dear sir, to accept the expression of my especial consideration.   Giers

And when the battles had begun, then the whole world again listened with the keenest interest. Yet this was noteworthy: little Japan proved to be more than a match for huge China. There was no little pride manifested in German military circles at these Japanese victories, since the complete system of armament and of tactics in the Land of the Rising Sun was the fruit of the instruction which German military instructors had given the Japanese army. We Europeans are the bearers of culture. Perhaps it is also going to be our province to make the Chinese into a first-class fighting nation. Attempts in this direction are not lacking; this comes under " unanimity of views and endeavors." Quite naturally, he who possesses a set of white chessmen and likes to play chess must provide for an opponent with an equivalent number of black ones.

In May, 1895, the Asiatic war came to an end. The Peace of Shimonoseki was signed, and secured to the Japanese important advantages from the victory. This the European Powers would not endure, and they united in advising the Japanese to renounce various fruits of their triumph over China; otherwise they would feel compelled to back up this request by recourse to arms. Fortunately Japan yielded, and this "recourse" was not required. But why did the Powers not unite *before* the war in intervening and demanding that the Korean question should be submitted to a court of arbitration?

The Interparliamentary Conference of the year 1895 met at Brussels. Although we were invited, this time we did not attend; but our correspondents kept us informed of the course of events. The principal features of this Conference were:

Submission and acceptance of the plan for a national tribunal determined upon the preceding year, and formulated by Houzeau, La Fontaine, and Descamps.

Resolution to send this plan to all governments.

Participation in the Union for the first time of a Hungarian group. At the head of this group, Maurus Jókai, and, as its most brilliant representative, Count Apponyi, whose eloquence makes a sensation.

Invitation of the Hungarians to hold the next — the seventh — Conference at Budapest at the time of the Millennial Festival; accepted.

All these tidings filled me with joy. Once more a few important steps forward had been taken; an elaborated plan for a national tribunal was now placed before the governments, and the project did not emanate from unauthorized dreamers in private life, but from statesmen, the representatives of seventeen countries; and the whole thing came from the initiative of one of the strongest and most distinguished men of his day, William E. Gladstone. Moreover, it could be seen how the nucleus of the peace endeavor was gaining new force — this time from the acquisition of Hungary, with one of her most influential statesmen, Apponyi, and her most celebrated poet, Jókai.

It was as if there could be seen on the horizon something still small and distant, but slowly growing bigger, and certainly ever coming nearer. No longer a vision of the fancy, no mere " pious wish," but something substantial, actual, which to be sure may still be attacked and hampered, but no longer flatly denied. And why attacked? Was it not good fortune and success drawing nigh? Ever larger would become the throngs of those who recognize it, and then they would all hasten to meet the approaching marvel and greet it with jubilation!

In our comprehension of this, My Own and I were happy, and we labored in the great work according to our feeble powers, full of joyous confidence. Not as if we did not see the obstacles in the way; we were painfully conscious of them, and we realized the opposition that was still to be overcome. Anything old and firmly rooted has very obstinate endurance, and the law of inertia gives it effective protection. Men do not like to be shaken out of their ruts; they avoid new roads, even though they lead them into paradise!

These were the thoughts that formed the basis of the novel *Sie wollen nicht.* The question of peace was not treated in it, but the question of social reforms in the domain of political economy: A landed proprietor introduces all sorts of improvements, desires to bring about conditions which shall give his laborers prosperity and independence, but "they do not want it"; they distrust him and ruin him.

Yes, the increasing, approaching ray of light on the horizon rejoiced us, but we had our trials in the immediate and the near which filled the world about us. Thus at that time terrible news began to arrive from Armenia, — butchery instigated, measures taken to exterminate a whole nation. From Spain also came gloomy tidings, — Cuba wanted to gain her independence, and, in order to retain her, her yoke was made ever more oppressive . . . and the Madagascan enterprise of the French . . . in brief, cause enough for horror and worriment all around! But also sufficient cause for hope and joy!

The Association Littéraire held its congress in Dresden. We were invited to attend, since my husband was a member of the society. I do not know what prevented us from accepting the invitation; but I find in my papers a report from there which at that time gave me great pleasure:

FURTHER VARIED RECOLLECTIONS

During a literary evening, at which the King and the Queen, the leaders of official society of Dresden, and all the participants of the Congress were present, J. Grand-Carteret, in an address on " German Women as judged by the French," said these words :

" Spiritually the German woman has been presented to us by Luther and Johann Fischart, later by Goethe and Schiller, until at last, like an incarnation of the human conscience she stands before us as the apostle of peace and civilization, and with the Baroness von Suttner utters the cry which long since ought to have found an echo in the heart of every mother, *Die Waffen nieder !* "

At the banquet in Leipzig, Grand-Carteret returned to the same theme in his toast :

" . . . I drink to the book, that is to say, to the general expansion of humane thought.

" To the book that had its origin in Germany, *en pleine nuit armée*, to the book born on crossroads and to-day casting a light on the highway of the future ; to the book which has arisen against the sword. . . .

" I drink to the feminine Volapük of the future, which all by itself, if men continue to want to kill one another, will permit the women of all countries to utter the cry, *Die Waffen nieder !* For the first time in thirty-five years we have felt the soul of the people here vibrating. I drink to that soul to-day ! "

At the same banquet Émile Chasles, Inspector General of Public Instruction in France, delivered a speech which closed with these words : " I salute the spirit of internationalism, which rises above the quarrels of men and governs nations with the aim of drawing them together."

We made an excursion to Prague, the city of my birth. The Concordia Union had invited me to deliver a lecture. Before this affair, which took place at eight o'clock in the evening in the mirror room of the Deutsches Haus, we were invited to dinner at Professor Jodl's. The famous philosopher—a friend of my friend Carneri — was then a docent in the University of Prague, while he is now a light in our Vienna Hochschule. It was a pleasant little meal, with few but choice guests. The professor's young wife, Margarete, was a fascinating housewife, who had already won my heart, because I knew her as the liberal-minded translator of Olive Schreiner's stories. This same Olive Schreiner, in her " Peter Halket," has said a wonderful thing, — a thing that expresses beautifully my profoundest belief: " With the rising and setting of the sun, with the revolving flight of the planets, our fellowship grows and grows. . . . The earth is ours."

Since I was to speak in a literary union, I had chosen the subject of peace literature, and as I was in Bohemia, I cited also Bohemian authors, — the two great poets Vrchlicky and Swatopluck Czech. In my absolute innocence I had no suspicion of the fact that it was something unheard of in Prague, so torn by national jealousies, to praise Czech geniuses in the Deutsches Haus. For a moment a certain feeling of restraint seems to have manifested itself in the hall, but when the splendid verses of the two princes of Czech poetry — paraphrased rather than translated into German by Friedrich Adler — rang out, the German auditors were disarmed and the ill-humor passed off. There is no field which would be better adapted to bringing about reconciliation between two contending factions than the field of supernational pacification.

FURTHER VARIED RECOLLECTIONS

At the banquet which followed the lecture I made the acquaintance of many interesting people, and particularly of the theatrical manager Angelo Neumann, and his wife, Johanna Buska. The latter was very much after the style of Sarah Bernhardt, — so delicate, so thin, so golden-voiced, so exquisitely elegant, and so many-sided in her art. There is no leading part in the repertory, from the naïve to the heroic, the sentimental, and the coquettish, which la Busca had not played and made the most of. That evening she recited a poem which Friedrich Adler had composed as a rejoinder to Carducci's " Ode to War."

The next day we went to see Vrchlicky. We were conducted by a maid into a little drawing-room, where we were kept waiting some time for the master of the house. When the door opened and he entered, I was rather disappointed. I have been so accustomed to find generally in the creators of beautiful works handsome people that I was literally horrified at Vrchlicky's ugliness — for he is ugly, his best friend must admit it. A flat, potato-like nose, tangled hair, — only from the eyes shines forth his clear intellect, and in the metallic tones of his voice vibrates his fiery soul.

" I am very much delighted," he said, as he shook hands with us, "that you have both come to Prague. You will find here a thoroughly intelligent public."

" Well, the public, because of national antipathies, is surely not altogether receptive of our cause, as we discovered only last evening."

"Oh!" exclaimed the poet, "there are no national passions in music."

We did not understand the significance of this remark, and after a while the conversation took all sorts of turns, during which sometimes we and sometimes Vrchlicky showed the greatest astonishment in our faces, until it finally transpired that we were taken for Mr. and Mrs. Ree, the well-known piano virtuosos, who were going to give a concert that evening in Prague and had promised to call on Vrchlicky. When the misunderstanding was cleared away we warmed up to each other, and I saw that he was as enthusiastic an adherent of my cause as I was an enthusiastic admirer of his genius.

Our next little journey took us to Budapest — of course also in the interest of peace. "You have become genuine peace-drummers" (*die reinen Friedens-Commis-Voyageurs*), said my father-in-law banteringly.

Just as in the year 1891 it seemed a necessity to found a society in Austria, that the country might be represented at the Congress in Rome, so now, since the Interparliamentary Union had invited us to the Millennial Festival at Budapest, it seemed likewise necessary for a private society to come into existence there and invite the other societies to take part in a Peace Congress. Our Vienna Society took up the agitation of this matter in the Hungarian capital. Leopold Katscher, the well-known publicist, who had wide-branching affiliations in Hungary, where he had

lived for many years, and who was now a member
of our Union, made a trip to Budapest, and called on
Maurus Jókai, and on the statesmen with whom I, for
my part, was assiduously corresponding. And the result? Instead of giving a detailed account of this I
will quote the text of the following dispatch which was
sent to the Vienna press:

Budapest, December 15. Peace Union established yesterday.
Meeting conducted by B. von Berzeviczy, vice president of the Reichstag. Addresses in Hungarian by Jókai, and in German by Baroness
von Suttner; a whirlwind of applause. Several hundred prospective
members come forward. Voted to accept the invitation to the Seventh
World's Peace Congress. Influential personages chosen to serve on
the directorate, among them two members of the former cabinet. Jókai,
president. Unexampled enthusiasm shown by the press; all the
Hungarian and German papers devote from four to ten columns to
the reports. Prime Minister Banffy declared to Baroness von Suttner
that both the Interparliamentary Conference and the World's Peace
Congress would be welcomed in Budapest, and that the government
would not only assist but would take the lead in the arrangements,
though they were not instituted by the government.

But simultaneously my diaries bring back the echo
of very gloomy events and voices from that time.
Under various dates of December I find the following entries:

"War in sight." So it is reported in all the papers
since this dispatch was received: "The President of
the United States has spoken insultingly and impera-
tively now that England has rejected arbitration in
the Venezuela affair." Now England has no alterna-
tive — so run the leading articles — but to pick up the

gauntlet. Fresh dispatches: All America aroused over Cleveland's message; all England in a rage; demands for many millions for warships, torpedoes, fortifications; a hundred thousand Irishmen have offered their services to the United States. The war-prophesying tone of the leading articles is accentuated; the familiar " inevitableness " of the conflict is demonstrated. Every journalist on the Continent is able to point out with certainty what England cannot put up with except at a loss of her honor, what all Europe cannot permit without imperiling its interests. . . . What is going to be the result? . . .

The result I chronicled ten days later in the following words:

It was a test of strength. Only a few years ago, when the peace idea had not as yet taken form and utterance, the misfortune would have inevitably occurred. The greater part of the press, the chauvinists of all countries, the military parties, the speculators, those engaged in the industries of war, adventurers of all kinds who expected personal advantage from the general scrimmage, — all these have assuredly left nothing undone to promote the breaking out of war. On the other hand, negotiations were instituted. Not only our Unions, but also chambers of commerce and mercantile corporations took a stand against the war, and in almost all churches sermons were preached against it, and statesmen, interviewed as to their opinions, revolted at the thought of settling the question by an appeal to arms.

Lord Rosebery says, "I absolutely refuse to believe in a war between England and the United States over such a question, for that would be an unexampled crime."

Gladstone says, "Simple human reason is here sufficient."

The English heir-apparent and his son telegraph to the *World*, "It is impossible for us to believe in the possibility of a war between the two friendly states."

How if the Prince of Wales had spoken out in as martial a tone for his nation as certain continental editors found it for their interest to do in the name of "all England"? How if he had sent a sword-rattling, fist-doubling dispatch? Or rather no dispatch at all? How did heirs to the crown happen to write to mere newspapers? The generality are gathered together, or at least recruits — so tradition likes to have it — and the requisite blunt threats are uttered. The future King of Great Britain acted otherwise.

My novel *Vor dem Gewitter* (" Before the Storm") was finished. The newly founded Austrian Literary Society issued it as its first publication in an edition of three thousand copies, and this inauguration was celebrated by a banquet given by the publisher, Professor Lützow. The actress Lewinsky, from the royal theater, read a chapter from my novel; congratulatory addresses were made, and when the champagne went round a great success was predicted for the enterprise; but in a few years — Austria is no field for literary establishments — the business failed.

When I had written the word "End" on the last page of the book *Vor dem Gewitter*, I began another under the title *Einsam und arm* ("Lonely and Poor"). And My Own, besides working at his two-volume *Sie wollen nicht*, wrote many stories of the Caucasus region. We were as industrious as bees, — that must be granted us. There we sat evenings at our common worktable, generally until midnight or later — and wrote and wrote. We used to talk about what we were doing, but we did not read our manuscripts to each other; we did give ourselves the delight, however, of reading each other's proofs.

Ah, those happy, lovely times! Even though they were full of cares, — for the Harmannsdorf stone quarries were getting more and more involved in difficulties, causing the whole family deep anxiety; for the fear ever increased that we should not be able to keep up the dear home. One sacrifice after another was demanded, — even the quite opulent rewards of our literary labors were swallowed up in the abyss, — all in vain; as I look back on those days the exclamation is nevertheless justified, — Oh, those lovely times! For I was sincerely happy and so was My Own, in spite of Venezuela, in spite of Armenia, in spite of Cuba, and even in spite of Harmannsdorf. Our kingdom lay elsewhere, — the kingdom of our closely united, laughing hearts.

And then our studies. It was our custom at that time to read aloud at least an hour every day to each other. We had then just discovered Bölsche. He introduced us into the halls of nature's marvels, initiated us into the mysteries of the splendid universe. It often happened that when the reading had brought us a new revelation we would stop and exchange a silent pressure of the hand.

XLVIII

POLITICAL KALEIDOSCOPE

Gumplowicz: father and son · The Italian campaign in Africa · Utterances of King Menelik · The defeat of Adowa · The warlike press · Demonstrations against war · Victory of the peace party · Correspondence with
Carneri · From Armenia and Macedonia · Insurrection in Cuba and a sharp
proclamation · Professor Röntgen's discovery · The Anglo-American arbitration treaty · Death of Jules Simon · A letter from Jules Simon.

AMONG the letters preserved from the year 1896
I find an interesting one from Gumplowicz, the
professor of philosophy. How I came to correspond
with him I do not remember. It is not to be supposed
that I could have been drawn to his works in admiration and sympathy, for, together with Gaboriau and
Joseph Chamberlain, he is one of the most influential defenders of that vicious race theory on which are
based Aryan pride and German and Latin conceit,
which are so hateful to my very soul. Probably his son
was the occasion of this correspondence. As radical as
the father was conservative, he had sent me for my periodical a series of poems, entitled "The Angel of Destruction" (*Der Engel der Vernichtung*), translated by
himself in a masterly manner from the "Slave Songs"
of the Polish poet, Adam Asnyk. Whether it was this
translation or some other publication which had aroused
the displeasure of the German authorities, all I knew

was that the young singer of freedom was condemned
to a long period of imprisonment. When, during my
lecture in Prague at the Deutsches Haus, I quoted various poems, I read also some stanzas from "The Angel
of Destruction." I see from an old account of that
lecture that I informed the public of the poet's fate in
the following words:

> A soul of fire . . . but not wise and prudent: what moved him —
> sympathy with human misery, indignation against human enslavement
> — he spoke out too clamorously and in the wrong place, and he is now
> atoning for it in state prison, with two years and a quarter of solitary
> confinement. . . . Do you realize what that means for a youth with
> exuberant powers of vitality, with a soul full of poetic inspiration, with
> eager yearning for work, for love, for helping the world to betterment,
> — seven and twenty months of solitude! . . . I believe it will rejoice
> his heart if word is sent him that his verses, so deeply penetrated with
> emotion, have been heard in this circle, and that his fate has touched
> a few noble hearts here — it will be to him like a greeting from free-
> dom, for freedom. . . . And if you now applaud this sentiment, may
> every handclap count as applause for our imprisoned colleague.

The hearty applause that followed vindicated the
defiant bard of peace in Plötzensee.

Here is the letter from the professor at Graz:

> Graz, April 21, 1896
> My dear Baroness:
> Your note caused me great embarrassment. I am asked to give
> my views on your article, "Two Kinds of Morals," which would
> necessitate uttering my opinion concerning your whole philosophy of
> peace. I will make you a counter-proposal, — fling me, together with
> the horrid Sighele, into a pot, and leave these naughty professors en-
> tirely out of consideration. There is nothing to be done with them.
> They only spoil your temper, drive you out of your dreams, and spoil
> that noblest enjoyment of yours which you find in agitating the peace

idea. I, at least, will not take it upon me to play such a rascally rôle in opposition to you. You desire to see the picture at Sais and I am to raise the curtain, am I? No, my dear Baroness, that I will not do. I have long made it my principle:

> " Where'er a heart for peace glows calm,
> Oh, let it be, disturb it not!"

Must I on your account go back on these principles? Again the poet warns me:

> " Believe my word, that were a fault!"

Not for a moment do I yield to the illusion that I could persuade you; the chasm is too wide for me to be able to throw a bridge across, and I am not convinced that by doing so I should do any good. It would be a better thing if *you* could convert *me;* but hops and malt are lost on me, — I am even worse than Sighele.

The difference between us bad professors and you, Baroness, is this, that we are stating facts, — among them the *fact* of the " Two Kinds of Morals,"—while you are preaching to the world how it ought to be. I always listen to your preaching with great pleasure. I should have no objection, on the contrary I should be very happy, if the world would change in accordance with your ideas. Only I am afraid that it does not depend on the world to slough off its skin, and that your moralizing is in reality a complaint lodged against the dear God in heaven, who made the world as it is. Yes, if you could stir him to bring out his work in a second revised edition, that would be really a success!

By all means believe that if the world will only "have the will," then everything will come out all right! Because of taking that very standpoint my son is in prison in Plötzensee. He, too, could not comprehend that the State is so "unmoral" as to let the unemployed go hungry while it has control of bread and nourishment in ample sufficiency, this being in direct contravention of the commandment about love for the neighbor. And so he went forth and gave the State a castigation, calling it a "band of exploiters," a "legally organized horde of bandits." From the standpoint of "the one and only morality" he was perfectly right. Since he has been in prison I have refrained from attacking this standpoint to his face. Why?

POLITICAL KALEIDOSCOPE

Because this enthusiasm for this "one and only morality," the bringing about of which he has been striving for, makes him happy and enables him easily to endure all the trials and privations of his dungeon. And just for the same reason I have no idea of attacking to your face the standpoint which you accept; for in your endeavor to make this clear to all the world you are certainly finding your greatest happiness. How could I satisfy my conscience if I willingly disturbed your happiness?

Go on your way, my dear Baroness, in peace; do not worry about the Sigheles; do not read Gumplowicz's "Conflict of the Races"; it might cause you sad hours; and do remain always what you are, — the champion of a beautiful idea! In order to fulfill that mission stick to the persuasion that this idea is the truth, the sole and only truth. And of this belief may no professorial chatter ever rob you!

With this wish, I remain with the sincerest respect

Your most faithful

Gumplowicz

I have inserted this letter in my memoirs because I like to let the opponents, especially such eminent opponents, have their say. What reply I made to the professor I do not remember, but assuredly I did not leave uncontroverted the idea that I was pleased by the condescension with which he regarded my views as pleasing delusions! The morality that to-day is already beginning to influence the lives of individuals is not a fact handed down by tradition from the creation of the world, but a phase gradually won by social development and beginning to react on governmental life and to work on quite different factors from mere "hearts that glow calmly for peace."

Italy at that time was trying to make war in Africa. It wanted to conquer Abyssinia; but that was not so easy. The Negus was victorious in many battles. The Italians had been obliged to withdraw from Fort Makoli. Then Menelik expressed his desire to enter into peace negotiations. General Baratieri sends Major Salsa into the enemy's camp. But no conclusion of peace is reached. The Negus demands the evacuation of the newly acquired territories; whereupon Baratieri sends word that these propositions can neither be accepted nor be taken into consideration as a basis of further proceedings. So then, further prosecution of the war. Reënforcements are sent. The *Riforma* declares that Baratieri has done well in refusing the Negus's overtures; they insult the dignity of the nation.

In place of Baratieri another generalissimo is to be shipped off, and the victory of Italy is assured. General Baldissera, Austrian born, who in the year 1866 had fought against Italy, is intrusted with this mission of conquest. So now let it be said that it can be something else than the most glowing patriotism that moves the mover of battles! . . .

And Menelik meantime? A French physician, drawn to the enemy's camp during a journey of research, wrote from Oboch:

The Negus received me. . . . Is he really sad, or does he only put it on? He keeps affirming that he is to the last degree troubled about this war which has cost and will continue to cost the shedding of so much Christian blood. He is attacked — he defends himself; yet if he is too hard pushed and they want to try it again, then — Menelik seems confident as to the upshot of the war, but why so much blood?

Why, O swarthy Emperor? Because the white gentlemen in the editorial offices declare that it is the
"duty demanded by honor."

In Italy the protest of the people against the continuation of the war continues to grow louder. But
since it is Republicans and Socialists who vote for the
discontinuance of the campaign, their demonstrations
are suppressed by the government. On February 29
a great anti-African banquet was planned in Milan,
but forbidden by the prefecture. And on the next
day comes the terrible news of the defeat in Adowa, —
eight thousand men fallen — the rest put to flight —
two generals killed — in short, a catastrophe; wild
agony in Italy and sympathy throughout Europe.
All the fury is concentrated on Baratieri because he
attempted such a sortie.

Out of the multitude of reports about Adowa I have
entered in my diary only one or two lines from *Il
Corriere della Sera* of the eighth of March: " The
soldiers of Amara, who are cruel brigands, hacked
down the Italian wounded, mutilated them, and tore
the clothes from their bodies."

Gentlemen of the press, who have demanded the
continuance of the war, does it not occur to your
consciences that you are accessories in the mutilation
of your fellow-countrymen? No, they demand that
the blood of the fallen shall be avenged, — in other
words, that still others, unnumbered, shall experience
the same misfortune. *L'Opinione* writes:

Baratieri's act was that of a lunatic; he wasted in a craven way the lives of eight thousand soldiers and two hundred officers. But our military honor remains unblemished. The material lost will be replaced within a month; our military power remains as it was. The country understands this and is ready to avenge the blood of the fallen. Those who think the contrary are a handful of people [that is to say, those who come out against the war — ah, why are they only a handful?], people without God and without a country. Nevertheless, these people can do no harm, for the nation is against them.

Was it? . . . A dispatch of March 9 says:

The anti-African movement is assuming great dimensions. In Rome, Turin, Milan, Bologna, and Padua, committees of ladies are active in getting signatures for a peace petition to Parliament. This has been signed by many thousand persons.

So acted the ladies; the women of the people were still more energetic. They threw themselves down on the rails before the cars that were about to carry away their husbands and sons to the place of embarkation, and thus actually prevented the departure of the trains.

Likewise in the barracks, a protest is made against sending more men to the African shambles, and large numbers of deserters are escaping over the border. What is beginning to take place in the whole country is a battle between the idea of war and that of peace.

The King, the first war lord, with a military education, grown up in soldierly traditions, sees only the possibility of continuing the war, of winning a victory, of brilliantly bestowing the honor of his arms, — would sooner abdicate than conclude peace *now!* . . . He would be glad to retain Crispi, but a storm is arising against him throughout the land and — Crispi falls.

POLITICAL KALEIDOSCOPE

A new ministry is formed. Rudini — that name stands
on the list of the Interparliamentary Union — becomes
Prime Minister. What will he demand in the name of
the government at the opening of Parliament? The
Crispi journals and the papers representing the war
party are fierce against any idea of peace: "Revenge
for Adowa!" *Guerra a fondo!* ("War to the bitter
end!") And had it been a lustrum earlier, this cry
alone would have come to the surface. Yet louder and
more impetuously now arise the voices in protestation
against the continuance of the unrighteous war. The
movement of protest was organized; hence it was
effective. Through Teodoro Moneta I learned all that
was going on in this direction. It was a victory; for
the new minister, Rudini, did not demand the continuance of the war. . . .

It might be urged that what I am relating is really
a political-historical chronicle, and not a biography.
But it *is* my life's history; for the very life of my soul
was closely bound up with these events. My thoughts,
my labors, my correspondence, were all filled with
those performances on the world's stage. And that I
am repeating what is for the most part a matter of
common knowledge, what was printed in the newspapers everywhere, and therefore is treasured in the
memory of all, — this I do not believe. The forgetfulness of the public is great. What one day brings, the
next swallows up again. I know from my own experience how, before I had begun to live for the peace

cause, political events, even though they were important, disappeared from my memory without leaving a trace, if indeed they had attracted my attention at all. But now I noted in my diary everything that related to the struggle that was taking place between the new idea and the old institutions; this was the red thread which I followed in weaving the history of the day, — a thread which assuredly has quite escaped those who have not kept their eyes expressly fixed upon it.

A letter from my friend Carneri, written during the Italo-African war, shows that I had vigorously complained to him of the pain which that tragedy was causing me. The letter ran:

My dear Friend, Marburg, March 5, 1896

Do not be vexed if I fail to attain my object, which is none other than to give you permanent comfort in your suffering over the present condition of the civilized world.

We two from the beginning have taken a quite different standpoint (you may still remember my hesitation at the first invitation to join the Peace Society, and that I yielded, much less won by the cause itself than by your own personal charm), and I should like to bring you to my way of thinking, which consequently *should* be yours.

"Consequently," — how so? I hear you say. Because you, like me, accept the theory of evolution. This knows nothing of a complete cessation of conflict, and recognizes only a gradual amelioration of the methods of the conflict. It also knows nothing of a complete disappearance of want — not to be confused with the wretchedness of poverty, which can very properly be checked; this theory holds rather that want is the great stimulus to progress. A cessation of all want would be absolute stagnation, and therefore it is just as little thinkable as a world of nothing but good people, which would be a contradiction in itself, just as it would be to think of a day without night.

I believe firmly in progress; but I expect it to come not in a universal improvement of men, but as a gradual refinement of the good. If you could be content with this modest but firmly established view of life, you would not need to make any change in your activity in the cause of peace, but you would look at the world with that calmness with which one must face what is unalterable, and you would be safeguarded against disillusions as painful as they are superfluous.

The movement toward the quickest possible establishment of a general arbitration tribunal is now on, and must take its course. At least do not promote it; for if it remain without results, this would be far more favorable for the cause of peace than if such a court, which would have to be preceded by an international agreement, should make a perfect fiasco. The only practical thing to-day is that the contending parties should themselves choose arbitrators in whom they have confidence. This custom is, happily, getting to be more and more generally adopted, and all attempts to push it can only endanger it. To win more and more advocates for this custom is the task which will bring the greatest blessings from the work of these peace unions; but all the peace unions in the world have not as yet in all this time performed such a service for the idea of peace as my Martha alone with her matchless tale.

This is one thing you have to keep ever before you, and if you will join me in smiling at the Utopias of those who believe it possible to have a world of angels, then you will share my indifference in the way you regard that ancient beast, Man, and his constant readiness to heap up inflammables on inflammables.

Do you remember how I warned you against an American who counseled disarmament? They will yet, in alliance with Russia, threaten Europe; and I am thoroughly convinced that it is only the enormous armies, which no one would be able to command and provide for, that are to-day an assurance of peace and are smoothing the way for the arbitrators.

The defeat of the Italians in Africa pains me; but it is a wholesome lesson. If I were Crispi's successor, I should have no scruple

in openly declaring, " Italy has been deservedly punished for a great
offense; let us not make the offense worse; we have something
better to do," and Italy would give jubilant ratification to

Your Carneri

I possess a copy of my reply, and I give some
extracts from it:

Harmannsdorf, March 10, 1896

Dear Friend,

Your letter is a new proof of your affection. I have known for a
long time that you are not one of us, — have known it from the day
when you discovered that it would be money ill spent to contribute a
legacy as a proof of respect to my life work. You find my work useless, — almost harmful; but at the same time you love Martha and
Löwos, and would like to spare Martha pain. But, my dear, if I did
not feel pain what would be the impulse for my work? Certainly
not, as my enemies say, vanity? You surely do not believe that?
No, pain at the way men stick to their barbarism is what penetrates
me and compels me to oppose my weak activity against the general
inaction. If one should keep waiting for the next century or so for
things to be done of themselves, they would never get done. After
the principle of railroads was discovered (they, too, were sufficiently
opposed), locomotives and tracks had also to be built, without waiting
until a future generation should be ripe for such a mode of travel. . . .

The war that does not break out because of worry over the responsibility, that is to say, because of the excess of armaments, is not
peace, for it is doubly precarious: in the first place, because the
armaments are in themselves ruinous, materially and morally, for they
exhaust all resources, they enslave and degrade men, and they *must*
keep alive the spirit of war and the worship of force, which is happening in all schools at the present time; secondly, because the explosion of the powder magazine is left to depend on the arbitrary
will of a few people. . . .

Of course disarmament — especially of a single state — cannot
begin immediately; but just as the interminable increase of armaments is the consequence of the anarchy that prevails in the mutual

relations of states, so would disarmament be the consequence of their mutual relations based upon law. . . .

And if only people would not keep saying to us believers in evolution that the progress of culture is slow, as if we did not know it! But, because of that, to leave the first steps to the next generations and stand still ourselves is not a correct way to apply our knowledge of the slowness of the general movement forward; for we ought also to know that this trifling advance of the whole mass is the result of the greatest haste and the greatest output of energy on the part of single atoms.

. . . Yes, you are right; one looks calmly into the face of the unalterable and is spared painful disillusionment; but you are not right in adding that with such a realization I could maintain the same activity; for I regard the present state of things as not unalterable, and my whole activity consists in nothing else whatever than in modest but steady coöperation, according to my ability, in bringing about the change.

Your scruples about the Universal Court of Arbitration now in process of establishment rest upon an erroneous conception of the plan. That is usually the cause of mistaken judgments. It is believed that Mr. X is aiming at something irrational, and one therefore hesitates about helping Mr. X. On the other hand, Mr. X knows very accurately all the objections to what is attributed to him; unfortunately, however, the real thing that he wants is not known. . . .

" Share your indifference in the way I regard that ancient beast, Man, and his constant readiness to heap up inflammables on inflammables." No, the " young God " in man cannot have this indifference if he is going to conquer the ancient beast in man. The great heaps of inflammables, which are to-day growing smaller and smaller, even though they are still predominant, must not be left under the illusion that their realm is inviolable; and besides,

> " He is guilty of half the harm
> Who, to stop it, will not lift an arm."

What separates us two is faith. If you believed, as I do, in the possibility of the result, you would suffer as keenly as I do from the inertia of the world around us, but you would yourself take hold and act, and you would find your own pain and grief a small price for the beckoning reward; at the same time you would have the additional joys which often stir me when I see how the work is advancing; how, here and there, ever more numerous and ever more determined, are arising those who demand the accomplishment of what is already granted theoretically by the majority.

May the difference of our beliefs in peace matters in no respect imbitter our old friendship, but do not attempt any more to free me from my worries; it is in vain. Only he can mitigate them who shares them and helps me in the battle, but helps not because he is " won by personal charm," but because he believes in the possibility, in the necessity, of this battle.   B. S.

At this period I had still other political joys and sorrows. The persecutions of Armenians in Turkey were ever assuming more grewsome proportions. The Balkan tribes, in their distress, put their hope in the peace societies. One day I was surprised by the following dispatch from Rustchuk :

June 28

Bertha von Suttner, Vienna :

A meeting attended by more than two thousand persons was held to-day to express the wish that the twenty-third article of the Treaty of Berlin might be made operative in Turkey. It was voted in the name of the freedom of all the peoples of Turkey, and with a view to putting an end to the continual shedding of blood and preventing a possible European war, to urge you to enlist the services of the Peace League in recommending to the European governments the enforcement of Article 23 of the Berlin Treaty.

The Macedonian Committee in Rustchuk for the
Freedom of European Turkey
Koptchef

The insurrection of the unhappy Cubans, and the Draconic method of subjugation employed by the

Spaniards, was a real paroxysm of the system of force. General Weyler, who was hated with a deadly hatred by the Cubans on account of his cruelties, was sent over as Governor General. On his arrival he issued a proclamation; the neat document is " sharp," that must be confessed:

The death penalty for promulgation, directly or indirectly, of news favorable to the insurrection; death for assisting in smuggling arms or for failing to prevent same; death for the telegraph operator who communicates news of the war to third persons; death for any one who verbally or through the press or in any other way lowers the prestige of Spain; death for any one who utters words favorable to the rebels, etc., — these punishments to be determined by a court martial without appeal, and all verdicts to be immediately executed.

Thereupon great indignation in the United States regarding the Spanish dictatorship.

And now the joyful things which my diary contains:

A great event has happened: a professor in Würzburg, — his name is on all lips, — Professor Röntgen, has discovered a way of photographing the invisible by invisible rays. O thou wonderful world of magic! What splendid surprises hast thou still in store for us? Invisible rays which disclose the hidden — utterly new horizons open before us. Thus science enriches the world without having caused any increase of poverty or destruction. This is the true expander of empire, — a contrast to the sword which enriches one person only by what it has snatched from another, mangling him into the bargain!

And another joy I found in the progress of the Anglo-American arbitration treaty for the settlement of all differences, without any reference to the limitations that later treaties contain. It was not yet adopted and ratified, but the negotiations were powerfully urged on both sides of the ocean. The editors of the *Review of Reviews* (William T. Stead) and the *Daily Chronicle*, in coöperation with the English pacifists, established inquiries, meetings, demonstrations, petitions — in short, a popular movement, in which the most distinguished men of the day were enlisted and induced to take part. At the meeting which, on the third of March, brought six thousand people to Queen's Hall, sympathetic letters were read from Gladstone, Balfour, Rosebery, Herbert Spencer, and others. The resolve of this meeting was communicated officially by its chairman, Sir James Stansfeld, a former member of the Cabinet and friend of Lord Salisbury's, to the latter, whereupon the Premier replied that the matter had the sanction of the government. On Easter Sunday three English Church dignitaries issued a manifesto to the people. The issuer applied directly to Cardinal Rampolla, and he replied with the approval of the pope.

On the other side of the ocean there was the same movement in favor of the treaty. A national convention is called in Washington for the twenty-second and twenty-third of April for the same purpose, and the signatories are statesmen, bishops, judges, governors.

President Cleveland is well known to be inspired with the same desire; in short, the conclusion of the treaty may confidently be expected to take place very soon; and a new epoch of the history of civilization will be thereby initiated.

Now death overtook the former French Prime Minister, in whom our movement had such a firm support, — Jules Simon. My friend Frédéric Passy was especially affected at this bereavement. It is a matter of common knowledge that Jules Simon had won the sympathies of Emperor William II.

I have a letter from the famous statesman and philosopher which shows clearly with what conviction and passionate eagerness he fought against the institution of war. I had written urging him to attend a festival meeting of our Union in Vienna, and received the following reply:

Senate, Paris, May 24, 1892

Madam:

You ask if I will come to the meeting at Vienna. Alas! no, and I am very sorry that I cannot. I have taken upon me all kinds of obligations which are devouring my life without any too great advantage to the causes I am serving. You thoughtlessly accept an engagement and discover the next morning that if you had not alienated your liberty you could make a better use of your energies.

I could do nothing which would be more in line with my ideas and my tastes, if it be permitted to speak of one's inclinations when it is a question of duty; no, I could do nothing that would satisfy me better than to go to Vienna and fight under your leadership and that of your friends against this eternal war from which we are suffering in the midst of perfect peace, and which is becoming a disease endemic in the whole human race.

RECORDS OF AN EVENTFUL LIFE

I know perfectly well that I should not say anything which has not been said and which ought not to be repeated again this time. I do not blush for our cause because of its antiquity, nor because of the necessity which rests on its defenders of reiterating unceasingly the same arguments and the same complaints. It is like a Catholic litany, which ceaselessly repeats the same words to the same music, and which, in its monotony, is none the less an energetic and passionate prayer. I should have liked to mingle my voice in that chorus of thousands of voices which will be raised in protest against the collective assassinations, against the official massacres, against the destruction of human life and property in this horrible hell.

As I am unable to go there and raise my voice, I find some consolation, madam, in sending you my lamentation; and permit me to add to it my perfect admiration for all you are doing, and the homage of my respect.   Jules Simon

XLIX

THE SEVENTH WORLD'S PEACE CONGRESS AND THE SEVENTH INTERPARLIAMENTARY CONFERENCE IN BUDAPEST

General Türr's visit at Harmannsdorf · Anecdotes from his life · Garibaldi's appeal to the governments · Our journey to Budapest · Reception and preliminary festival · Opening of the Congress · From Türr's address · The historical Millennial Exposition · Élie Ducommun gives a report on the year's events · Debate: Armenian horrors · Address to the pope · Letter from Dr. Ofner · Excursion to the Margareteninsel · The youngest member of the Congress · Exciting debate about dueling · Nepluief and his institution · Deputation from the Society for the Protection of Animals · Conclusion of the Congress · Preliminary festival of the Conference · Soirée at the Parkklub · Opening session in the House of Magnates · Second session · Soirée at the Prime Minister's · From the protocol · Apponyi on the participation of Russia in the conferences · The Russian consul Vasily and his action · Excursion into the future · Visit at Maurus Jókai's · Gala operatic performance · End of the Conference · Opening of the "Iron Gate"

NOW we were getting ready to start for Budapest, where, during the Millennial Festival, the Seventh World's Peace Congress and the Seventh Interparliamentary Conference were to be held.

General Türr was chosen as chairman of the Congress. On the twenty-sixth of August we were surprised by a dispatch from Türr announcing that he was coming to Harmannsdorf. He had arrived in Vienna from Rome, and before continuing his journey to Budapest he wanted to fulfill a promise made long before to visit us in our home.

It gave us great delight, and in order to show it we prepared a grand reception for him. Before the entrance to the palace a triumphal arch was erected, adorned with the inscription

WELCOME, STEPHAN TÜRR

and when the carriage that brought him from the station, whither My Own had gone to meet him, drove up, a double line of our foresters performed a fanfare. Türr was greatly pleased with the fun.

Although he was then seventy-one years old, he was as fresh and martial and elastic in his bearing as if he had been only fifty at most. At our house he added another to his conquests. Not to speak of myself, our pretty niece Maria Louise, who was twenty-two, was so fascinated by him that she begged a cousin who was a painter and happened to be with us to make a life-size portrait of the handsome old warrior. The portrait was painted and she hung it in her boudoir.

My diary has the following entry under date of August 26:

On arising I find a dispatch from Türr. Wire reply and make preparations. Arrival at four o'clock. Much fun over triumphal gate, banners, and fanfare; looks fine. At the very first, long chat in the billiard room about the Congress. Still much to be done in preparation, but the larger part has already been begun by his friends, and through his influence many advances by the government. Dinner with the whole family.

Then black coffee in the garden. Very interesting stories. On the whole, he is full of gayety, goodness, and wit — like all men of the highest distinction who have been condemned to death two or three times!

Of the anecdotes from his experiences, which he intermingled with his conversation, I jotted down a few afterwards in a condensed form:

In the year 1868 he came to Vienna, commissioned by King Victor Emmanuel, whose adjutant general he was, to bring this message to Emperor Franz Joseph: "Tell the Emperor that in me he has not only a good relative but also a good friend." Türr told us in what a friendly manner the Emperor received the message and the messenger — although he had once been proscribed and under the ban as a revolutionist.

Türr had no specially good things to say of Bismarck. From his conversations with the Chancellor he quoted the following remarks: "After supper I brought Rechberg to the point of letting me buy Lauenburg — I wanted to prove that this Austrian would sell what he had no right to." And again: "I have not succeeded very well in persuading my king that we must wage war against Austria, but I have brought him to the very edge of the ditch, and now he must leap."

Türr was once talking with a Chinaman about civilization. "Do you know," remarked the man from the Middle Kingdom, "that your *liberté, fraternité, égalité,* are very fine, but a fourth thing is necessary."

" And that is — ? "

Un harmonisateur.

" What is that ? "

The Chinaman, making a gesture suggestive of whipping, said, *Le bambou.*

Türr is also somewhat of the opinion that it would be a good thing if men could have some of their bad qualities whipped out of them, especially some of their stupidity. *La bêtise humaine est in-com-men-su-ra-ble* . . . and *that* word is still too short !

Ach Götter,
Schneidt's Bretter !

With this sigh of resignation he used to conclude his observations over this or that piece of immeasurable stupidity among men.

He told us ever so much about his life as a soldier. He had already passed his fiftieth year in military service, for he had entered the army in 1842. During this half century he had seen so much that was horrible on the various battlefields, that he had consequently become an enemy of war:

It was in May, 1860. We were marching with Garibaldi's thousand heroes against Palermo. In the neighborhood of the market place of Partenio we had a glimpse of something that filled the hardest-hearted of us with horror. Beside the road a dozen Bourbon soldiers lay dead, and a pack of dogs were gnawing at their bodies. . . . We approached and saw that the soldiers had been burned. Garibaldi expressed his indignation at this in a terrible outbreak of rage. He could hardly hold in till he entered the little town. The inhabitants received him with joy, but he shouted to the exulting people in a voice trembling with wrath :

"I have seen here a barbarous deed — the partisans of freedom have no right to give way to such inhumane cruelty. . . ."

The people listened in deep silence to the general's outburst of passion. Finally some one came forward and said:

"We must acknowledge that we have done wrong, but before you condemn us, listen to what happened here; perhaps you will find our action comprehensible. . . ."

And the people conducted the general to a group of houses. He was taken into four or five of these houses and shown a heap of women and children, all scorched and burned to cinders. "This is what the Bourbon soldiers have done," they cried; "they drove the women and children into these houses, set the houses on fire, and would not let one escape. They guarded the doors until the wretched creatures struggled with death in the flames. We heard their screams of agony and hurried to help them; but it was too late. . . . In our bitter indignation we could only wreak our vengeance for the innocent victims by hurling the monsters into the fire in turn, and then we brought them out into the road."

Türr told us also of the document that Garibaldi, after the campaign was concluded, sent to all the crowned heads of Europe, urging them to form a league of peace. No notice was taken of this action and it is generally unknown. The only trace of it still remaining is the remark in the encyclopedia under the name Garibaldi: "Brave, patriotic, disinterested, warm-hearted, but *without deep political insight, a visionary.*" But it was really General Türr who suggested that attempt. Again I quote his own words:

One evening at Naples I was with Garibaldi on the balcony. The general, according to his usual custom, was contemplating the sky full of glorious stars. For a long time he was silent; at last he said:

"Dear friend, we have again done only half a job. God knows

III

how much blood will still have to be shed before the unity of Italy is established."

"May be . . . but, general, you can be contented with the great result that we have brought about within six months. The shedding of much blood might be avoided if better views should obtain among the rulers. . . . If, as far as it were possible, an agreement might be entered into by the European countries; if what Henry the Fourth and Elizabeth, Queen of England, centuries ago dreamed, and what Minister Sully so beautifully described, could be brought about, — who knows but the king's noble idea might even then have been realized, if a fanatic's dagger had not struck him down. But it would seem as if the time had now come to carry it out, so as to save Europe from other dreadful massacres and battles. General, you have accomplished a great work; you would seem to be the very one to bring an appeal to the rulers and the nations in the interest of peace and confederation."

We talked for a long time about this, and the very next morning Garibaldi brought the appeal which, with a few modifications, we sent to the powers. Since that time I have often had that appeal printed. Whenever opportunity has offered I have striven to call the attention of those in power and the great public to Garibaldi's lofty ideas. And now, when the peace workers and the representatives of the nations are about to assemble on the occasion of the Millennial Festival, I am going once more to bring forth the never-to-be-forgotten leader's inspired words of exhortation. It will not fail to be interesting — amid the conservative tendencies — to hear ideas of the so-called "revolutionists and subverters," dictated as they were by the purest philanthropy; for those men sought to overthrow nothing except the dikes that block freedom and progress.

General Türr pulled out of his pocket a copy of Garibaldi's appeal and handed it to me. It is an interesting document, and it makes one realize how thoughts which are regarded as new have been conceived many years back, and how they are swallowed up in forgetfulness, no matter how eloquently they may have been spoken. Ever again and ever again they have to emerge, like something new, surprising people, until at last they become common property.

In this appeal Garibaldi points to the enormous armaments of the sixties (what would he say to-day!); he laments that in the midst of so-called civilization we fill our lives with mutual threats against one another. He proposes an alliance of all the states of Europe; then there would be no more fighting forces on land and sea (that we should be now building air-fleets he did not foresee), and the enormous funds that have to be withdrawn from the necessities of the nations for unproductive, death-dealing purposes might be made available for ends that would improve property and lift the level of human life; these latter are then enumerated.

The document also gives satisfactory answers to possible objections. "What will become of the multitude of men who are serving in the army and in the navy?"

Rulers would have to study institutions of common utility if their minds were no longer absorbed in ideas of conquest and devastation. . . . In consequence of the advance in industry and the greater stability of commerce, the merchant service would soon take care of the whole personnel of the navy; the immense and innumerable works and undertakings which would spring up because of peace, the alliance, and security, would employ twice as many men as are serving in the army.

The appeal concludes with warm words addressed to those princes to whom "the sacred duty is intrusted of doing good and cherishing that greatness which is higher than ephemeral false greatness, — that true greatness the foundation of which would be the love and the gratitude of the nations."

General Türr returned that same evening to Vienna and went the next day to Budapest, where he finished the laborious preparations for the Congress.

Two days before the Congress opened we three followed him there. I say "we three," for we took our niece Maria Louise with us; we wanted her to enjoy this journey and the social festivities with us.

I see us on board a Danube steamer. It was a beautiful, sunny September day. There was quite a little peace band of us, — Malaria, Dr. Kunwald, the Grollers, husband and wife, and Countess Pötting, "die Hex"; of friends from abroad, — Frédéric Passy, Gaston Moch and his wife, Yves Guyot the former Minister, publisher of *Le Siècle* and a great free trader before the Lord, the Grelix couple, and M. Claparède from Switzerland.

So we had already a little Congress on deck; even at meals our company clung together. We passed by Pressburg, by Gran with its proud episcopal palace, and at Waitzen a deputation from Budapest which had been sent out to meet us came aboard, — three members of the Congress committee, and with them a reporter of the *Pesti Napló* (the "*Budapest Journal*"). It was already evening and all the lights were ablaze when we slowly came into port. On the dock stood other members of the committee, among them Director Kemény, who greeted us with an address; and gathered about was a dense throng shouting *Éljen!* (" Hail!") at the top of their voices. Carriages in waiting whirled us all to the Hotel Royal, where General Türr and a number of other colleagues were already awaiting us. That was the day of our arrival, September 15. By the entries in my diary I will now bring in review before my memory the week of the Budapest Congress and Conference.

September 16. Interviews the whole morning. Leopold Katscher brings me newspapers and tells about the preliminary labors. Luncheon in the Hotel Hungaria given by General Türr with only a few intimate friends. Visits with Karolyi, Banffy, and others. In the evening of this day before the opening of the Congress all the delegates are invited to a reception in the great drawing-rooms of the Hotel Royal. Türr and Count Eugen Zichy, the great Asiatic traveler, act as hosts. At supper various addresses: Pierantoni, a giant in stature, with a stentorian voice, speaks in Italian, and as fascinatingly as if he were a famous reader rather than a famous teacher of international law. I make the acquaintance of Dr. Ludwig Stein, professor in Bern University, whose philosophical feuilletons in the press have long been a delight to me. Frédéric Passy and Frédéric Bajer speak, and the " Peace Fury " is also obliged to take part.

September 17. Opening session in the council chamber of the new City Hall. Before the door, in the entrance hall, and on the stairs are stationed pandours, splendid in their lace-adorned uniforms and armor. It reminds one of the reception at the Capitol. The hall is packed. The galleries are densely crowded. Türr takes his place on the platform between the Minister of the Interior and the Mayor. He opens the Congress with a brief, vigorous address. Here is a passage from it:

> Not so very long ago there were princes and noblemen who fought one another and exercised jurisdiction over their subjects and serfs. If any one at that day had told them that the time would come when they would be required to bring their quarrels before a judge, they would have declared that person a dreamer, a Utopian, or something worse. And now these great lords are compelled to appear before the judge, where all their former serfs stand on the same footing with them.
>
> This change might be brought about also in the relations of the powers, and all the easier since it does not here concern two or three hundred princes and thousands of members of the high and lower nobility. We have to-day six great powers; and even these have united, — some in the Triple Alliance, the others in a friendly union; and all for the purpose of preserving peace.
>
> Now then, only one further step is required. If these two groups unite, then the smaller states will join, and the free confederation of the European powers is accomplished.

After the session the participants in the Congress are conducted to the Millennial Exposition, — the " Historical Exposition," . . . a thousand years of Hungarian history, from the primitive simplicity of the semibarbarous time of Arpád down to the refined industry of the highly developed — let us say only quarter-barbarous — to-day. And if another thousand years pass by and again an exposition illustrates the course of development, will the little medals with the word *pax* on them, such as we all have attached to our clothes as tokens, at that time be found perchance among the articles of apparel?

In the evening a garden party in Oes-Budavar. Everywhere at the appearance of the troops of peace ring forth from the densely encircling public hearty shouts of *Éljen!*

September 18. An interesting session. Élie Ducommun reads the report about the events of the past year. In the first place the progress of arbitration and the other successes and labors of the League; then a survey of the military events in Egypt, Abyssinia, Cuba, and Madagascar; finally, the latest events in Turkey. " Whoever may have been the originators of the atrocities, every civilized man must condemn them, just as he must condemn those who permitted the atrocities."[1]

James Capper, the sympathetic Englishman with the white, apostolic head, with the hearty, ringing voice, gets the floor. "The report of the Central Bureau," he says, "shows so clearly the absurdity of the so-called armed peace ... What! The many armies, the terrible

[1] The first series of massacres extended from October 3, 1895, to January 1, 1896. On the part of the Armenians, as is shown by documentary evidence, there was no provocation whatever. In spite of that, 85,000 people were killed, about 2300 cities and villages were laid waste, more than 100,000 Christians were compulsorily converted to Islam, and 500,000 were reduced to starvation. — B. S.

engines of destruction, are for the purpose of furnishing and maintaining peace, are they? and yet six million soldiers have not sufficed to prevent the infamies that have been taking place in the Orient! We should not look idly on while brigands trample down a whole nation! If I see in the street a child attacked by villains, I consider it my duty to interfere with both fists in defense of the one attacked, and if in the struggle I should have to lose my life, I would do it willingly!" Loud applause. We all feel it would be a legitimate use of force to protect the persecuted against force.

A young French priest, Abbé Pichot, moves that the Congress send an address to the Pope, begging him to grant the movement his support: it is known to him that Leo XIII had the peace cause much at heart, and that a word of approval from that quarter would be of the highest value. I spring to my feet and second the motion. I also know for a fact that the Pope has frequently of late years spoken against preparations for war and in favor of the international arbitration tribunal; but it is not sufficiently well known, because these utterances were made to a Russian publicist and an editor of the *Daily Chronicle*. The Catholic press and the Church generally, as well as the whole Catholic world, have failed to hear those words. How very different would be the effect if the Pope should direct these observations of his directly to the millions of his faithful. So then, I urged, let the respectful request be submitted to him that he embody in an encyclical the expressions of encouragement already often pronounced by him in the presence of the advocates of peace. Some one objects: the motion could not fail to offend those of other beliefs, especially freethinkers; no religious tendency should be introduced. Frédéric Passy explains that we are dealing not with religious but with humanitarian demonstrations. The motion is carried.

In the evening, gala performance of the opera *Der Geiger von Cremona.*[1]

I receive a letter from Dr. Julius Ofner, deputy to the Austrian Parliament. I give the text of it here:

... I should gladly have taken part in the deliberations on the international arbitration tribunal. The talk that is made on this point seems to me too timid, too much directed to the welfare of the states and too little to their duties; *apostles do not flatter.*

From a legal point of view there can be no doubt: no law without a judge; no one can decide in his own cause, and history teaches that if states desire even the most unrighteous things, they have always found crown jurists to defend them and declare them lawful. As long, therefore, as there is no tribunal erected for international differences, there will be international politeness, international morals, but no international justice. The strong is infallible; injured justice turns only against the weak. The appeal to sovereignty, which, it is said, must not be curtailed, is nothing but a cloak for the desire to be permitted to do arbitrary wrong. For all law limits the single individual for the advantage of the rest, limits arbitrariness for the advantage of universal liberty. Law and righteousness are at the foundation

[1] *Der Geiger,* or rather *Der Geigenmacher, von Cremona,* a one-act opera by Hans Trneček, born May 16, 1858, at Prague. Text by Leopold Günther, after Coppée. First produced at the Court Theater of Schwerin, April 16, 1886. — TRANSLATOR.

of all culture, and what Kant said in regard to mankind in general applies to states, — " If there were no law it would not be worth while for men to live on earth."

There is nothing sensational in the session. The afternoon is spent at the Othon, a journalists' club. In Türr's company my niece and I make a call on Prime Minister Banffy.

September 20. Outing for the members of the Congress. We are taken on special steamboats to the Margareteninsel, where the committee provide a luncheon. The weather is splendid — the tables are set in the open air, surrounded by the wonderful grounds of the park. " Do you know, my dear colleagues and friends," said General Türr, " this island was formerly a wilderness. The owner, Archduke Joseph, by clearing, cultivating, and decorating it, has made a paradise of it. So may that wilderness which to-day prevails in international life be turned by the civilizing power of the work of peace into a blooming land like the Margareteninsel."

Of course others also speak. Deep emotion is caused, however, when an Italian delegate, a former captain on the general staff, Conte di Pampero, lifting up his eight-year-old son and standing him on the table, asks permission to speak in the name of the youngest member of the Congress, and, laying his hand as if in blessing on the lad's head, adjures those present to bring up their children, just as he is doing, to hate war and love humanity. . . .

September 21. Very lively debate over dueling. A delegate — Félix Lacaze from France — makes the motion that all Peace Societies shall require their members to agree to decline all duels. A great controversy arises. Count Eugen Zichy declares that if this is carried he must as a matter of honor resign from the Union. Such an obligation cannot be undertaken in certain countries and in certain circles. The English members, who are indignant that the duel is being discussed, are provoked and refuse to allow Count Zichy to have the floor a second time, although he declares he wishes to speak in the line of conciliation. Finally Houzeau de Lehaye, the ever conciliatory, offers a compromise resolution which, although declaring that nothing can be mandatory upon the members, nevertheless urges them to make every effort to discourage the use of the duel, as contradictory to the principles which they are supporting, and to secure the execution of the laws that relate to it.

I have made an interesting new acquaintance, — a Russian by the name of Nepluief. He introduced himself to me during a recess in the proceedings, and is urging me to support his ideas. He has founded in his country an institution based on the principles of education for peace. He gives the impression of being a *grand seigneur*, and at the same time a deeply religious man. His idea in coming here is to acquaint the Congress with the institution which he has called

into life, and have it imitated everywhere. He called
himself on his visiting card " Président de la Confrérie
ouvrière de l'Exaltation de la Croix." In this way he
imparts an ecclesiastical tinge to his socialistic undertaking. A multimillionaire, possesser of wide landed
estates and numerous factories in the Government of
Chernigof, he began his career as a diplomat, but gave
it up in order to devote himself wholly to the task of
elevating the Russian peasants morally and materially.
At his own expense he founded popular schools for
industrial and agricultural training, and peasant unions
which he calls "Brotherhoods." From the first he
gave these unions a share in the profits of his undertaking; later he turned over his whole property to
their complete control, reserving for himself only the
title of life president of these enterprises. But things
did not run smoothly. For years he had to contend
with the ill will of the Russian bureaucracy, which suspected him of being a socialist. Finally, however, his
work of education brought him satisfactory results.
He has explained his methods and experiences in a
pamphlet, which he distributed to the members of
the Congress. He himself departed from Budapest
the same day.[1]

In the evening a banquet is given by the city.

[1] In 1904 Mr. Nepluief called upon me in Vienna. He had remained faithful to himself and his apostleship. He had also succeeded in interesting the
Czarina in it. It was his desire that the peace societies everywhere should
establish such fraternities among the common people; but, to say nothing of
other objections, these societies, above all, lack the means for doing so.

September 22. A deputation from the Society for the Protection of Animals call upon me and beg me to support their endeavors. I reply that I have at that moment a book under way, entitled *Schach der Qual* ("Check to Suffering"), in which there is to be a chapter pleading for our poor dumb fellow-creatures, that are so cruelly treated.

Final session. At half past one General Türr ends the Congress with the greeting *Auf Wiedersehn*. The "meeting again" takes place two hours later, in the Hotel Royal, where a farewell dinner is given to the president and the committee and the rest of us. Malaria — Olga Wisinger — had taken charge of the arrangements. But even now there is no general breaking-up, for many of the participants remain here in order to be present at the opening to-morrow of the Interparliamentary Conference.

We were also among those who were going to remain a few days longer. As early as the sixteenth of August the following letter had reached us at Harmannsdorf:

Interparliamentary Conference, Hungarian Group
Budapest, August 15

Your Highness:

The useful zeal and the self-sacrificing and profitable labors which you have undertaken in the interest and service of universal peace make it a pleasant duty for us to invite you, as well as your husband, and your niece the Baroness von Suttner, to the Interparliamentary Conference which is to open at Budapest on the twenty-second of September.

123

As you are aware, only members of legislatures can take part in the Conference; yet it may interest you to follow the sessions from the gallery and to participate in the festivities and excursions.

In this hope, etc.

Koloman v. Szell, Chairman
Aristide v. Deszewffy, Secretary
of the Executive Committee

I return to my Budapest diary.

September 23. Yesterday, as on the eve of the Congress, a great soirée in the Parkklub, cards of invitation for which were sent out by Koloman von Szell. This clubhouse is really beautiful — massive, splendid, with English comfort. All the members of the Conference are present; we have a joyous meeting with old acquaintances, — Stanhope, Beernaert, Cremer, Descamps, and others. Many ladies of Hungarian society and the wives of the members of the Conference are there. Almost all the Hungarian ministers, Baron Banffy at their head; Counts Eugen Zichy, Albert Apponyi, Szapary, Esterhazy, and many journalists and artists. Our old Passy is closely surrounded. Maria Louise looks wondrously pretty and, it seems to me, is turning the heads of several of the Magyars! Also that northern maiden, Ranghild Lund, the beauty of the conference days at Rome, is here and arousing much admiration. John Lund comes up to me and brings me a message from Björnson. I make the acquaintance of a young Countess Kalnoky (unmarried and very independent), and her free and broad-minded views greatly appeal to me. Then we are joined by a

124

Countess Forgac; she has much to tell us of Empress Elisabeth, among other things the following: Some spirit communications had been made (presumably at a spiritualistic séance) to the effect that the place where the Crown Prince Rudolf is staying is worse than hell and no prayers are of any avail; the Empress is full of despair about it. Melinda Karolyi and I exchange glances equivalent to many exclamation marks.

Servants bring round delicious edibles and drinkables. A journalist remarks, "One need not be a member of a peace league to find this sort of international meeting decidedly pleasanter than those where bombs and grenades are served."

To-day the opening session takes place in the House of Magnates. Before the building, on the edge of the street, fastened together with garlands of flowers, stand masts, from which float the flags of all the nations that participate in the Conference, — an object lesson for the passers-by. That conception of a " European Confederation," still so strange, is here expressed in the language of emblems.

We reach our places in the gallery before the members of the Conference make their appearance in the hall, so we watch them as they come in deliberately and take their places. In the ministerial chairs, where of late the King's Hungarian councilors sat, now the foreign parliamentarians are taking their seats. Frédéric Passy is between Cardinal Schlauch and Minister Darany. Gobat mounts the platform and proposes

that the president of the Hungarian House of Deputies, Desider Szilagyi, be chairman of the Conference.
He accepts and delivers the welcoming address. Now
follow the speeches of old acquaintances, — Pirquet,
Descamps, Beernaert, Von Bar, Bajer, and others. Apponyi is new and surprising to me. What a speaker!
He has a tall, elegant figure, a powerful barytone voice,
and an easy mastery of foreign tongues.

At the second session at four o'clock begin the actual
transactions. Point I: "Permanent International Arbitration Tribunal." Descamps reports that he has sent
to all the sovereigns and governments the memorandum in regard to this question, drawn up in accordance with the motion of the previous year. Most of
the governments had replied favorably to the principles, but the most decisive answer came from St.
Petersburg, from the recently departed Prince Lobanof.

In the evening a great soirée at the Prime Minister's.

I see that my diary has not kept a very strict account of the various phases of the transactions of the
Conference. But the official protocol lies before me
and I will here dwell upon something that seems to
me important in the historical development of the
peace cause. In that session of September 22, 1896,
the following resolution was offered by Pierantoni:

The Seventh Interparliamentary Conference requests all civilized
states to call a diplomatic conference in order that the question of an
international court of arbitration may be laid before it; at this conference the labors of the Interparliamentary Union shall serve as a
basis for further resolves.

126

A Conference of Diplomatists. In this term does there not already ring — how shall I express it? — a note suggestive of the conferences at The Hague, in which, indeed, the labors of Descamps and La Fontaine served as the foundation of the establishment of the Hague Tribunal.

And still another debate of historical interest. During the session of the twenty-fourth of September the order of the day contains the question whether those nations that have no parliament may be able to participate in the Interparliamentary Conferences, and what their status shall be. Count Albert Apponyi, who has composed a memorial on this subject, which is distributed through the hall, makes the report. He refers to the memorial, and confines himself to a brief exposition. He reserves the privilege of again expressing his views at the conclusion of the debate; now he will only state the motion:

That an amendment be added to the statutes to the effect that the Conferences shall admit to their deliberations also the delegates of sovereigns, rulers, and governments, as well as of the Russian Imperial Council or any similar institution in nonconstitutional countries, in so far as such delegates are accredited by their governments. The Management (*Bureau*) shall be authorized to inform the rulers and governments of nonconstitutional countries that the Conference would be pleased to welcome their delegates to its deliberations.

Lewakowski, member of the Austrian Parliament, opposes Apponyi's motion; its aim is wholly and solely the admission of Russia.

" We are here," he declares, " as the representatives

of the people, and we are working here in the spirit of our commissions. The Russian nation cannot send any representative that can have the same authority as we have. Norton, Snape, Pirquet, Rahusen, and Passy speak in favor of the motion.

M. G. Conrad[1] opposes the motion in the most violent terms: " Either we are a parliamentary conference or we are not. We do not need to know what the governments say; we want to hear the views of the people themselves. And the views of the Russian people you surely will not be likely to hear from the mouths of the delegates of the Russian government."

Stanhope favors the adoption of the motion. The magnificent object of the Conference, he declares, would only be furthered by it. There actually exists in Russia something that corresponds to a parliamentary body, and, who knows? some day, directly through the influence of our Conference, something may develop that will lead to constitutionalism.

Then Count Apponyi brings the debate to a conclusion. He takes strong issue with his opponents. In reply to Lewakowski he declares that numerous gentlemen are sitting here who have not received their credentials from their nation and indeed are members of the upper houses appointed by their sovereigns. In the one scale are placed the objections that have been adduced, in the other the immense importance of the

---

[1] Our old friend the literary Hotspur, so full of mettle, from Munich, recently elected to the Reichstag.

fact that such a great empire as Russia, occupying a third of all Europe, ought to share in our deliberations. This question came up for the first time in the Hungarian Group, and was agitated in the interest of those countries that have, to be sure, no parliaments, and yet desire to participate in our labors and to battle for the peace of the world. These also have the right to collaborate with us in the great work of civilization. We are all pursuing the one aim of helping a righteous cause to victory, and any kind of assistance can be welcomed by us. The honored president of the former Conference has sent to all the governments his memorandum regarding the Court of Arbitration, and the most sympathetic reply was that received from the late Prince Lobanof.

Descamps: " That is correct."

Apponyi: " In Russia, as may be seen by many indications, the tendency to take part in European affairs is strong; for some time Russia has been represented at most Congresses. We must give her the opportunity to share also in our labors; it is indeed not beyond the bounds of possibility that the development of affairs in Russia will be in this way favorably influenced. At all events the sympathy of such a powerful state could only strengthen our endeavors."

It is interesting to connect with this debate of September 24, 1896, the fact that on the 24th of August, 1898, the manifesto calling the Peace Conference at The Hague emanated from Russia.

One other circumstance must also be mentioned here. The then Russian consul, Vasily, was present at the sessions and exercises of the Conference at Budapest, and communicated to his government accurate and sympathetic reports. He was an unhesitating friend of peace. His report was, as I afterwards learned, cast in the form of an impassioned plea for cessation of war preparations. The suggestion did not receive the approval of his superiors, and remained for some time forgotten. A year later, however, when Lord Salisbury in his Guildhall address animadverted on the endless increase in armament among the nations, and declared that the only hope of escaping general ruin lay in the union of the powers in some kind of an international constitution, then M. Vasily presented anew his idea in behalf of an attempt to bring about an international understanding on this point. Vasily was attached to the ministry of foreign affairs ; he naturally communicated his ideas to his chief, Count Lamsdorff, who, in turn, laid them before the Emperor.

When, in 1906, the Interparliamentary Conference met in London, a parliament was sitting in St. Petersburg which sent its representatives to England, not in the name of a group, but of the whole Duma. To be sure, on the very day when, at the opening session in Westminster Hall, the Russian delegate was to deliver his salutatory, the news arrived that the Duma was prorogued. The Russians were obliged, therefore, to quit London with their business unaccomplished, and Campbell-Bannerman, who opened the Interparliamentary Conference, was given the opportunity of perpetrating his *mot*, which afterwards became so famous: *La douma·est morte, vive la douma !*

After this brief excursion into the future I return to the Budapest notes in my diary.

September 24. After the morning session, when the Russian debate was on, in which Apponyi distinguished himself and which Vasily and Novikof followed with great interest, we make a call on Maurus Jókai. An attack of indisposition prevented him from taking part in the Conference, but he is well enough to receive us. He lives in a villa of his own, not large but very beautiful, and surrounded by a garden. He shows us all his treasures, — his worktable, his books, and the gifts which he received at his Jubilee; among them the splendid offering from the Hungarian nation, the de luxe edition of his complete works, for the publication of which subscriptions of a hundred thousand gulden were paid in advance, — a gift of honor presented to the poet by his fellow-countrymen. Two very interesting hours. Jókai tells us much about his life. He gives me his photograph inscribed with his name.

In the evening a gala performance of the opera *Bank-Ban*, by Erkel[1]; Bianca Bianchi trills like a nightingale.

[1] Erkel Ferenz (1810–1893), creator of the national Hungarian opera. *Bank-Ban* is regarded as his best work. — Translator.

131

September 25. Final session. Closing banquet in the festival hall of the Exposition. Eight hundred participants. On both sides of the vestibule stand Haiduks in gala uniform. At the table of honor, with the leaders of the various foreign groups, are Beernaert, Passy, Stanhope, Descamps, and others; and the Hungarians, Szilagyi, Szell, Apponyi, Szapary, Berzeviczy, Franz Kossuth, and Mayor Ráth as host. My neighbors are the English General Havelock and Count Koloman Esterhazy. After the toast to the King, offered by the mayor, Koloman Szell toasts the members of the Conference, "the masters and banner bearers in the greatest question in the progress of civilization."

The exercises were not at an end even on the last day of the Conference. The participants were invited to help celebrate the opening of the "Iron Gate," which was to take place in the presence of the Emperor. On the twenty-sixth of September, in the evening, two special trains took us to Orsova, where comfortable quarters were assigned to each and every guest. On the morning of the twenty-seventh, radiant with unclouded sunshine, we all went aboard the special steamboat *Zriny*, which, occupying the fourth place in the column, accompanied the imperial ship down the Danube; the second boat carried the generals, the third the diplomats. After the flotilla reached the Kazan pass, the imperial ship cut through a cable of flowers stretched across the Danube canal — the "Iron Gate" was opened.

" This festal occasion," said Emperor Franz Joseph, " which brings us together to celebrate a great work of public utility, fills me with happiness, and in the conviction that this work will give a powerful and healthy impulse to the peaceful and advantageous development of international relations, I drink to the happiness and prosperity of the nations."

The four steamboats now moved slowly past and sailed back to Orsova.

L

OTHER EVENTS OF THE YEAR 1896

Jingo criticism of Budapest · A prophetic chapter from Schach der Qual · A poem by Hoyos and a letter from Nathaniel Rothschild · Visits of the Tsar · Extracts from diary · Correspondence between the Austrian Peace Society and the English Department of Foreign Affairs · Treaty of peace between Menelik and Italy

AGAIN at Harmannsdorf. The days at Budapest had left a joyous feeling of exultation. The meeting had given conspicuous testimony to the growth of the movement and to the impression that it was making in powerful political circles. Perfectly amusing and indeed comical in its malicious perversion of facts, its absolutely bottomless ignorance, was an article in the jingo press that I found in a mountain of press notices which had collected at home during our absence. The *St. James Gazette* of September 18 wrote:

There are more important transactions in progress at this moment in Europe than the Seventh Peace Congress, which has just met in the Grand Hall of the Municipal Palace in Budapest. None are more odd, or, in a way, better worth looking at. The good men who have met on the initiative of a most excellent lady, the Baroness Bertha von Suttner, author of " Down with Arms," and creator of the Peace Congress, represent the fine flower of all that vaguely well-meaning, emotional, and unpractical class of persons which is to be found in most countries, and nowhere in finer feather than among ourselves. To see that there is something wrong in the world, and to propose a remedy which, on inquiry, turns out to be a radical change in human nature, is the same thing with them. They are active in many fields, or, to speak with more accuracy, they talk at large on many subjects; but they are nowhere seen in more complete beauty than when in congress assembled for the purpose of speaking of peace. . . . Carlyle wanted to know the meaning of the moralist who, in the conflict between Gods and Giants, put out his hand armed "with a pair of tweezers." At this moment, when it is really not too much to say that all Europe is "a town of war, the people's hearts yet wild, brimful of fear," the good Baroness Bertha and like-minded persons come forward at Budapest with their pair of tweezers. . . . The value of the Baroness von Suttner's picnic becomes fully conspicuous when we turn, etc., etc.

I sent Alfred Nobel a careful account of the events at Budapest, and corresponded also with Egidy about them. I worked steadily on my book, *Schach der Qual,* an imaginative story. A chapter in it is called *Frohbotschaft* ("Good Tidings"). It describes an "international conference for securing peace." In his opening address the chairman speaks these words:

This meeting is called together at the initiative of one of the most powerful sovereigns of Europe, and after the assent to its principal object has been obtained from all the other governments; and almost all countries, great and small, with very few exceptions, have declared their agreement and are here represented.

The book was begun in 1895 and was published by Pierson at the beginning of 1897, so that the words here cited cannot be a reminiscence of the Hague Peace Conference, which was first summoned in 1898 by "one of the most powerful sovereigns of Europe"; but they are a prophetic announcement of it. This was a coincidence rare enough to make it worthy of remark.

Other incidents that interested me during the year 1896 I find jotted down in my diary:

October 2. No letter from Hoyos in a long time. He must be ill. I hope he will soon be well again, the splendid man! There are not many in our aristocracy who are so free and grand and magnanimous in their thoughts, and who are so entirely opposite to reactionary — almost socialistic. Note this example of it: Lately a collection was taken for the unemployed. Hoyos added the following verses to his contribution:

Sammlung für die Arbeitslosen

For the unemployed, collections, —
  Coal, old clothes, and doles of bread,
Linen, hose, — they 're no corrections
  For the want so widely spread!

Do not mitigate starvation;
  See that hunger you expel;
Then you 'll make the demonstration
   . That you love your neighbor well.

Give not alms to your poor neighbor;
  Stop the source of poverty;[1]
Do not limit, hamper Labor;
  Make its course forever free!

[1] As a contrast to this idea (*Hebt den Grund der Armut auf!*), which is not current among philanthropic financiers, I append the following letter:

My dear Baroness:

  I have had the pleasure of receiving your esteemed favor of the nineteenth. Highly as I esteem the work to which you are devoting yourself with such self-sacrificing assiduity, I regret that I cannot be of assistance to it by acceding to the wish that you express. The great number of demands made upon me in behalf of humanitarian objects forbid my considering them all. You will, therefore, my dear Baroness, understand and will not feel offended with me, if I give the preference to such associations

OTHER EVENTS OF THE YEAR 1896

In the Code's indwelling spirit
Let not Law o'er Duty stand;
Let them the same place inherit;
Let all men the Law command!

October 10. The Emperor of Russia has been in Vienna. From there he went to Breslau, Balmoral, Paris. The result of it is *Pax et Robur.* So at least some remark; others say the result is *Revanche;* still a third think that everything remains as it was before. But this last is not correct. It has brought about something new, to wit, — that in divided and split-up and hostile Europe the sovereign of one country travels to another and goes everywhere as a friend and is everywhere received as a friend. Indeed, if Europe were a civilized complex of states, that would be as natural and as much a matter of course as it is for a landed proprietor to make a series of visits among all the neighboring families. Not in half a century, perhaps, has the word "peace" been so frequently, so emphatically, so solemnly, so universally repeated in speeches and newspapers as it has been in consequence of this journey. That shows the tendency of the *Zeitgeist;* but it is still far from the peace that we mean. For the whole affair abounds in contradictions, especially the contradiction that exists between the new tendency and the old institutions, views, and political

as not merely have in view an ideal purpose but pursue practical ends connected with real life.

Regretting that I am not in a position to give you an affirmative answer, I beg you to accept the expression of my distinguished consideration.

Bn. N. Rothschild

137

constellations still intrenched in power. Here is a monster of contradiction, such as the history of the world has never before displayed: two mutually opposed shields loaded with explosives; two hostile guardians of the peace, or two peaceable guardians of enmity, — *Dreibund* and *Zweibund.* Why not equally well *Fünfbund?*

October 15. Already 165,000 men in all have been sent to Cuba. The Spanish Ministry of War intend to dispatch 40,000 more, because yellow fever and other diseases have already greatly reduced the number of the effective. A loan of a milliard is planned.

October 18. Rear Admiral Tirpitz has elaborated a naval budget of 150,000,000 marks. The *Post* writes: "Tirpitz has made use of a long leave of absence, under orders from the supreme authority, to formulate from the strategic-technical standpoint a plan for organizing our fleet so that from the military standpoint it shall correspond to the demands of the present time." When shall we ever plan from the ethical-humane standpoint how circumstances may be shaped so that from the standpoint of the philosopher they may correspond to the demands of a better future?

November 9. Yesterday our beloved Rudolf Hoyos departed this life at his Castle Leuterburg in Silesia. Ever more and more numerous the graves!

November 10. Telegram from Washington: "The English ambassador Pauncefote lays before Secretary of State Olney the proposals for the Anglo-American treaty pertaining to the settlement of all future controversies through arbitration."

This news may announce the dawn of a new epoch of civilization. Yet our "serious" politicians do not touch upon it in their leading articles.

The following letters were exchanged between the Austrian Peace Society and the Department of Foreign Affairs at London on this occasion:

Austrian Peace Society

My Lord Marquis: Vienna, November 17, 1896

The Committee of the Austrian Peace Society venture to express to your Lordship their deep gratification in the treaty passed at Washington, November 9th. This is the greatest triumph which the cause of civilization has hitherto attained, and posterity will never forget the part which, in this happy achievement, is due to your Lordship's wisdom and energy.

We have the honor to be, respectfully

Baroness Bertha Suttner (president)

To the most Honorable   Prince Alfred Wrede (vice president)
the Marquis of Salisbury
   London, Foreign Office

London, Foreign Office

Madam: November 21, 1896

I am directed by the Marquis of Salisbury to acknowledge the receipt of your letter of the 17th inst., expressing the gratification of the Austrian Peace Association in regard to the negotiation between Great Britain and the United States on the question of arbitration, and I am to express his Lordship's thanks for your communication.

I am, Madam, your most obedient humble servant

The Baroness of Suttner, Vienna   F. H. Villiers

November 20. The papers are full of the Bismarck disclosure.[1] The explanations given right and left in

[1] Secret guaranty with Russia.

139

the Reichstag by Prince Hohenlohe and Herr von Marschall set a limit to further extension. Yes, much was certainly disclosed in this affair, and particularly the rascally face not of this or that politician but of that folk-cheating intrigante called " high politics."

November 25. Good news. Italy and Menelik have concluded peace. Only a few days ago the Trieste *Picolo* learned from a diplomat of high rank that the chances for a treaty of peace with Menelik were small; he was unwilling to submit to the condition that he should not put himself under the protection of any European power. " Let the Roman government circles take into account the probabilities that the prisoners must be left to their fate (!) and hostilities resumed." But the diplomat of high rank was fortunately mistaken. The treaty of peace is signed. In a letter which Menelik on this occasion addressed to the King of Italy he said that it was a pleasure for him, on the twentieth of November, the Queen's birthday, to be able to restore their sons to the Italian mothers; and thus he showed a tenderer feeling for the prisoners than the above-mentioned Roman government circles.

According to the tenor of the treaty Italy renounces the (falsely interpreted) treaty of Utshili, and the two belligerents resume their former boundaries. Consequently the *status quo ante* — why, therefore, the great sorrow, the gigantic expenditures, the heaps of corpses mutilated and putrefying in the torrid sun? Why? why?

LI

ALFRED NOBEL'S DEATH AND WILL

News of his death · His last letter to me · The will · Letter from Moritz
Adler · The will is contested · Letter from the executor · Emanuel Nobel's
noble act · Fortunate solution · Distribution of the peace prize up to date

DECEMBER 12. Alfred Nobel is dead.
I recorded this loss in my diary with this single
line. The news — I found it in the newspapers —
was a bitter blow to me. The tie of a twenty years'
friendship was snapped. The last letter which I received from Nobel was from Paris, dated the twenty-
first of November, and ran as follows:

Dear Baroness and Friend: Paris, November 21, 1896
   " Feeling well " — no, unhappily for me, I am not, and I am even
consulting doctors, which is contrary not only to my custom, but also
to my principles. I, who have no heart, figuratively speaking, have
one organically, and I am conscious of it.
   But that will suffice for me and my petty miseries. I am enchanted
to see that the peace movement is gaining ground. That is due to
the civilizing of the masses, and especially to the prejudice hunters
and darkness hunters, among whom you hold an exalted rank. Those
are your titles of nobility.   Heartily yours,   A. Nobel

The ailing heart on which he touches playfully
brought him to his death. On the tenth of December
— he was then at his villa in San Remo — he was suddenly snatched away by angina pectoris. No one was

141

with him when he died; he was found in his work-
room — dead!

Some time after the report of Alfred Nobel's death
the newspapers announced that he had left his millions
for benevolent purposes, a part to go towards promoting the peace movement. But the details were lacking.
I received, however, from the Austrian ambassador in
Stockholm a copy of the will; and the executor of it,
Engineer Sohlmann, entered into correspondence with
me. So I became accurately informed as to the provisions of this remarkable last will and testament:

After payment of legacies to relatives, amounting to about a million crowns, the residue of the property — thirty-five millions — was
set aside for the formation of a fund, from the interest of which five
yearly prizes should be assigned to such as had contributed some
notable service to the benefit of mankind. These were specifically:

1. For the most important discovery and invention in the realm
of physics;

2. For the most important discovery and invention in the realm
of chemistry;

3. For the most important discoveries in the domain of physiology
or medicine;

4. For the most distinguished productions of an idealistic tendency
in the realm of literature;

5. To that man or woman who shall have worked most effectively
for the fraternization of mankind, the diminution of armies, and the
promotion of Peace Congresses.

The Stockholm Academy is intrusted with the assignment of the
first four prizes, the Norwegian Storthing with that of the fifth.

After the publication of the provisions of the will I
received the following letter from the faithful collaborator on my *Review*, Moritz Adler, the author of the

valuable essays *Zur Philosophie des Krieges* ("The Philosophy of War").

My dear Madam: Vienna, January 4, 1897

Allow me to congratulate you with all my heart on the New Year's delight which the splendid Nobel foundation must have given you, of course modified by the drop of wormwood which the death of such a spirit and heart mixed with the nectar. *Multis ille bonis flebilis occidit* can be truthfully said of this great man now passed away. He left behind no sanitary train for future gladiatorial baiting of the nations, for it was far from his idea to wish to put to sleep the consciences of the mighty and to make them believe that he thought it possible for the disgrace to be repeated. He has not founded a hospital, either, for the other sick, who are not innocently condemned by society to wounds and death. But millions in days to come will rejoice in brighter life and health, and perhaps not one in a thousand will ever suspect that he owes it to Nobel alone that he is not a cripple or a candidate for an infirmary. Could we have believed it possible that Mammon, Mammon sprung from dynamite, should be so ennobled ? I am happy to have lived until this day ; it has been the richest joy of my life.

I kiss your hand with the profoundest respect.

Moritz Adler

Indeed, yes ; this foundation was a deep gratification to me ; again something new had come into the world: not the donors of alms, nor the lawgivers, least of all the conquerors, have been held up as the benefactors of mankind, but the discoverers and explorers, and the poets inspired by high ideals, and, in the same category, the workers in the service of international peace. Already the news of this last will and testament has aroused general attention ; and every year, at the time when the prizes are awarded, this sensation will be repeated. It has been openly declared to the world, not by an overexcited dreamer, but by an inventor of genius (an inventor of war material into the bargain), that the brotherhood of nations, the diminution of armies, the promotion of Peace Congresses, belong to the things that signify most for the well-being of mankind.

Thus a guiding star is fixed in the sky, and the clouds that have hitherto obscured it are breaking away more and more; the name of this star is Human Happiness. But as long as men legally threaten one another's lives, as long as they are at feud instead of being helpful one to another, there will be no universal happiness. Yet it must and will come. The increasing spirit of research puts into man's hand a nature-controlling power which can make of him a god or a devil.

" Here you have a material," said the living Nobel to his own generation, " with which you can annihilate everything and yourself as well. . . ." But the dead Nobel compels us to look at yonder star and says to future generations, " Grow nobler, and you will attain happiness."

It was five years before the distribution of the prizes began. It took this length of time because a lawsuit which was brought by certain members of the Nobel family against the validity of the will had to be decided, and then the estate had to be liquidated. If the then head of the family, Emanuel Nobel, had joined the rest in the protest, the will would have been broken, to his own great advantage; but Emanuel Nobel refused his consent to this step. He declared that his uncle's will was sacred to him, and he took the ground that it must be faithfully carried out in all respects, even in regard to the fifth clause, which was especially endangered.

A letter dated April 13, 1898, from the executor of the will, brought me interesting particulars regarding the whole matter. Mr. Ragnar Sohlmann wrote:

... As you will have learned from the papers, certain members of the Nobel family have been attempting to break Herr Nobel's will in the Swedish courts, and especially on the ground that no residuary legatee is constituted. The Nobel fund as created by the will itself lacks the necessary elements — so they claim — for performing its functions, — that is to say, administrators.

To this we shall reply that all necessary elements have been provided by the will, namely, the capital, the scope of action, and the institutions designated to perform the action, — the Swedish Academy and the Norwegian Storthing. The mere organization — so we shall urge — belongs evidently to the task conferred upon the executors and the Academy.

Originally the complainants conceived the plan of bringing the suit before a French court by endeavoring to prove that Herr Nobel's legal residence was not in Sweden but in Paris. They regarded the French laws as more favorable to their claims than the Swedish, and this undoubtedly would have been the case. We have so far succeeded in preventing the execution of this plan, and only a few days ago the highest court of Sweden rendered the decision that Bofors was Herr Alfred Nobel's legal residence.

The fact that Herr Emanuel Nobel, of St. Petersburg, and the whole Russian branch of the family decline to take part in the suit forms a very important factor in the coming trial. This circumstance assures the fulfillment of the will in so far as it concerns the corresponding portion of the property. In consequence, the will may be regarded as established regarding eight twentieths of the whole estate.

That diminishes also the chances for a judicial declaration of the invalidity of the remaining twelve twentieths.

The chief danger for the will lies in the actual animosity which at the present time obtains between Sweden and Norway, and in the fear here entertained — even among the members of the government — that the whole thing might give rise to further irritation between the two countries. The conservatives especially believe — or pretend to believe — that the Norwegian Storthing might use the prize to " bribe " other countries to oppose Sweden. And they have certainly been given some ground for their fears by the appointment of Björnson, who is regarded as Sweden's worst enemy and is on the committee which is to award the prizes. The truth of the matter is that the members of the Nobel family who are trying to break the will are supported by the conservatives here, even by some members of the government.[1]

So far my correspondent, who indicated that these communications were confidential, not designed for publication. Of course, as long as the matter was un-decided I did not give out the above information; but now, since the lawsuit was long ago decided in favor of the validity of the will, and the accompanying circumstances have become an open secret, I may be permitted to regard the injunction of privacy as removed. But it is a matter of universal interest to see how picayune politics everywhere harbors suspicions and enmities, and how, in general, the " conservatives " are distrustful of the peace movement and kindred matters. Now the Swedish-Norwegian controversy has been settled; Björnson is no longer counted as an enemy of Sweden. He received from the hand of the King himself the

[1] Also, as I have learned from other sources, by the King himself. — B. S.

Nobel prize for literature, and, in company with Eman-
uel Nobel, dined at the royal table, on which occasion
Oscar II conversed in the most friendly spirit with the
Norwegian bard.

The first distribution of the prizes took place on the
tenth of October, 1901, the anniversary of Nobel's
death. At commemorative exercises in Stockholm the
King himself delivered to the laureates the four prizes
assigned by the Swedish Academy. The peace prize
was awarded by the Nobel committee of the Storthing.

In the eight years that have passed since then the
peace prize has been awarded as follows: 1901, Frédéric
Passy and Henri Dunant;[1] 1902, Élie Ducommun and
Albert Gobat; 1903, William Randal Cremer; 1904,
Institut du droit international; 1905, Bertha von
Suttner; 1906, President Theodore Roosevelt; 1907,
Ernesto Teodoro Moneta and Louis Renault; 1908,
K. P. Arnoldson and M. F. Bajer.

[1] I observe that the division of the prize corresponds neither to the letter
of the will nor to the testator's intentions, which I knew well.

LII

FIRST HALF OF THE YEAR 1897

HERE let a few specimens from my collections of letters be reproduced. Some weeks before the annual meeting of my Union, which took place early in January, 1897, I applied to various personages, asking for communications to be read; and I received numerous replies, among them the following:

Political Department of the Swiss Confederation, Bern

December 10, 1896

My dear Madam:

Your letter of the fifth instant was duly received, and I thank you most sincerely for the congratulations therein conveyed from the Austrian Society of the Friends of Peace to the Swiss government.

The Parliament indeed follows with genuine interest the philanthropic endeavors to spare the civilized world the horrors of war, and it joins with great sympathy in the demonstrations that aim to make nations comprehend the priceless advantage of peace.

In expressing to you the best wishes for the complete success of your general assembly, permit me, my dear Madam, once more to thank you heartily and to assure you of my distinguished consideration.

The President of the Swiss Confederation

Lachen

FIRST HALF OF THE YEAR 1897

International Peace Bureau
Secretary's Office
Honored Colleague: Bern, December 9, 1896

Every isolated effort of the friends of peace resembles those tiny globules of mist, the condensation of which will afterwards form the rain for which the caravan is yearning. These particles are not noticeable; no one heeds them, and when the cooling rain is falling the atoms that so patiently worked to constitute it are no longer remembered.

"Who cares for that," say our faithful prophets, "if only it rains?"

For more than five years the Austrian Society of the Friends of Peace has been resolutely pushing forward, and its efficacy has been gaining in breadth without losing anything in depth. It will have a significant share in the final success of our united effort, and it desires, just as we all do, nothing else than that the law of international peace may some day appear as much a matter of course and as self-originated as the law of gravity and the light of the sun.

In those happy days the peace unions and peace bureaus will exist only as mere traces in the recollection of a few archivists, who will have made the discovery that there were, in that strange epoch of cannons, anti-cannon endeavors also.

Accept for yourself, honored colleague, and for your worthy fellow-workers, the assurance of my perfect consideration and high attachment.   Ducommun
Honorary Secretary of the International Peace Bureau

Brussels, Chamber of Representatives
My dear Baroness: Office of the President, October 13, 1896

I was absent from Brussels when your letter of the fourth arrived, and I reached home too late to be able to send in season the lines desired for the meeting.

It is now certain that Brussels will have the sequel of Budapest in the course of the coming summer. I hope that on this occasion we shall have the honor of seeing you again. This would greatly delight Madame Beernaert as well as myself.

Accept, etc. Beernaert

Nice, December 6

. . . King Humbert told me that he had heard with great pleasure the fine results of the Peace Congress in Budapest. "I am for peace," said his Majesty; "Italy needs peace, and you see that now a more friendly understanding with France is coming about."

My best greetings to all of the old fellow-combatants

S. Türr

At that time somewhat strained relations existed between France and England. I had learned that Gladstone's friend, our proved fellow-worker Philip Stanhope, was introducing an act which had for its object the improvement of the relations between the two countries. I wrote him asking for detailed information and received the following reply:

Dear Frau von Suttner: Algiers, December 11, 1896

I am unfortunate in always being away from home when you do me the honor of writing me, and so it happens that your letter of November 23 reached me only day before yesterday.

It is correct that I am among those who are at the present time working for a combination to improve the relations between France and England. You, who follow with such keen attention the development of public opinion, are in a position to appreciate the dangerous tendency in those relations which has recently developed, especially in a portion of the press. These influences are difficult to resist, and the work required will demand much time and energy. The combination [1] of which you have heard is as yet only sketched in very indefinite outlines; but on the reassembling of Parliament on the twentieth of January we hope to make some progress, and I will send you accurate details.

As regards the Venezuelan affair, the treaty in settlement of it

[1] The union, *Entente cordiale*, for the bettering of Franco-English relations, due to the initiative of Representative Thomson and the Honorable Philip Stanhope, under the chairmanship of Lord Dufferin. — B. S.

has been definitely concluded between England and the United States; and we are just in receipt of the news that it has been accepted by the government of Venezuela. So this question is in a fair way to be settled by arbitration; and as regards that far greater question, namely, the conclusion of a general and permanent treaty between the two powers, President Cleveland in his message to Congress of December 7 announces that the negotiations touching it are on the point of coming to a favorable and definite conclusion.

So as soon as I reach London for the opening of Parliament, I hope to be in a position to send you a fuller résumé of this question, — which we may expect will then be definitely decided, — together with all the details that you may desire.

Accept, etc.

Philip Stanhope

The contents of these letters have a historical interest, as they show how leading men in influential positions were all the time working to bring the postulates of the peace movement to validity. On the other hand, these varied and occasional fragments from my extensive store of letters have also a biographical interest, for they mirror the course of development of that cause which ever more and more was becoming my vocation, my very life, my "one important thing"! And I was enabled to find therein such profound contentment for the reason that I knew I was in harmony with so many and such a rapidly increasing number of noble contemporaries, and especially in complete unanimity of soul with an endlessly beloved and loving life companion. Every inward experience and every outward event aroused in us both the same feelings. And therewithal was that full consciousness of peace, that absolute sense of security against all that might happen, which we feel when we know that there is a heart in whose fidelity we may have absolute confidence, a breast in which we may find a refuge from all the bitterness of fate — in a word, the boundless happiness of unconditional unity of love.

On the eleventh of January, 1897, the permanent arbitration treaty, which had been so long in preparation, between England and the United States was signed by Ambassador Sir Julian Pauncefote and Secretary of State Olney. President Cleveland designated the event as the beginning of a new era of civilization. The golden pen with which the treaty was signed was deposited in the National Museum. Queen Victoria said in her address from the throne that she hoped the example would be imitated in other countries. In the daily press and among the general public the news attracted no attention whatever.

It is true this first attempt did not come to fruition. The treaty had to be ratified before it could be made effective. In order that a law may be passed or an agreement become valid a two-thirds majority in the American Senate is required. When the arbitration treaty with England came up for ratification, three votes were lacking of this two-thirds majority, and thus it was defeated.

This in no respect altered the main significance of the fact that it was signed by the representatives of both governments; the forces that brought about the drawing up and signing of the treaty would in time also overcome the opposition of the Senate.

An insurrection breaks out on the island of Crete. Kanea is burning. The villages in the vicinity are on fire. Skirmishes between Turks and Greeks are taking place. Who began it? No matter; the island of Crete declares that it will shake off the Turkish yoke and join Greece. Street demonstrations in Athens; tremendous excitement. The Chamber in its session of February 25 votes to send war ships to Crete.

Something new makes its appearance, — the "Concert of the Powers." The powers unite to restore order and quiet in Crete and guarantee Cretan autonomy.

In the entries in my diary during April, 1897, I find an echo of the way in which these proceedings were conducted. Let me introduce a few passages here:

That was an Easter gift! — the outbreak of hostilities between Greece and Turkey. So then the "Concert of the Powers" was unable or *unwilling* to hinder the misfortune? Probably both. In the circles of diplomacy and the regents neither power nor will are as yet sufficiently developed in the direction of the spirit of peace; they still remain under the curse of the thousand-year-old Genius of War.

That the war was so long controlled, that it is now to be localized, that the "European Concert" will prevent the general conflagration, — this is a victory of

the New. That the war broke out at all, that the
powers look on and hesitate to interfere, — this is a
victory of the Old.

It is clearly shown how necessary and advantageous
at the present time an effective European code of laws,
a European tribunal, *one* European army, would be.
The embryo of these things has shown itself, to be
sure, but the development into a strong, healthy, living
thing is yet to be.

Yes, tendencies toward a federation of the civilized
countries are included in the "Concert." If this has
gone forward with little harmony and unsteady step,
the fault lies in this fact: it is the might of the mighty,
not the rights of the weak, that they want to support.
Much stress is laid on the consideration that is due
the will represented by the great powers, not on the
consideration that should be given the cause of the
weak. Compassion, righteousness, and liberty, — that
is the triad that must lie at the basis of a genuine
peace concert!

A picture from the campaign: Wild flight of the
Greeks. For miles and miles around the darkness of
the night was illuminated by the flashes of the shots
which the fugitives in wild confusion fired at one
another. Horses, becoming unmanageable under the
blows of the whip, dashed off and overturned the
wagons with all their contents. Helpless men and
wailing women everywhere, over whom the fugitives,

impelled by despair, like wild hordes, recklessly trampling everything and everybody under foot, dashed away through the night. . . .

In the meantime, while the war is raging on one side, in perfect silence the conflicts obviated by arbitration are increasing in number. The controversy between the United States and England as to the Guiana boundary, and a similar controversy between France and Brazil, have been submitted to arbitration, the former on the fifth, the latter on the tenth, of April.

A war cloud, however, is rising between Great Britain and the Transvaal. Will public opinion be influenced strongly enough by our friends in England to avert the danger?

Egidy writes me that he has applied to the Spanish ambassador in Berlin with regard to the cry for help from Barcelona.[1]

About that time I received the following letter from Prince Scipione Borghese, the same who ten years later was to make the great automobile trip from Pekin to Paris:

London, April 28, 1897

My dear Baroness:

Accept my heartiest thanks for your most encouraging letter, which was sent to me here from Rome.

[1] Prisoners charged with being anarchists were tortured in the fortress of Montjuich. A letter, dated March 11, and signed Sebastian Sunjé, addressed to "all good men of the earth," came to light: "Oh, by all that is sacred to you, rescue us from the hands of our torturers." But alas! the "good men of the earth" are not organized, are not ready to be mobilized. They can only shudder.

The trifling service that I have done for the ideal of peace is only a shadow compared to what in greatness and brilliancy other and better men have done for the progress of mankind. In my opinion this perpetual struggling forward toward a better and more righteous life must be the end and aim of all our actions.

I am happy to be able to come into direct alliance with you, and I hope very much to make your personal acquaintance soon.

In the meantime, my dear Baroness, I remain respectfully,

Your most devoted Scipione Borghese

Our literary labors do not rest. My husband is putting the last touches to *Sie wollen nicht*, and I am beginning the novel *Marthas Kinder* ("Martha's Children"), the second part of *Die Waffen nieder*, having just finished the translation of an English book, "Marmaduke, Emperor of Europe." *Die Waffen nieder* is appearing in a French translation in the *Indépendance belge*.

This same translation two years later was issued in book form by Zola's publisher, Tasquelles (Charpentier). From the French public came now many newspaper notices and private letters which showed me that the theme treated in that book was waking a loud echo among contemporaries in other countries.

In May, 1897, I received from London, from the ecclesiastical Arbitration Alliance, a letter asking if I would be willing to present to the Emperor of Austria a copy of an address which a hundred and seventy dignitaries of the Church were sending to all rulers. I assented, and thereupon received the document, a beautifully engrossed copy of the text in a tasteful roll, with the autograph signatures of the petitioners. A special copy was provided for every potentate. At the head of the hundred and seventy names, which comprised only high ecclesiastical dignitaries, were the Archbishop of Dublin, the bishops of Ripon, Durham, and Killaloe, Queen Victoria's chaplain, and others.

I applied at the office of the cabinet for an audience, and it was granted for the third of June at ten o'clock in the morning. I was obliged to state the object of my desire in my request for an audience.

On the day set, at the appointed hour, I presented myself in the imperial palace, accompanied by the vice president of my Union. There was a perfect swarm of uniforms in the anteroom to the audience chamber. Generals and staff officers were awaiting their turn to be summoned. We were not kept waiting long. When the door opened to permit the personage who had just been with the Emperor to pass out, we were immediately summoned. This preference was not at all due to the fact that the presiding officers of the Peace Society were bringing an "arbitration petition," but simply because my escort was a prince (at court everything goes by rank and title).

I had my artistic-looking roll in my hands and a well-prepared speech on my tongue, — which at the crucial moment completely failed me, — and we passed through the door, which was held open by an adjutant and closed behind us. The Emperor was standing by

his writing table and he took a few steps to meet us.
After a low, courtly bow, which I am under the impression was a success, I gave utterance to my desire. My
escort added a few explanatory words, and I handed
the Emperor the document; he received it with a
kindly smile. When I told him that the address was
concerning an international arbitration tribunal he
replied: "That would indeed be very fine . . . ; it is
difficult however . . ." Then a few questions to us both,
the assurance that the document would be carefully
read and considered, an inclination of the head, with
a gracious "I thank you," and we were dismissed.

Here is the text of the petition which we presented,
and which is now buried in the archives:

> To his Majesty Franz Joseph I
>
> Emperor of Austria, Apostolic King of Hungary
>
> Blessing and Grace and Peace!   King of Bohemia, etc.

In common with other organizations of the Christian Church we
are taking the liberty of appearing, in all humility, before your Majesty,
as the monarch of a great and mighty people, for the purpose of calling your Majesty's attention to the method of peaceful solution of
such difficulties as may arise between the nations of the earth.

The spectacle which Christian peoples present as they face each
other with portentous armaments, ready at the slightest challenge to
go to war and settle their differences by the shedding of blood, is, to
say the least, a stain on the glorious name of Christ.

We cannot, without the deepest pain, look upon the horrors of war,
with all the evils which it brings in its train, such as unscrupulous
sacrifice of human life, which should be regarded as sacred; bitter
poverty in so many homes; destruction of valuable property; inter-
ruptions in the education of the young and in the development of
the religious life; and general brutalization of the people.

Even when war is avoided, the presence of a powerful army withdraws vast numbers of men from family life as well as from the productive occupations of peace; moreover, in order to support this state of things, heavy burdens must be laid upon the people. It is also true that the settlement of international differences by force of arms does not rest on the principles of right and justice, but on the barbarous principle of the triumph of the stronger.

What encourages us to recommend this matter to your Majesty's benevolent consideration is the fact that already so much has been accomplished; as, for example, in the settlement of the *Alabama* question by the Geneva Court of Arbitration, or in the deliberations of the American Conference at Washington, not to mention other important cases. Happy for the world will be the time when all international controversies shall find their peaceful solution!

This is what we are earnestly striving for. Regarding the ways and means for attaining this end we refrain from all special suggestions, confidently intrusting to your Majesty's superior intuition and wisdom all details in the domain of political life.

We offer our prayers that the richest blessings of the Prince of Peace may rest upon your Majesty's realm and people, and especially on your Majesty.

I learned how the petition was presented to the other rulers. Frédéric Passy presented it to the President of the French republic. In Switzerland the President received it from Élie Ducommun; the President of the Confederation declared that the contents of the address corresponded perfectly with his ideas and those of the Parliament. Dr. Trueblood, of Boston, undertook the service for America, Marcoartu for Spain, and the address was presented to the Queen of England by Lord Salisbury. The Tsar also received it, but I do not know through whom.

The petitioners themselves could scarcely have expected that the action would have an immediate effect. Words of this kind scattered abroad are seeds of grain, or, by a better figure of speech, hammer blows. New ideas are like nails; old conditions and institutions are like thick walls. So it is not enough to hold up the sharp nail and give it one blow; the nail must be hit hundreds and hundreds of times, and on the head too, that it may be firmly fixed at last.

LIII

SECOND HALF OF THE YEAR 1897

THE enthusiasm for the peace cause which had flamed up at the Millennial Festival in Hungary had not proved to be merely a fire in the stubble, as so many pessimists had predicted it would be. I kept getting news of the progress and growth of the group in that country. The following letter bears witness to the opinions of one of the most brilliant members of the Congress, Count Eugen Zichy:

My dear Baroness,   Vienna, December 4, 1897

Most honored President:

To-morrow our delegations break up, and it has not been my good fortune, during our several weeks' *séjour* here in Vienna, to see you. Twice I have made the attempt — alas! in vain. You were out of town — still in the country! So I will at least send you in writing my hearty respects and greeting. You must have read with delight Berzeviczy's utterances in our delegation, and have rejoiced, likewise, at the reply made thereto by our skillful and masterly (*takt- und sattelfest*) Minister of Foreign Affairs. Great ideas are realized only slowly, but a healthy seed always brings healthy fruit, even if, as often happens, it takes a long time ; so it is with the idea for which you, dear

161

Baroness, and all of us are fighting. *Gutta cavat lapidem !* Over and over, and ever unweariedly, we must renew the battle, and at length it will, it must, win the day; for our aim is humanitarian, — the welfare of mankind.

And an idea that has this for its only object is not to become effectual? Impossible! That is the answer that hovers on my tongue, and "impossible" will at length be the shout of all reasonable human beings! And we shall be victorious! And the victory will then really be — universal peace! And even if the present does not recognize it, posterity will remember with gratitude those who turned the first sod.

I understand that in a few days — I believe about the middle of December — you are to hold your annual meeting in Vienna. Permit me, dear Baroness, to send my sincerest respects, and to beg of you to communicate to our peace friends my warmest greetings and good wishes. May your work be blessed!

I hope, dear Baroness, that you may for a long time to come have the most abundant health and strength to share in bringing your work to completion. And for my own self I desire that you continue to grant me your favor and good will, which I so highly prize.

May the Angel of Peace be with you and your work!

Your most faithful fellow-worker and admirer

Eugen Zichy

This year the meetings of the peace workers were not held, as hitherto, in the same place, but in different towns. The Congress met from the twelfth to the sixteenth of August at Hamburg, and the interparliamentarians had their sessions a few days earlier in Brussels.

We took part in the Hamburg gathering. Again we met all our old friends, — Passy, Türr, Bajer, Émile Arnaud, Dr. Richter, Moneta, Hodgson Pratt, Ducommun, and others. We had anticipated that the chairmanship of the Hamburg Congress would be taken by the writer of exquisite verses, Prince Schö-naich-Carolath, but he declined to take it, though he was suggested for the office. What his reasons were may be seen from the following letter:

Haseldorf, July 19, 1897

Highly honored, gracious Baroness:

Allow me to thank you cordially for your friendly lines. The expectation that in all human probability I should be permitted to greet you in Hamburg has caused me much happiness, even though I look toward the Congress with a kind of solemn enthusiasm. Your kindly supposition that I have been intrusted with the chairmanship is in so far correct that the Hamburg local group at first, as I heard, thought of conferring that honor upon me. Later, I believe, a more official personage was found, and this saved me from declining with thanks; for I have not the gift of speech and the acquaintance with parliamentary usages requisite for the performance of the duties of such a position.

My wife and I regret that we cannot have the honor of seeing you and your honored husband at our house; my wife's health unfortunately makes it impossible for her to entertain company in Hamburg as she had hoped. If ever Copenhagen should be selected for a peace gathering, we shall venture to ask you again, either before or after the Congress, to honor us with a visit in our more hospitable Danish home.

Begging you to remember me most warmly to the Baron, and with regards to yourself, gracious and kindly Baroness,

I sign myself yours devotedly

E. Schönaich-Carolath

A new fellow-champion came upon the arena, — Moritz von Egidy. It was a source of pride and satisfaction to me that I had won him over to take part in the Congress and to assist our cause by the fascinating

power of his eloquence in the public meeting which
had been arranged by the Congress.

At the first session, — all present being under the
influence of the painful news, just received from Spain,
of the assassination of Prime Minister Cánovas by an
Italian anarchist, — Teodoro Moneta, in conjunction
with R. Raqueni, editor of *Il Epoca*, in the name of
the Italian group offered the following resolution:

The undersigned, citizens of the country from which, unhappily,
came the fanatic who has murdered the Prime Minister of Spain,
urge that the Congress, before it begins its labors, transmit to the
widow of Cánovas del Castillo the expression of its profound sympathy. Devoted to doctrine which involves the harmonization of
politics and morals, we insist that under no conditions must the
principle of the inviolability of human life be transgressed, for on
this principle our whole existence and the lofty aims that the Peace
League has in view are based.

The public meeting, which took place on the first
evening, brought together in the hall of the Sagebiel
establishment an audience of five thousand of all ranks.
Otto Ernst made the opening address. Then Richard
Feldhaus recited a poem by Schmidt-Cabanis. And
then Egidy. This was the first time I had ever heard
him speak. Clear, assured, deliberate, vibrant, powerful.
The real voice of command. " Be good ! " is an injunction which is usually whispered mildly or spoken in an
unctuous, preachifying tone; Egidy thundered it out
like a command. The gist of his address was:

We must grow into the unmilitary age which we are fighting to
bring about. A new mode of thought must take possession of our

inmost being. War predicates the hostile opposition of man to man. We must oppose this hostility and put in its place the feeling of solidarity (*Zusammengehörigkeit*). In this soil is to grow the natural equality of all people and all peoples. This equality of birth leads to the right of every one in the nation, and of every nation taken collectively, to determine its own career under the limitations made by the duties that each one has in turn toward the whole. In a certain sense we have already entered upon the warless age; but we do not realize its blessings because we have not the courage to meet the transformation.

Egidy spoke also of other conflicts besides those of war:

The conflict between employers and employees, between consumers and producers, must cease. To every person in the community must be assured a dignified existence. Then every conflict will cease. In the unions we already have the beginnings of it. . . . Credal relationships must become different. The faith of the individual must be respected, but the discrepant evaluation and persecution of individual forms of belief must cease.

The French artillery captain, Gaston Moch, who was present at the Congress, was so delighted by the former Prussian lieutenant colonel that he subsequently published a book, *L'Ère sans violence*, in which he introduced Egidy's doctrine and way of looking at things, together with several translations from his articles and speeches.

At the second session I announced that a new adherent had joined us, — Jean Henri Dunant, the founder of the Geneva Convention of the Red Cross. I stated that he would use his influence in the Red Cross societies so as to work through them for our cause, especially in the Oriental nations, amongst whom the Red Cross numbered many adherents and to whom a special appeal was to be directed in all the Oriental languages. I presented the text of this appeal. Dunant had sent it to me with a request that I should give it my signature and win the sanction of the Congress.

General Türr announced that he was prepared to procure its translation into Turkish and to have it disseminated.

Here are a few extracts from my diary:

August 14. Banquet given by the city at the Horticultural Show. My neighbors are Egidy and a senator. Three hundred persons present. Egidy as a table companion does not show his apostle or popular-preacher side; he is a jolly, amusing companion, versed in the usages of the best society.

August 16. Yesterday, after a session which was adjourned early, about five o'clock in the afternoon, we took a trip down the harbor and made an excursion to Blankenese. What a rush of traffic in the colossal harbor! What a host of ships docking and discharging! Our party had supper on the Süllberg; My Own was toastmaster. Novikof, Trueblood, and Ducommun made addresses. A general feeling of enthusiasm. It was after eleven o'clock when we got down to the float. The road was illuminated with Bengal lights. As the steamboat put off, the Süllberg

Restaurant was so brightly lighted up that it looked as if it were bathed in fire. Music on the ship; as we sailed along, rockets flew up into the air against the cloudless, moonlit sky. These are the old instruments for celebrating, — toasts, music, fireworks, — which are indeed also employed in the celebrations of battle anniversaries; but how differently they act when they are accompaniments to the feelings of fraternity, of prospective redemption, — redemption from the curse of slaughter and hatred. . . .

I will also copy the advice which Dr. Wagner, a Hamburg author and journalist, gave us. "It seems to me of dubious value," he said, "for the Congresses to indulge in long and tedious debates over resolutions for the future, and merely to vote on them, perhaps with trifling majorities. Debates bring to the main issue more confused rubbish than serious, valuable thoughts. It would seem to me a far more useful activity for the cause if the members were presented with a series of vigorous reports and speeches, which, when accepted by the Congress after discussion, should be printed and disseminated as pamphlets in tens, nay hundreds, of thousands of copies, and also brought before the governments and parliaments."

At the final session Lisbon was suggested as the next place for holding the Congress. The Interparliamentary Union, which had met at Brussels, decided upon Lisbon as the place for their 1898 meeting. But it was to result differently.

How did things look in the rest of the world while the debates regarding arbitration and peace were going on in Brussels and Hamburg? Of the "peace negotiations" between Turkey and Greece no end is in sight. Spain also is still a prey to discords. Fresh troops are constantly being sent off to America, and the reports from there announce terrible and increasing losses through sickness. Protests are raised in the country, among them that of Silvela, that concessions ought to be made to the Cubans, that a *convenio* with them should be entered into. But the government remains inexorable: First surrender, then talk of reform may be in order. This attitude wins much applause in the European press. "Liberal policy," so run the leading articles, "is admissible in times of peace; in times of war it is equivalent to abdication. Besides, the moment would be ill chosen to make the United States any gift or concessions. All Europe is stirred by her aggressive and extravagant policy, and all Europe has an interest in seeing Spain stand firm. The government is, therefore, right in paying no heed to timorous and interested proposals. The undeviating policy which the Prime Minister has chosen, and to which he clings, is alone worthy of a statesman."

So stubbornness, despotism, uninterrupted sacrifice of the country's sons and the country's money, — that is the only worthy attitude! And such views are borne out in millions of sheets from the editors' tables. Lucky for these gentlemen that there are no great public scales in which their responsibility might be weighed!

The Minister Plenipotentiary of the United States, General Woodford, came to Spain in order to offer the services of his government for intervention, so that an end might be made of the Cuban war. The press and public opinion (it is well known how that is created!) assume a very hostile attitude to the American ambassador, who cannot understand it. Why should Spain decline mediation which would put an end to a war ruinous to the country? — Yes, why? As if ruin of country and people were to be taken into account when national pride is involved!

The Emperor and Empress of Russia were to spend the month of October in Darmstadt. I find in my correspondence a letter from Frau Büchner, the daughter-in-law of the author of *Kraft und Stoff*, who was *persona grata* with the late Princess Alice of Hesse, mother of the young Tsaritsa.

Gracious and honored Lady: Darmstadt, Feburary 13, 1897

Your very charming letter has made me more than happy, and I should have willingly answered it immediately to tell you how ready I am to fulfill your wish; but only to-day do I get to it. I have considered the matter from every side; it can be managed only in case the Empress should be here. It is expected here that she will take up her residence this summer at Castle Seeheim, near Darmstadt. If that should happen, my husband thinks that he might smuggle the book[1] in through a chamberlain with whom he is personally acquainted.

[1] *Schach der Qual.* I had cherished the wish to bring to the Tsar's attention the chapter entitled *Frohbotschaft* (" Good Tidings ") containing the invitation to a conference of the powers. — B. S.

But I myself have no confidence in this scheme, for the gentleman in question seems to me not at all equal to the responsibility. I think the book should be sent directly to the Empress here in Germany, where watchfulness and exclusiveness are not so absolutely punctilious. Then the name of a Baroness Suttner would assuredly help it to make its own way.

That would not work in Russia, even through the mediation of the court here, — that is to say, of any person connected with it. Our sovereigns here are still young and take little interest in anything in particular, and consequently play no great rôle.

Oh, if a Grand Duchess Alice were still alive who made it her special purpose to support noble efforts, to look out for the general good, and to establish truly benevolent institutions! That wise woman had sympathy with the burgher class, and from it she selected her most efficient forces; and a Luise Büchner was her right hand in her useful undertakings. How easy such a matter would have been then! And yet even at that time my father-in-law did not get on with her sister, the Empress Frederick; she was very much interested in his works, and caused this to be intimated to him, and so he sent her the book of the two crowned Liberals, but she never again let him hear from her. And she was a comparatively liberally educated English princess!

Even here little is known about the character and opinions of the young Empress of Russia. From all that is heard it seems that the dowager Empress there wields the scepter, and it is said she has not become reconciled to the fact that her daughter-in-law is a German princess.

So the young woman will have little to say in her country. Nevertheless, I will let no opportunity pass of executing your commission; perhaps it will be more successful than I can now count upon. Perhaps, also, the Empress has inherited something of her mother's energy and capacity and will be able in time to win a position and to maintain it. In that case I am firmly convinced that her influence will be good, since nothing but good has ever been heard regarding her character.

I have not lately told you that I know and prize your husband's works also — especially the fresh, thrilling tales in *Die Kinder des*

SECOND HALF OF THE YEAR 1897

Kaukasus. Those wonderfully beautiful descriptions of nature have constantly brought before my eyes your own idyllic life there. It must be splendid to live in such a lovely land when you have the genuine, inspired feeling for such beauty. In fact, I think often of your life, your habits, your environment; just because you are both such talented people you must get double the enjoyment out of everything. Only I had always imagined that you lived in beautiful, gay Vienna; so I was greatly astonished that you were in the country. I was obliged to overturn your whole surroundings, — that is, as they existed in my imagination, — and conjure up a quite different frame for the picture of your life. In doing this I was helped by your *Einsam und arm*; that must have been written at Castle Harmannsdorf.

I should so like to know whether you took for Karl Binsemann a model out of real life. This interested me so very much because generally in real life it is just the opposite : As a rule a man who is in unfortunate circumstances is a reformer in his youth ; it is then he has the genuine sacred fire for righteousness. By the time he reaches old age he becomes weary, indifferent, and selfish, by reason of cares or the eternal monotony of his days. Then he says to himself, " What is the use of puzzling one's brains over insoluble enigmas, what is the good of becoming indignant over injustice — it does not prevent it ! "

Of course I am speaking of men of the same rank in life and the same grade of culture as a Binsemann. If this figure were taken from life, or at least suggested by a prototype, it would make the book much dearer to me, because I have always believed that it is not in accordance with life for any one to be thoughtless of such things in his youth, and in old age to begin, for the first time, to think rightly. The descriptions are so true to reality, and everything is so vivid, that one cannot help feeling, just as in reading *Die Waffen nieder*, that they must be taken directly from life.

My father-in-law was greatly delighted to hear from you again. All the cordial greetings from yourself and your husband are most cordially reciprocated.

In the hope of being able to carry out your commission success-fully, I am   Yours with deepest respect

    Marie Büchner

During the month of November the Dreyfus case made the whole world hold its breath. My Own and I followed the affair with the greatest interest and sympathy. At that time Scheurer-Kestner, Bernard Lazare, and Émile Zola came out in favor of the reopening of the trial. The *Figaro* had published Esterhazy's autograph; it was an ocular demonstration that the handwriting was the same as that on the *bordereau*. All the military, and especially the Anti-Semitic circles, were against a new trial. The interest which I took in the course of the affair is frequently reflected in my diary:

November 18. Probably the case will be taken up again. The mere possibility that the man banished to Devil's Island is innocent would be horrible, supposing the sentence should stand . . . and we are bound now to believe in this possibility. The public conscience would remain forever oppressed by this thought. . . . Again it has been strikingly shown that there is such a thing as a "European soul." A French journal remarks, in a peevish tone, about the many comments in other countries, " In the last analysis, the matter concerns France only."

No, no! such national exclusiveness has ceased in our day. If a catastrophe occurs in any country, — the assassination of a ruler, the burning of a charity bazaar, — expressions of sympathy stream in from all directions, making the afflicted country glad. But if it permits other countries to share in its good and evil fortunes, then it must also be willing that its right and wrong actions should be judged everywhere. The partisans of justice all over the world have an equal interest in the conquest of justice and truth over tyranny and concealment. And, vice versa, the partisans of authority, the race persecutors, are in the same camp all over the world; not only in France but also in Austria and everywhere are to be found passionate anti-Dreyfusards!

The two camps are growing more and more clearly divided. But the forces are very unequally distributed. The party that champions the right has certainly on its side the overwhelming power that is peculiar to its object, — universal human happiness; the other party has the actual power, however — has the cannon behind it. . . .

Power engenders pride. Everything is permitted to it — so it thinks — and it wishes to make manifest that it is bold enough to attempt anything. So the whole Esterhazy investigation, the Esterhazy trial, and the shameful Esterhazy apotheosis are a pure satire on every judicial proceeding, a slap in the face of august Justice, — even more, a trampling of her scales under the spur-armed heel of the soldier's boot! The people must knuckle under, — that must be borne in upon them so that another time the desire may pass of pulling down the General Staff's sacred ensign of error! You wanted to run up against a *res judicata*, did you? Very well, now you have two of them. And quite right; the people knuckled under. "The affair is at an end " (*Affaire liquidée* is the heading over the leading articles in the papers); but a man got up and uttered the cry of his soul, — *J'accuse*, — one man against an army! The far-distant ages to come will praise this heroic action.

Even in our family circle there were disputes about the affair. My father-in-law, the conservative-minded, ardent reader of *Das Vaterland*, would hear nothing of the proofs in favor of the exile. He also believed in the "Jewish syndicate" that was bent on buying the rehearing. And my mother-in-law had nothing good to say about Zola; she had even gone so far once as to make a great auto-da-fé of such of his books as had strayed into the house.

The year 1897 closes with an event that might well arouse much anxiety among the partisans of peace. We know how it began, but we can never know how it will end; it carries war in its womb, for it is once more something undertaken under the emblem of force, — the voyage of the fighting squadron to the Yellow Sea.

So then . . . Port Arthur besieged by the Russians, Kiauchau by the Germans, — that is the newly created situation. High Politics, that is fifty or sixty men and a following of newspapers, see to it that there shall never be any rest, that no progress can ever be made toward the healing of internal troubles, the elevation of human society. A cruel state of things for the champions of peace! For years there have been perpetual wars and rumors of wars, even while in the governmental circles there were constant assurances of peace. Japan and China, the Venezuela controversy, Spain and Cuba, Armenian massacres, Italy and Africa, Greece and Turkey, England and India, and now this East-Asiatic expedition! And all the time constantly increasing armaments and paroxysms over fleets. No wonder that the slow, as it were subterranean, peace movement remains unobserved by the masses.

LIV

A STIRRING HALF YEAR

Outbreak of the Spanish-American War · Article in mourning borders ·
Fridtjof Nansen's lecture in Vienna · Extracts from diary · Bereavement
in the family, Countess Lotti Sizzo's death · Johann von Bloch's book ·
Death of Bismarck · End of the Spanish-American War

THE beginning of the year 1898 brought me much
anxiety. Not domestic anxiety or heart sorrow or
worry about money. My troubles — faithfully shared
indeed by my husband — were far away from Harmannsdorf; they were on the distant ocean.

The United States warship, the *Maine*, blows up.
The suspicion is rife that the ship was destroyed by
the Spaniards; can it be true? In heaven's name, what
is not possible among men, who in general regard hate
and slaughter as "political" weapons? In American
jingo circles there is a mad craze to declare war on
Spain as a punishment for this — "unproved" — crime.
I have direct information that in government circles
(with McKinley at the head) as well as in wide circles
among the people, the peace sentiment is strong. In
Spain also there is excitement, in the name of national
honor. The journals *Globo* and *Liberal* (how everything
calls itself liberal!) regard any concession in the Cuban
question, any acceptance of an indemnity, as out of
reason, — rather, utter ruin, "rather let us all perish!"

And the Bishop of Madrid heads a subscription for the purchase of battle ships.

Long the scales waver this way and that. Our friends in America and also in Europe put forth their utmost efforts. Petitions are sent to McKinley, to the Queen Regent — but in vain. The May number of my magazine appeared with a black border, and printed the following text on the front page:

Bordered with mourning black we present here the tidings that in the last week of April, 1898 — so short a time before the entrance of a new century — the grewsome fury and bearer of the old barbarism is again let loose.

What makes our trouble harder to endure is this: America, the cradle and shelter of the peace movement — America, which scarcely a year ago was on the point of putting into vigorous actuality the long-cherished ideal of the first permanent arbitration treaty — America, which is unacquainted with militarism — America must be the field where war is let loose!

By that outbreak the signal for a universal war may have been given, for who can foresee the consequences? There is a fire; the burning rafters are flying, and all our roofs are thatched with straw — with petroleum-soaked straw.

Once again has the mighty Ancient won the victory over the as yet not sufficiently strengthened New. Again Force chooses to set itself up as the judge and avenger of sins committed by Force, and heaps up sins on sins all calling for revenge. Cruelty and oppression in Cuba; that was the long-continued accumulation of the "unendurable." Why could not the European Concert have swept this "unendurable" off the face of the earth? Because they will not grant the principle that peoples may be allowed to throw off the yoke.

Our movement has thus suffered a heavy blow. All the opposing elements are triumphing, yet we must not allow the results of the work that has already been done to be obscured. The forms of those — both individuals and corporate bodies — who stand for the ideals of a time free from manslaughter and oppression, remain unbowed; their voices still ring out loud and clear; their light, be it the torch swung high or a modest spark, still shines into the darkness. The present, though still so dark, must not make our faith in a brighter future grow faint.

Yet even this faith does not help to deaden the pain of the days that are before us. Misfortune — though perhaps deserved, yet none the less severe — has overtaken our poor race during these spring days.

On the sixth of May the famous Arctic explorer Fridtjof Nansen came to Vienna, and gave a lecture that same evening in the hall of the Rathaus before two thousand people. We were prevented from going to the city, but I wrote Nansen the following letter, to reach him a few hours before the lecture:

Dear Sir, Harmannsdorf, May 5

Highly and sincerely honored:

You have no time to read long letters; so I can only indicate, without offering reasons, what I desire to ask. You will, I know, meet with perfect sympathy what is only half said.

A new era must be dawning for the world, — after the old heroic age of war comes the heroic age of knowledge and investigation. Who would be better authorized than you to point out the way thither? This evening thousands of my fellow-countrymen will listen to you. I beg of you to weave into your lecture two lines which shall express this thought: the reign of war must yield; the future must belong to the right. The impression will be immense, just at this moment, when the sea is again desecrated with burning and exploding ships. Speak words like these and you will thus give the work of peace a powerful impulse forward.

With the most profound respect

Bertha von Suttner

The text of the lecture was published, from the manuscript, on the seventh of May, by the *Neue Freie*

Presse. In it there was no reference to general questions of civilization. On the other hand, *Das Tagblatt* published a report taken stenographically, and there it said:

Nansen brought his lecture to a close as follows: "People will ask, what are the results of polar explorations? I reply, science desires to know everything. There must be no spot on the earth unseen by a human eye and untrodden by a human foot. Man's lot is to fight the battle of light against darkness. There are still many problems to be solved. The time for great wars of conquest has passed; the time for conquests in the land of science, of the unknown, will last, and we hope that the future will bring us many more conquests, and thereby forward the interests of mankind."

Further entries in my diary during May echo all kinds of events from abroad:

. . . The great sea fight which the public of the arena is so anxiously awaiting is still unfought. Epidemics are breaking out in Cuba and the Philippines, and "the red cock," that dreadful bird, is flying from place to place. . . .

. . . The craze for fleets has also reached Austria. Enormous plans for strengthening the navy have been broached. Unions of the great industries are pleading for it. The slogan "Protection for exports" is throwing a mantle of political economy around the wish to pocket great profits from manufacturing and furnishing supplies. Nevertheless Switzerland has an export trade, and without a fleet, either!

. . . Debates over the increased price of grain. Of course the price of bread is not raised by the American war and the closely guarded boundaries! Oh, no! Our political economists know better. The Stock Exchange is to blame for everything; and a sure means for relief of the distress has been proposed by a friend of our mayor, — hang three thousand Jews; or, still better, grind up all the Jews for artificial fertilizer. This last proposition was only meant humorously — gentlemen can also be witty. . . .

. . . [The Dreyfus Affair.] The Zola case is to be brought once more into court. Esterhazy threatens to kill Picquart; the mob insults Zola—*à l'eau ! à l'eau!* — and the persecuting press again resumes its system of abuse and slander.

. . . In England the Colonial Secretary gives utterance to a speech which has brought the whole European press into turmoil. He said that war should have been declared against Russia long before. . . . The speech is universally pronounced unstatesmanlike. Well, yes, the accepted course is to prepare for war, make plans, bring it on, and scheme for it, — that the diplomatists do; but to call it by name in times of peace, oh, never! The customary method demands that one must speak of the familiar " good relations."

Chamberlain also jostles the Transvaal; he is bound that the sovereignty of England shall be recognized there. Kruger produces the text of treaties which make such a demand untenable, and suggests submitting the matter to an arbitration tribunal. Chamberlain and his organs haughtily announce that a question regarding Great Britain's right of sovereignty shall never under any conditions be submitted to arbitration. How far below par has the splendid thought, " Right instead of Might," everywhere fallen! The waves are hissing and roaring around it on all sides, are threatening to swallow it up; but this thought is a rock, — the billows will dash into spray and fall back, and the thought will tower on high.

Up till to-day (May 28) the two hostile fleets have not met. The great naval battle for which the whole body of spectators is waiting (glass-house owners who anxiously want to see how the stones fly) has not as yet taken place. Only a privateering game is played on the ocean. A prize court has been instituted in order to decide whether a ship is rightfully captured or not. Why not a court that shall discontinue the whole business of official piracy?

The month of June brought an unexpected bereavement into our family circle. One afternoon, I remember, my sister-in-law Lotti, the Countess Sizzo, came into our room and sank with a groan into an easy-chair. She held a great bunch of roses in her hand and had just come in from the garden, where she had got overheated in picking and watering the flowers. After a while she felt better, chatted quite gayly, and left us to go to her own room. There, as we were immediately informed, she fainted. She was put to bed. It was a slight stroke of apoplexy. A physician was summoned from Vienna. When he arrived she seemed better, and he announced that the invalid would be well in three weeks. It was about the twelfth of June, and with minds at rest we took our usual wedding anniversary excursion. When we got back our poor " Hendl " — this was my sister-in-law's nickname, but I do not know why she was called so — had grown decidedly worse. The Vienna doctor had come again and was now ordering constant application of ice bags to her head. The sisters took turns in caring for her, and My Own also spent many hours by Lotti's sick bed, for she seemed most grateful and happy to have her brother near her. On the eighth or tenth day the death agony began. The death rattle lasted from four o'clock in the afternoon until one at night. We were all gathered around her bed and in the next room, — the aged parents, the two sisters, Marianne and Luise, the families from Stockern, and also a cousin who had loved Lotti for years. I still see him before me as, hearing from the next room the heavy breathing, he staggered, leaned against the wall with outstretched arms like one crucified, and cried, " That is the end — the end ! "

And it was the end. The pastor was summoned. Then it lasted an hour or two longer; the rattling grew more subdued, the breathing less frequent, and the last sigh was drawn gently.

The next day the body was borne into the castle chapel. Clothed in white satin, with her golden hair unbound, roses in her folded hands, a celestial smile on her lips, she looked as young and as lovely as a bride.

Although I had lived so long, it was the first time I had ever seen the dead body of one whom I had known in life. All those whom I had lost from my own circle—my mother, Elvira, Fritz Fürstenberg, the Dedopali, Mathilde—had died when I was far away, and I had always avoided looking upon the dead who were indifferent to me.

Very soon indeed I was to see more dead—among them one who was my world. . . .

In July the news came of the appearance of a great work, in six volumes and in Russian, against war. The author was said to be a Russian state councilor, named Johann von Bloch. The book was entitled "The Future of War in its Technical, Economic, and Political Relations." A German translation was shortly to appear. Permission to publish it had been granted only a short time before, after the author had had an audience with the Tsar.

News of hunger riots comes from Italy and Spain. For a time the danger has been acute that a United States squadron would attempt to land troops in Spain.

The Dreyfus affair takes its course: ever clearer proofs of Esterhazy's guilt on the one hand, ever more insane adherence to *la chose jugée* on the other.

On the thirtieth of July comes the following entry in my diary:

Bismarck dead. The question arises whether the statesman is as yet born who shall be for the thought of humanity what Bismarck has been for German thought.

And a few days later:

In the cathedral 'at Berlin a funeral service is held at the Emperor's command. Court preacher Faber quotes from the favorite psalm of the departed. The text[1] runs:

> Let the high praises of God be in their mouth,
> And a two-edged sword in their hand;
> To execute vengeance upon the nations,
> And punishments upon the peoples;
> To bind their kings with chains,
> And their nobles with fetters of iron.

Sword and chains — well, yes, those were the Iron Chancellor's ideals. Now he belongs to the past. The future requires other symbols, — instead of blood-dripping iron, the light-streaming diamond.

The Spanish-American War is at an end. The hostilities ceased on the fourteenth of August.

And ten days later the world was surprised by an event, the account of which I must give in a new part of these memoirs.

[1] Psalm cxlix, 6–8. — Translator.

PART EIGHT
1898–1908

THE TSAR'S RESCRIPT

I WAS sitting in the summerhouse one beautiful August day, waiting for the arrival of the mail. My Own was in the habit of going himself to the postman to get the letters and newspapers that he brought. This was to me always the most interesting hour of the day.

This time he came back with flying steps and shining face and shouted, while still at a distance, " I am bringing the most magnificent, the most surprising news to-day . . ."

" What is it ? Have we made a ten-strike ? "

" Almost — listen ! ·This is what some one wrote in last evening's paper."

He sat down and read:

" ' The maintenance of general peace and a possible reduction of the excessive armaments which weigh upon all nations — ' "

" That is what we are always saying," I interrupted.

" ' present themselves in the existing condition of the

whole world as the ideal toward which the endeavors of all governments should be directed.'"

" Should be, but are not — "

"'The present moment would be very favorable for seeking, by means of international discussion, the most effectual means of insuring to all peoples the benefits of a real and lasting peace,— ' "

" That article must be by Passy or one of our friends."

" What a clever guess! — 'and, above all, of putting an end to the progressive development of armaments.' "

" Well, indeed — "

"'Hundreds of millions are devoted to acquiring terrible engines of destruction, which are destined to-morrow to lose all value in consequence of some fresh discovery in this field.' "

" That is nothing new."

"' National culture, economic progress, and the production of wealth are either paralyzed, or checked in their development. Economic crises, brought on in great measure by the system of developing armaments to the utmost, and the constant danger that lies in this massing of war material, are transforming the armies of our days into a crushing burden which the peoples have more and more difficulty in bearing.' "

" That article must have been written by a social democrat!"

" More clever than before! — 'It appears evident, then, that if this state of things is to be prolonged it will inevitably lead to the very catastrophe which it is desired to avert, and the very thought of whose horrors makes every man shudder.'"

" Not *every* man — "

"'To seek the means of warding off the calamities that are threatening the whole world is the supreme duty that is to-day imposed on all states.'"

"Yes, if only the rulers of states thought so!"

"Well, read for yourself — and rejoice!"

He handed me the paper — and what did I see? That was no article from socialistic or peace circles — it was an official document, addressed in the name of one of the highest war lords to all governments, with an invitation to meet in a conference which should have to deal with this "serious question" — a conference which — I cite the actual words — "would unite in one powerful combination the efforts of all states which are sincerely seeking to make the great idea of universal peace triumphant."

Was not that like a dream, like a fairy tale?

I recollect that hour which, after receiving these tidings, — truly "Good Tidings," as the chapter heading of *Schach der Qual* expressed it, — My Own and I spent together discussing the marvelous event from all sides; it was one of the loveliest hours of our lives. It was actually like counting over the amount of an unexpected windfall.

In the September number of my periodical I expressed my views regarding this event in the following words:

The news that stands at the head of this number, the Tsar's rescript, is the greatest event which, up to the present time, the peace movement has had to show. It has filled us all with jubilation, for the colossal, and at the same time the unexpected, overpowers. The tidings filled the rest of the world with astonishment, and indeed many (especially the friends of war) with apprehension.

Deep feeling is expressed in the young monarch's words. The conventionality of ordinary diplomatic phrases, which say nothing, is abandoned once for all. So the peace movement — and we have lived to see the day — has passed over into the sphere of accomplishment.

But the *raison d'être* of our societies is not abolished thereby. The Tsar's act proceeded only from the public spirit which of late has been so strongly wrought upon; and the support of public spirit, the organized demonstration of the popular will, is required in order to support this action which has come from so high a source, in order to overcome the hostile forces which will assuredly even now stand in the way.

On the whole, from our standpoint, the event cannot be estimated highly enough. One of the most powerful of rulers acknowledges the peace ideal, comes out as an opponent of militarism; from this time on the movement is incalculably nearer its goal; new ways are opening before it, and it is to be carried on to a new basis of operations.[1]

And in the next issue:

. . . Other periodicals may have already to a certain degree lost interest in the subject and may only treat it as a reality when the suggested conference takes place; but for us it does not mean a merely ephemeral event, but the most significant milestone in our history so far.

One of the most important and most difficult tasks of the peace societies — the making their purposes known — has been given a mighty boost, for from this time forth the knowledge thereof has not only penetrated into the masses but has also compelled the attention of every politician.

[1] *Die Waffen nieder*, VII, 344.

So in this respect the work is accomplished; but now comes the equally difficult task of assisting, according to our abilities, to secure the success of the conference, for the bringing about of which we have preached and voted so much.

Already pessimists and doubters and dealers in spiteful insinuations have arisen on all sides. "As if by a silent conspiracy a large part of the daily press has banded together for the annihilation of a plan which embraces the dearest hopes of humanity " (*Concord*). The great masses are as lacking in discretion and understanding regarding the rescript as they were in regard to the endeavors of the peace movement, the whole programme of which is contained in it in concentrated form.

One thing is forgotten in this controversy and dubiety. There is always an attempt made to calculate what is to be the result of the conference, and the marvelous fact is left unnoticed that the invitation itself — from such a quarter and with such a motive back of it — is really a triumph for the cause and instantly renders nugatory the hundreds of objections which have always been brought up against our endeavors under the pretext that it would be impossible for autocrats and the most powerful war lords ever to give up the growing armaments.

The settling up of the goal is now the great and cheering element in the event; the discussion of ways and means may be confidently left to those who are sincerely aiming to reach the goal. This is what our enemies feel, and that is why they throw doubt on the sincerity of the invitation. As if one could lie with such words ! The rescript is absolutely lacking in the vague sinuosities of diplomatic verbosity. As if anything said should not be directly examined and accepted for what it is ! That is the first right of every utterance of every ingenuous man who has not as yet been seduced into rascality.[1]

During the days following the publication of the rescript numberless congratulatory letters and telegrams came to me. I, too, sent congratulations to

[1] *Die Waffen nieder*, VII, 377.

true-hearted allies. Egidy likewise received many tokens of rejoicing. He afterwards told me that a lady, a friend of his, put a copy of the newspaper containing the rescript in a cover and laid it on his writing table, with the inscription *Geburtstagsgeschenk* (" a birthday present "); it chanced that Egidy's birthday coincided with this event.

Here is a selection from the letters that I received:

Highly honored and gracious Lady:
Ischl, August 29

Warm and most respectful congratulations to you and your husband from the depths of my heart! What feelings it must arouse in you! the noblest of all joyful emotions!

That I have lived to see this day I regard as the most incomprehensible and the most surprising delight of my life, which has been so rich in sorrows and so lean in hope. I could not have dreamed of this most noteworthy *ex oriente lux*, when in *Wenn ich Kaiser oder König wäre* (" If I were Emperor or King") I attempted to bind the laurel of this day around the temples of William I, or when in " The Strike " I let a wise prince pour out his heart as he stood facing the unripe nations. Now the dream has come true, and may these forever sleeping nations and inert consciences be aroused with the sound of the trumpet! Goethe hit it:

> Thy spirit world is not forbidden;
> Thy heart is dead; thy wits are slow!
> Wake! student, lave thy breast unchidden
> Within the ruddy morning glow!

I consider myself happy to be able to share your delight.

Most respectfully yours
Moritz Adler

Porto Rose near Pirano, August 31

My heartiest congratulations that your indefatigable endeavors continued throughout long years in the interest of universal peace

THE TSAR'S RESCRIPT

have suddenly, by means of a word on the Neva, brought such a sur-
prising and brilliant victory into happy prospect!
With heart and hand
Dr. Karl von Scherzer
Minister Plenipotentiary (retired)

Munich, August 30
. . . The Tsar has done a splendid thing. Whatever may come
of it, from now on the air is throbbing with thoughts of peace, —
even where yesterday they were deemed impossible. This will bring
great and unexpected results. Now the Anglo-American treaty will
be ratified, and ultimately all Germans will be at one — in such an
air all things can come about. You see! it is worth while to preach,
to have faith, to be a prophet, energetically and incessantly!
Björnstjerne Björnson

Vienna, August 30
Congratulations from the bottom of my heart! Salvos of victory!
Now will the great socialist politicians still continue to scorn us!
Balduin Groller

Sondja, October, 1898
. . . I know from a very trustworthy source of information that
the Emperor wrote this document after he had read *Die Waffen nieder*.
Consequently this fortunate event is to be ascribed wholly to your
influence.[1] I learned quite incidentally, through the newspapers, of

---

[1] *Post hoc* is not *propter hoc*. Although it delighted me to hear that the
Tsar had read my book shortly before the appearance of the manifesto, yet I
was firmly convinced that a long chain of many influences, among which that
of reading a novel could have been of only small effect, must have preceded
such an action. Later I learned that Bloch's book had made a deep impression on the Tsar; at that time I suspected that Professor Martens had helped
inspire the document and wrote him to that effect. His answer follows:

Villa Waldeuse near Wolmar
Livonia, September 9, 1898
My dear Madam:
I make haste to present my sincerest thanks for the friendly letter of the
4th inst. with which you honored me. I do not know to what degree my
teaching could have influenced his Majesty the Emperor or his councilors in

193

the rescript which has caused all the friends of peace so much delight, for I have, during the last few years, been very little in St. Petersburg. I take no part in political activities, as I have devoted myself to the interests of the zemstvo, which at the present time demand a great deal of labor and ever claim more and more the intellectual powers of the country. However, a few years ago I made the attempt to organize a Russian peace society. This attempt failed, either because a favorable soil for such a union had not been sufficiently prepared in advance or because I myself lacked the necessary qualifications for promoting it.

As far as the public opinion of the province is concerned, I can from personal observation assert that the most progressive element of society regards the plan of the peace conference from the same standpoint as the leading article of the inclosed newspaper, — favorably and hopefully. As is always the case while public opinion is forming, this is divided into two extreme camps, — the Utopians and the skeptics; the latter, unfortunately, in a majority. I am nevertheless persuaded that our young monarch will draw from the bosom of Russian society the same strength which his grandfather Alexander II thirty-six years ago had to help him in the accomplishment of another solemn deed, — the enfranchisement of the peasants from serfdom, — although then, too, there were many skeptics and people who were even strongly opposed to the reform. The labor and active effort in the question that is interesting us fall, in the present hour, both in Europe and in America, on the parliamentary forces, whose

the noble task which they have imposed on the governments and nations of the civilized world.

I had no direct part in the celebrated rescript of August 12 (24), having been for some time in residence on my estate in Livonia, far from the capital. But I have applauded with the keenest sympathy and the sincerest admiration the generous action taken by my august master for the well-being and happiness of all civilized nations.

As to the bibliographical notes, I shall make it my duty to communicate them to you after the meeting of the *conférence de la paix*. At this moment I am too busy with my official duties.

Reiterating my very respectful thanks, I beg you, Madam, to accept the assurance of my high consideration. Martens.

duty it is now to compel their governments to express themselves sincerely and without reservation in regard to the conference proposed by Count Muravieff.

By a strange irony of fate I learned of the imperial manifesto just as I was taking part in the maneuvers in my capacity as reserve officer. The officers regarded the matter without excitement, although the best among them could not help recognizing the correctness of the ideas embodied in the rescript. The others were of the opinion that all the peace projects concerned them very little, and that the military service to which they had been brought up would still for a long time fill their lives.

Our society was deeply moved and grieved by the death of your Empress. What a sad madness speaks in such deeds, and how much to be pitied is mankind when, besides the battle against war, we must also in the midst of peace think of the pacification of the classes.

Accept, etc.

Prince Peter Dolgorukof

Soras near Eperies, August 30

A storm of delight is rushing through the world in view of the mighty aurora that is shining from St. Petersburg. Whatever the result be, the mighty word of one of the mightiest can never be unspoken. The Lord bless your efforts!

Vice Admiral Semsey

Velden, August 30

Hurrah for the morning glow in the East!

Hedwig Pötting

Budapest, August 29

Can it be possible, can it be true? Now the thing is to use this victory wisely. Something must and will be done. Now it is a pride and a joy to be a friend of peace.

I congratulate us all, and first of all, you. This will rouse many.

Kemény
Secretary of the Hungarian Peace Society

Beckenhorn, September 12

. . . What do I think of the manifesto? A thousand things. I was at the Lake of Lucerne. I had been enjoying a delightful walk, and in the evening after dinner I took up the *Indépendance*. I confess I did so almost reluctantly — politics is such an unsavory dish. One would willingly forget it when yielding to the witchery of lovely nature and recovering from the miseries of humanity in the undisturbed purity of the lofty mountain peaks. So, then, imagine my amazement! Instead of the usual diplomatic commonplaces, the Emperor's manifesto! That absolutely staggered me!

But what do I think of it? In the first place, that we all, those of us who are of one mind with the spirit of the manifesto, ought to support Nicholas II with all our might, not only against his opponents but also against his own person. The undertaking is of great difficulty. He might lose courage in face of the obstacles. Then it will be necessary for liberal opinion in Europe, and especially for the peace unions, to give him unwearied, never-failing assistance.

Secondly, even if the manifesto should have no immediate results, it will undoubtedly have gigantic indirect influence. It establishes a new epoch in the history of Europe. That can never be changed.

Are you coming to Turin? That will be the place for us to lay out a complete plan of campaign. Though I do not belong to the Bureau, yet I am going there at any rate. If I do not have the good fortune to see you in Turin, I will on my way back make you that promised visit at Harmannsdorf.

Yours, etc. J. Novikof

Heiden, September 21

. . . Allow me to express my congratulations on the great step which the Tsar has taken on the path to which your most zealous apostleship has been devoted. It is a gigantic step, and, whatever may happen, the world will not shriek, "Utopia!" Disdain of our ideas is no longer possible; even if accomplishment does not immediately follow the work of the conference, which will assuredly take place, still, at all events, a beginning will have been made. This initiative will forever serve as a precedent.

The Empress Elisabeth's death has greatly saddened me — ah! if only our ideas had been made effective ten years earlier, there would not be any anarchists now.

Henri Dunant
Founder of the Red Cross

196

THE TSAR'S RESCRIPT

The replies of the governments to the manifesto soon began to be received, — almost all in the affirmative. But sincerity was lacking in the tone of the acceptances and in the whole treatment of the invitation. Everywhere, simultaneously, an increase in armaments was seen to be under way. Very deplorable was the attitude of the German Social-Democratic party, which holds that only by this party can militarism be driven from the world; if any one else tries to do it, one who — *nota bene* — has the power to do it, then it is fraud and farce.

The *Neue Hamburger Zeitung* sent a note to distinguished contemporaries, requesting opinions on the Russian manifesto. Very interesting replies were received. Among those who were in favor, many of them enthusiastically in favor, were Leo Tolstoi, Maurus Jókai, Otto Ernst, Ernst von Wolzogen, Peter Rosegger, Dr. M. G. Conrad, Cesare Lombroso, and General Türr. I am going to introduce here, however, only some of the replies sent by opponents of the peace movement, because it seems to me most instructive, for understanding the development of universal ideas and social conditions, to learn the obstacles which had and still have to be overcome.

Small differences, like the Caroline Islands question, can be settled by arbitration; greater differences will continue to lead to tests of power . . . perpetual peace is in heaven. There is no heaven on earth.

Friedrich Naumann
Retired Pastor

RECORDS OF AN EVENTFUL LIFE

The history of many thousand years unfortunately argues against the possibility that war will ever cease. . . . At all events the Russian proposal for disarmament is one of the cleverest diplomatic moves of modern times.   B. von Werner

These are questions of high politics with which I have nothing to do. In my opinion, so far as our trade is concerned, all interests are subordinated to one that is paramount, namely, that Germany be respected and feared, but so far as possible without being hated, in the world. Therefore the mercantile class has a vital interest in seeing the safety of the empire assured in the ways understood by those who are responsible for it.   Ferdinand Laeisz
                       Chairman of the Hamburg Board of Trade

I cannot assent to the general notion that armies prepared for battle are unproductive. Armies are a protection to the nations against attacks. . . . The idea of disarmament is unfortunate. We should be glad that slouchy men can be trained in a manly education.
                                          Reinhold Begas, Sculptor

This noble enthusiasm will miscarry, just as in 1890 the International Assembly of Workingmen did under Emperor William's auspices. A mighty state will never, without a struggle, submit to a verdict which offends its rights or merely its essential desires. A glance at the map is sufficient: our empire can resist the ever-possible double attack of France and Russia only by having all its powers in readiness.

I do not waste time thinking of Utopias. France lays down as a condition for every debate the return of the imperial lands; we lay down as our condition the exclusion of every discussion of this question. I think this is a sufficient answer. The talk of the private friends of peace is mere nonsense; the Tsar's advocacy of peace is perhaps a stimulus to war.   Felix Dahn

Gastein, on the anniversary of Sedan
    (September 2, 1870)

The present proposal of Tsarish Russia for disarmament is a fraud.   W. Liebknecht

THE TSAR'S RESCRIPT

The stronger the armaments the greater the fear of assuming the responsibility of starting a war. Disarmament would make wars more frequent. Reduction of the present force would withdraw a part of the people from the school of "military discipline and very generally diminish their efficiency. . . . The vital questions of the nations will always be settled by war. Germany must always lead the great powers in its armaments, because it is the only country that has three great powers as neighbors and may at any time be exposed to the danger of waging war on three frontiers. With the increasing solidarity of states, wars will naturally become more and more infrequent. It is a dream to expect anything more, and not even a beautiful dream; for with the guaranty of perpetual peace the degeneracy of mankind would be confirmed.   Dr. Eduard von Hartmann

The reply that most unctuously dripped with wisdom was that furnished by Herr W. Metzger, the Social-Democratic delegate to the Reichstag from the third electoral district in Hamburg. He wrote to the editors that " he did not feel the slightest inclination to waste even a quarter of an hour on that Russian diplomatic trick." So the third electoral district may be at rest — its representative is saving his time for higher interests than those that are moving the whole civilized world !

Those are the utterances of single individuals. As regards the voice of the newspapers, I collected a great number of clippings at the time. The following are typical of the tone of those opposed :

The Tsar's proposal for disarmament goes against nature and against civilization. This alone condemns it. Baroness von Suttner, who a few years ago gave the command *Die Waffen nieder*, and thereby won among all men a brilliant success, is now indeed experiencing the great triumph of having the Tsar join in her summons; but there will be only a short-lived joy in this for Frau von Suttner and

RECORDS OF AN EVENTFUL LIFE

all good souls, for, as we have said, disarmament is contrary to nature and inimical to civilization, etc. — *Heidelberger Zeitung*, August 30.

When the Russian disarmament rescript appeared in August, one of the severest criticisms made upon it was this: " Prince Bismarck has been dead twenty-eight days." This was as much as to say that care had been taken not to submit this question to European statesmen for discussion during this great stateman's lifetime, but they waited until after he was dead to spring it. We do not question the correctness of this interpretation, but are of the opinion that if Prince Bismarck had lived to see the publication of the Russian note he would have used the full weight of his authority to prevent Germany from relinquishing at a conference even the very smallest part of its right and duty to regulate its armament absolutely according to its own discretion. — *Hamburger Nachrichten*, September 18.

A stranger official document than the Tsar's peace manifesto, his summons to disarm and his proposal for a general conference, has never before thrown official and unofficial Europe into astonishment. The question rises to the lips, Is this an honest Utopia, or is there hidden behind it a deep calculation of Russian politics, which, as is well known, is excelled in slyness by the diplomacy of no other state? It remains at all events a Utopia, in spite of all the European " Friends of Peace," and all the other chatter about international brotherhood. — *Grensboten*, Number 37, September 15.

Our officials believed without any kind of real investigation that they must applaud that manifesto with drums and trumpets, solely for the reason that it had the mighty Tsar as its originator; and they kept up this policy of groveling when there was no more possible doubt that the originator of this manifesto was not the Tsar, but those international peace enthusiasts of the stamp of Suttner and her allies, whom hitherto no one has taken seriously. Our Emperor has found the only correct answer to the Tsar's proposal; we can wait until his answer is taken to heart in the quarter for which it is intended, and then the Utopian idea of an international conference for disarmament, which is of no earthly use, will disappear finally from the programme. — *Staatsbürgerzeitung*, September 9.

THE TSAR'S RESCRIPT

At the banquet of the Westphalian Provincial Diet, on the eighth of September, Emperor William said:

" Peace will never be better assured than by a thoroughly drilled army ready for instant service, such as, in detachments, we at the present time have had opportunity to admire and to rejoice over. God grant us that it may be ever within our power to conquer with this always keen and well-cared-for weapon. Then the Westphalian peasant may go to sleep in peace."

LVI

EVENTS AND MEETINGS

THE Empress Elisabeth assassinated! An infamous dagger thrust into a quiet, proud, unworldly, and generous heart. Once again mourning and terror flashed through the whole civilized world with lightning speed. More and more it is shown that this civilized world has only *one* soul. The memory of this princess, so opulent in sufferings, so endowed with beauty, will go down in history as a radiant and poetic vision. And that vision will be haloed with a tragic charm — so shockingly sad though it is, so hateful the deed that was responsible for it — from the fact that she did not die in her bed of illness or old age, but fell under the deadly blow of a fanatic madman, just as she was setting out on a new voyage into the splendor of nature which she loved so well. Out of the gray monotony of the commonplace thou standest forth for all time, — a figure in shining black, — Elisabeth of Austria!

My father-in-law, then seventy-nine years of age, had been for some time, especially since Lotti's death, very much shattered in health. He no longer took his daily walks, often dropped off to sleep, sometimes began to wander in his speech, — in short, his demise was evidently near at hand. Nevertheless he had his secretary and faithful attendant — my husband's former tutor — read the newspaper to him every day. When the news of the assassination of the Empress arrived we made haste to warn Herr Wiesner (that was the secretary's name, though at home we always called him "Dominus") not to read to the old gentleman the passages regarding the tragedy. Attached with the deepest devotion to the imperial house, Old Austrian to his finger tips, an enthusiastic admirer of the beautiful Empress, — the news of her death would have terribly shocked him, and we desired to spare him that.

Only a few days after this event he died in My Own's arms. At five o'clock one morning we were summoned to his bedside. The nurse thought that he was dying, but he soon rallied and lay peacefully. About nine o'clock — meantime the doctor had been called and all the members of the family stood about the bed — he sat up and took my husband's hand.

"Artur," he said, "you know I have always been an industrious worker—I must write a few letters to-day; . . . there the Dominus stands waiting for me to dictate—but, Artur, I should like to rest to-day—I may, may I not? — just a little sleep — yes?"

My Own laid him gently back on the pillow. " Dear father — sleep ! "

The old man thrust his arm under the pillow and turned his face to one side. With a satisfied sigh he closed his eyes, and after a few minutes he fell asleep — in the sleep that knows no waking.

Egidy wrote me as follows regarding the Empress Elisabeth's death :

> . . . The most affecting word that has been spoken about your Empress's death is that from her own husband's mouth : "It is incomprehensible how a man could lay his hand on this woman, who in all her life had never harmed any one and had done nothing but good."
>
> A touching truth is to be found in this thought, and àt the same time, also, the earnest call to think the thought again. Possibly the innocent woman had to die this sudden death in order that deep sorrow might come upon the best of all peoples, in order that all might mourn with the bereaved husband and Emperor, and also in order that we might repeat that lamentation in our thought, and comprehend, should the grief-stricken Emperor in humble realization come to the following resolution :
>
> " Henceforth men who have never done any one any harm shall cease mercilessly thrusting the deadly steel into one another's hearts. Henceforth I will not allow men whose lives are confided to my protection to march to fields of battle ; no longer will I train to war the nations that are under my scepter. The labor of the remaining years that Providence shall vouchsafe me belongs to internal and external preparation for the warless epoch."

Egidy still further elaborated this idea in the October number of his *Versöhnung* (" Reconciliation ").

The plans for the meetings to be held in Lisbon in the year 1898 fell through. The Iberian peninsula seemed little fitted to arrange for peace congresses as long as the Spanish-American War was in progress; so this year the two Bernese councils met for consultation in different places, having for their object the decision of what attitude to take regarding the Russian circular. The Interparliamentary Union met in Brussels, the International Peace Bureau in Turin, where a World's Exposition was being held.

We went to Turin, My Own and I, in spite of our bereavement, starting a fortnight after the old baron had been laid away in the family tomb at Höflein. A letter which I wrote to a friend tells of our visit to the capital of Piedmont:

Turin, Grand Hôtel d'Europe,
September 28, 1898

The committee which has been assembled here concluded its labors to-day. The manifesto of the Emperor of Russia naturally formed the basis and suggested the direction of the proceedings.

On Sunday, the twenty-fifth, the Turin " Peace Days " began with the centennial jubilee of the Piedmontese statesman, Count Federigo Sclopis. In the vast Aula of the Royal University the festival committee and a great audience were assembled. The hall was packed.

General Türr conducted me to the front row and introduced me to the Mayor of Turin, Baron Casano, the governor, Marchese Guiccioli, — I could not help thinking of Byron, who loved a Guiccioli whom I used to know in Paris, — and the Minister, Count Ferraris. We sat in front of the desk. The cards of invitation bore the names of twenty-four eminent men as patrons of the festival; among them were Biancheri, President of the Chamber, Minister Vigliani, the presidents of the Roman and Bernese Courts of Cassation, the rector of the University, the president of the Academy of Sciences, and others.

Lawyer Luzatti was the first to take the platform, and he gave us a biographical sketch of Federigo Sclopis. He eulogized his services, and particularized as most glorious the part he played as chairman of the Alabama Court of Arbitration. Then the vice president of the Roman Senate, who is also chairman of the Roman Peace Society, spoke, and he was followed by our Frédéric Passy. He had been in his youth a friend of Sclopis's, and was therefore able to tell much that was fresh and interesting about the life of the great man.

The meeting was over at noon. The rest of the day was devoted to social intercourse and the Exposition. Such visitors as had any taste for art were here afforded more delights than are often found in displays of this kind, for the galleries of sculpture and painting are better filled than usual, and in a great edifice, built like a coliseum, an orchestra of two hundred artists gave wonderful concerts.

But if I prove unable to tell much about the Exposition in general, who will blame a member of the Congress for that? Here old friends are discovered and new and congenial acquaintances are made, and this fact serves to promote serious conversation; so the Exposition park, with its many pavilions, is neglected; you sit down with your comrades round a café table and talk of the things that are in your heart. The manifesto first of all, but also everything else that is going on in the world; among other things, the Dreyfus affair, which just at this moment every one has more or less in mind. A delegate from Paris, Gaston Moch, who himself had been a cavalry officer and had served in the same corps with the exile, has much interesting information to give. Even as early as 1894 he had looked behind the scenes in the affair and had realized that the Jewish officer would not be endured on the general staff. A peculiar thing was also told us: In the summer of 1894, and thus before the charge was brought against Dreyfus, *Le Journal* published a novel as a feuilleton, in which a plot for the extermination of an unpopular comrade was devised and carried out: the smuggling into the intelligence bureau of a forged document and the like, — a whole chain of intrigues such as was actually adopted against the innocent man, just as if Paty, Henry, and the rest had taken the novel as a pattern to go by.

On Monday, the twenty-sixth, the delegates met for their first session in the Palazzo Carignan. The splendor of the Italian princely palaces is well known. The hall where we met is of sheer gold; the

EVENTS AND MEETINGS

wall coverings are of gold, the doors and window shutters heavily gilded; adjoining, and also glittering with gold, is the historic chamber in which Victor Emmanuel was born.

As the president of the Bureau was obliged to go to Brussels to attend the session of the Interparliamentary Directorate, the chairmanship of our meetings was intrusted to the lawyer Luzatti. Though many letters of greeting arrived, I will cite only the Italian Prime Minister's:

"Our country—on the ground of the principles that have inspired its regeneration, on the ground of its ideals of civilization as well as of its political interests—our country must desire that in international questions juristic reason may win the day over the appeal to force.

E. Visconti-Venosta"

The first subject for discussion is expressed clearly in the text of the resolution that was passed:

"The Meeting is of the opinion that the societies throughout their spheres of activity should organize demonstrations of every kind, in the form of petitions and meetings designed to promote a favorable result of the Tsar's rescript; it invites the societies to communicate the effects of these demonstrations to the International Bureau in Bern, which will give them the greatest possible publicity."

The English delegates were able to report that in their country numerous demonstrations in this direction had already taken place. Political leaders in Parliament had joined in the movement, among them Sir William Harcourt, Morley, the Marquis of Ripon, Earl Crewe, Bryce, Sir John Lubbock, Sir Wilfrid Lawson, Spencer Watson, and others; also many bishops, and the three English cardinals, Vaughan, Loyne, and Gibbons. The Congress of the Trade Unions, which had until recently held aloof, voted unanimously and enthusiastically as follows:

"This Congress of organized laborers, representing the industrial classes of Great Britain and Ireland, greets the Tsar's message with satisfaction and calls upon the government to employ all legitimate means to promote its success, since militarism is a great enemy to labor and a cruel burden for the slaving millions."

RECORDS OF AN EVENTFUL LIFE

This attitude of the English workingmen — be this observed in parenthesis — is at all events more beneficial than that of the socialists of other lands, who are distrustful of the Russian Emperor's views, and who say, "Peace and disarmament, yes — but *we* want to bring it about, we alone, and in our own way." But what is destined to benefit all mankind must be done by all; it cannot be the work of a class and against other classes.

Élie Ducommun gave a report on the events of the year, which he claimed would have marked it as one of the most unfortunate and discouraging for the movement, had it not ended with the Russian Emperor's proposal of official investigation of means for bringing about assured peace and the reduction of armaments. Moreover, to the assets of the year were to be reckoned the agreement of France and England on the Niger question, the arbitration between France and Brazil, and, finally, the conclusion of a permanent arbitration treaty between Italy and the Argentine Republic.

The assembly sent a congratulatory dispatch to the Italian government on this treaty, — the first of its kind and likely to prove of the greatest blessing as an example to be followed.[1]

On the other hand, apprehension was felt regarding the danger that threatens on the part of Argentina, which is on the point of declaring war against Chile. It was suggested that a trustworthy person might be sent in the name of the Peace Bureau to Argentina and Chile to urge both their presidents to submit the unsettled controversy to a court of arbitration. Perhaps they would turn a deaf ear to our delegate, but more probably a word spoken in the name of two hundred societies, representing both the New World and the Old, would turn the scale in their deliberations. Dr. Evans Darby suggested, on the other hand, that, as the outbreak of hostilities was already imminent and the delegate would assuredly arrive too late, a cablegram should be dispatched instead.

Accordingly two dispatches were sent on that very same day in the name of the Turin assembly, one to Valparaiso, the other to Buenos Aires, earnestly urging the two governments to avoid a war,

[1] A treaty without any limitations. (Observation of 1908. — B. S.)

EVENTS AND MEETINGS

which, just at this present moment, would be a lamentable setback to the approaching conference summoned by the Russian Emperor.[1]

The cable dispatches cost nine hundred francs. Prodigal Friends of Peace! when one thinks how penurious the war boards are!

On the evening of the twenty-ninth the general public of Turin were invited to listen to addresses in the Circolo filologico. There was not a vacant place in the vast auditorium. General Türr made the first speech and cited passages from Garibaldi's appeal to the governments. Then I followed with a reading of my short story, *Es müssen doch schöne Erinnerungen sein*, translated into Italian for this occasion, under the title *Bei ricordi* ("Beautiful Recollections"), by the poet F. Fontana. Then Émile Arnaud, Professor Ludwig Stein of Bern University, Novikof, and others spoke.

The audience was in such a high pitch of enthusiasm and sympathy at the end that I mustered courage, amid the storm of applause, to mount the platform again and make a brief appeal that the listeners should not reward our words with mere clapping of hands, — we were not artists hungry for approbation, we were plain champions of a holy cause, — but rather should join our organization; they might come up and sign their names. This invitation was accepted, and by reason of the addresses that evening the membership list of the Turin Peace Union was increased by many and influential names.

This Union has also a special section in the Exposition building. The autograph entries in the book that is there are very interesting. Even Arabic and Chinese signatures are among them; also dialogues: some one wrote in French, "I do not believe in it"; some one else wrote underneath, "I pity you with all my heart." Tolstoi's son wrote in the register, *Quale è lo scopo della guerra? L'assassinio—* ("What is the object of war? Massacre!").

[1] It is a fact that a few days later the question at issue was submitted to the arbitration of the Queen of England. Later the two republics concluded a standing agreement to bring every future controversy before the Hague Tribunal, and as a result reduced their armaments and sold their war ships. As a memorial to this agreement a gigantic statue of the Christ has been erected on a peak of the mountain boundary, the Andes. (Observation of 1908. — B. S.)

Our first care after our return to Austria was to organize a meeting to agitate in behalf of the Russian circular. Lieutenant Colonel von Egidy came at my request to address this meeting, which took place in the Ronacher ballroom on the eighteenth of October. It was the first time he had ever spoken in Vienna. Although our Viennese did not fully realize how distinguished he was, they were in a high degree curious about the famous man who had once been an officer of the empire. It was universally known that he had been compelled to leave the military service on account of his convictions as expressed in his pamphlet *Ernste Gedanken* (" Serious Thoughts ").

An acquaintance, Count X., whom I had invited to hear the address, wrote me:

I have never read a line by Egidy. But I cannot share your opinion regarding him, for in the first place I cannot endure the Prussians; secondly, if a soldier has done anything so unseemly (!) that he can no longer serve, I am compelled to reject what he says, even were he as wise as Aristotle.

Well, now, there are figures in history who have done such unseemly things that they have been compelled not only to doff their uniforms but also to empty the cup of hemlock or die at the stake or on the cross; these would probably have been subjected to a still severer criticism at the hands of my friend the count.

An hour beforehand the doors of the hall were thrown open, and the throng which had long been waiting rushed in. The great room was soon packed; people stood in the gallery behind the last seats. Entrance was free, "every one invited," — such was Egidy's wish.

The representative of the government took his place at the chairman's table near me. I made a few prefatory remarks; then Egidy stepped forward, and his words rang out like bell tones. It was ever so when this orator spoke, — bronze in his voice, gold in his words, consecration in the room.

The Tsar's rescript furnished the text. After he had explained what was contained in this manifesto, Egidy passed in review the various kinds of misunderstanding and misinterpretation it had met in the world. The doubts and questions raised in various quarters, the difficulties of detail enumerated by civilization brakemen (Kulturbremser, a word of characteristic Egidy coinage), — all this he answered and explained in clear, occasionally witty language, and always with logical conciseness. And the audience vibrated with him. Every satirical point was punctuated with a laugh, at every allusion a murmur of appreciation ran through the assembly. You might have believed that all were penetrated by the orator's meaning, yet how many of those present had probably expressed, only an hour or two before, ideas which were current as the view of the majority: " A proposal for disarmament? . . . Hm ! . . . political move — a trap set — practically unfeasible idealism. . . ."

Most characteristic of this prevalent skepticism remains deeply engraven on my memory the picture of a deputy, — a member also of the Interparliamentary Union, — who, after I had spoken for a time about the manifesto, turned his head in my direction and said, with a sly wink, "Do you believe that story?"

This phrase became a catchword between My Own and me; whenever either of us communicated to the other anything perfectly unquestionable and simple, we would look as sly as we could and hiss out, "Do you believe that story?"

After the address Egidy was our guest at a supper which, together with Baron Leitenberger and a few other friends, we gave in his honor at Sacher's. At the supper a pretty scene was enacted. One of our company was a former officer, now a deputy and also vice president of the Austrian Interparliamentary Group, Herr von Gniewocz. He turned the conversation to the campaign of 1866, in which he had taken part. Egidy then told how he also had been there, and then the two men recalled certain incidents, one of which, as it appeared in the comparison of details, had brought them face to face as opponents. And now here they were, both as adherents and champions of the peace cause, united in joyous festal mood.

Mark Twain happened to be in Vienna at this time and was present at this supper. The American humorist used the Edigy-Gniewocz incident for a brilliant improvisation, full of wit and feeling. He had been present at the lecture, had been recognized by the audience, and was asked to speak. He mounted the platform and declared that, as far as he was concerned, having only a penknife with him, he was ready to disarm!

A few days later I was permitted to make the personal acquaintance of a man who has taken a most important part in the peace movement, and with whose activity I had long been acquainted, — William T. Stead. A telegram from Vienna signed with his name invited me to make an appointment for a meeting with him as he was passing through the city. With delight I acceded to his wish, and on the following evening I spent several hours with the famous English journalist, enjoying with him a frugal supper and the most exhilarating conversation. We talked about a hundred things.

His external appearance is that of a gentleman; his hair and full beard are turning somewhat gray; he has noble, intelligent features, is forty-nine years of age, and his conversation is full of witty turns and comprehensive views of the world. His characteristics, one might say, are the energy of gentleness, tenderness, and capacity — also humor; those seem to be the predominant elements of his nature.

The son of a Protestant clergyman, he was brought up in strict orthodoxy. And since then, although he has attained spiritual emancipation and discarded every sign of dogma, he has kept a deeply religious spirit and is penetrated with the conviction that the spirit of goodness — God — is gradually bringing this world to perfection and using for this purpose inspired men as his instruments, — men who, being conscious that they are working in the service of a lofty principle, feel strengthened and elevated by it, full of joyous and courageous reliance in the support that is behind them in their divine mission.

The object of his journey was to ascertain how the Russian Emperor's manifesto was received in different countries, and especially in official circles, and, above all, to learn what direction the Tsar himself and his ministers intended to give to the coming conference.

He had been on a journey through Europe, and was now on his return from Livadia, still under the impression of two extended interviews which the young Tsar had granted him. He had not been received as a journalist, but as a privileged guest in accordance with the wish of the late Emperor, Alexander III. About ten years before, a perfectly false idea of the Russian autocrat had gained currency with the British public. He was described as morose, violent, and insincere. And it was particularly supposed that he was all ready to let loose the horrors of a universal war. Stead, the journalist, had succeeded in dissipating this impression. In the year 1888 he had been accorded an audience at the imperial court at Gatchina, and the Emperor had engaged in an exceedingly frank conversation with

214

him. When Stead returned to England he was able
to announce with the utmost particularity that Alexander III was quite the opposite of the popular conception of him; that he was an enemy of all false-
hoods, and imbued with the strongest detestation of
war. These representations entirely changed public
opinion, and must have helped to avert the ever-pres-
ent danger of war.

From what Stead told me of the impression made
upon him during his audience with Nicholas II, I felt
warranted in concluding that the young Emperor was
thoroughly in earnest in the matter of the manifesto.
I complained to him of the lack of comprehension, the
stupidity, and at the same time the hostile spite with
which the message was received, for the disappointment to me had been unprecedented; I had so firmly
believed that, with the exception of a small circle, the
world would surely break out into jubilation at having the hope so nearly fulfilled of being freed from
the mountainous weight that oppressed it. To this
Stead replied:

"The manifesto is a mirror — a kind of magic
mirror. You hold it up before men whose nature you
wish to learn, and according to the judgments they
pronounce on it, it reflects clearly the image of their
spirit and their character."

"But since almost everywhere a petty, ugly picture is shown," I went on complaining, "since the purpose manifested by the Tsar is to be counteracted by

mistrust, indifference, open and secret resistance, the lofty work may fail . . ."

"Are you of so little faith? . . . You? . . . Such a declaration may be delayed. But can it be silenced? Never! I myself, as I have made this journey through the cities of Europe, began to grow faint-hearted, but what I learned in Russia has restored my courage. The Emperor, I have faith to believe, now that he has put his hand to the plow, will draw the furrow, and his three ministers are with him in the matter. One is Kuropatkin, the Minister of War, whose ambition it is to reduce armaments; the second is Witte, Minister of Finance; the third, Count Lamsdorff, pupil and follower of Giers, the efficient force in the Ministry of Foreign Affairs.

"As regards the questions to be discussed at the coming conference," continued Stead, "of course neither the Tsar nor any of his ministers thinks of disarmament in the literal meaning of the word; such a proposition is not to be made at all. The practical purpose of the discussions is to bring about a cessation of the ever-increasing preparations for war."

During his journey Stead had also visited Councilor von Bloch, author of the great work "War." This work is said to have made a marked impression on the Tsar, even when he was still crown prince, and very possibly it gave him the impulse to issue the rescript. Upon Stead's asking him what results he expected from the conference, Bloch replied:

" In my opinion the most useful thing that can be done is for the conference, after its preliminary session, to appoint a committee of its ablest members, who shall be intrusted with the duty of investigating the degree to which modern warfare under present social conditions has become practically impossible — impossible, that is to say, without hitherto unheard-of loss of life on the battlefield, absolute destruction of the social structure, inevitable bankruptcy, and threatening revolution."

Stead proceeded from Vienna to Rome, where he heard that he might expect some encouraging words from the Pope, all the more as Leo XIII had already many times expressed himself in sympathy with the peace cause. He did not, however, succeed in securing an audience at the Vatican.

The Russian Minister Muravieff also came to Vienna in the course of a journey he was making through Europe, and he remained there two or three days in order to hold conferences at court and with the ministers, just as he had done in other capitals, and to get a personal notion as to what reception the rescript had met with; also under what premises the rulers would be ready to send delegates to the conference.

I requested an interview with the Minister, and he sent me word by return mail that he would be glad to receive me the following forenoon at the Russian Embassy, where he was staying.

We had scarcely entered the drawing-room (my husband accompanied me) when Count Muravieff came in by another door. He was of medium height, wore a gray mustache, and had a round, kindly face. In spite of a certain coldness and dignity he appeared sympathetic. Like all Russian *grands seigneurs*, he showed the most gracious courtesy and spoke faultless French. It gave him infinite pleasure, he said as he greeted me, to make the personal acquaintance of so zealous a champion of the idea for which the Tsar and his government had now enlisted as apostles, — an idea which he confidently hoped would gradually conquer the world.

On my return home, after a conversation which lasted almost an hour, I noted down the following utterances of the count in my diary:

" It is not to be expected that the end will be reached in a short time. Think only of the Geneva Convention; that also took years before it became the comprehensive organization that it is to-day. Only one step must be made at a time. For the present, the cessation of armaments is the first stage. It is not to be expected that the states will consent to complete disarmament, or even to a diminution of the contingent; but if we could reach a common halt in the ' race to ruin,' that would be a favorable beginning. Henceforth the endeavor must be made to put universal peace on a safe basis, for a war in the future is surely a thing of horror and of ruin, — really an impossible thing; to take care of the present huge armies in the field is impracticable. The first result of a war waged between the great powers will be starvation. . . . "

I detected the echo of Bloch's doctrine in those last words, and that justifies the assumption that the work of the Russian councilor had helped to give the impulse to the drawing up of the rescript. Only Bloch had added to the word "starvation" two others, "revolution" and "anarchy."

From what Muravieff told us of his journey through Europe, it was evident that his presence and intervention had as a result the blunting of the edge of the Fashoda conflict. From his conferences with the different sovereigns he had evidently become convinced that there was no inclination at present to adopt any measures toward the reduction of armies, or to accept the principle that war and the military establishment should be done away with, and that, in face of this difficulty, a basis must be found on which the first step, — stopping the increase in armaments, — might be taken in common. "It cannot be expected," he said, "that at this very first conference the great final object will be attained."

"It would be sufficient," I remarked, "if the powers would make an agreement not to wage any war in the next twenty, or even in the next ten, years."

"Twenty years — ten years! *Vous allez trop vite, madame.* We could be satisfied if such an agreement were entered into for three years. But I believe even that will not be demanded. First and foremost there must be a pledge not to increase the contingents or make any new purchases of instruments of destruction. The constant demands for more money always mean a conflict between the ministers of war and the ministers of finance."

"They ought to appoint ministers of peace," said my husband, interrupting.

"Ministers of peace?" he repeated thoughtfully. "Well, yes, courts of arbitration, national tribunals —" And he began to talk with great practical knowledge about all the postulates of the peace movement.

"In my youth," he told us, "when the movement was in its infancy, — I was then an attaché in Stockholm, — I enrolled myself as a member of the League."

I gave him some details as to the condition and progress of the movement. Much of what I told him he already knew. The names of the prominent representatives whom I mentioned were familiar to him. He spoke first of Egidy. I handed him Houzeau-Descamps's pamphlet, with a few appeals and articles. He asked me to keep him informed as to the course of events.

When at the end I expressed my delight at being able to press the hand that had written that epoch-making manifesto, he replied, "*Je n'y suis pour rien;* its only author is my august sovereign."

The Spanish-American treaty of peace was signed in Paris. Our colleague, Émile Arnaud, addressed to the commission that was intrusted with this transaction a memorial, in which, among other things, it was suggested that a way should be made for establishing a Spanish-American arbitration treaty. The following reply was received from the chairman of the Spanish Commission:

My dear Sir:

I am in receipt of your valued letter of the fourth instant, in which you do me the honor of communicating to me the resolutions of the Turin Meeting of Delegates. The desires of the commission of which I am chairman, as well as my own personal feelings, are in full agreement with the ends so nobly pursued by the Peace League. All right-thinking men, whose souls are elevated above the conflicts arising from the passions and interests of colonial politics, are to-day at one in recognizing the necessity of settling controversies between nations by the only means worthy of reasonable and free beings. Our commission has been, and will continue to be, inspired by these ideas, and if these noble endeavors fail, it will not be our fault. I thank you infinitely for the amiable offers which you make in the name of the Peace League, and remain

Yours most respectfully,

Montero Rios

The Dreyfus affair is settling down more and more to a forlorn hope; the military system is fighting for its threatened authority. With it all one thing that is good has taken place, namely, the union of the intellectual class with the laboring men.

General Türr had an audience with King Humbert. Apropos of the conference called by the Tsar, he spoke of the necessity of combining the *Zweibund* with the *Dreibund*, and forming a European confederation. I wrote in my diary, together with this bit of information, " This fact deserves to be noted."

I find a very sad entry under date of December 30 : Egidy dead !

Early yesterday, on his return from a lecture tour, he succumbed to an acute heart trouble. That is all I know as yet; I only know that a gap is made in my life, for I have had a warm love for this noble man, and have looked up to him in grateful admiration. His influence will continue, but what he would have yet done and accomplished with the magical power of his personality — that is lost. Moritz von Egidy, farewell !

Some time afterwards I received the following letter from his son :[1]

My dear Baroness :   Marine School, Kiel, March 17, 1899

Pardon me for my long delay in thanking you for the February number of your periodical ; now the receipt of a second copy impels me to write to you at once.

---

[1] It was not his first letter to me. A few months before, young Egidy surprised and delighted me with the following communication from a distant part of the world :

On his Majesty's ship *Seeadler*

My dear Baroness :   Tulear, Madagascar, April 20, 1898

As the first German naval officer who, since the war of 1870, has left a war ship to step on soil now French, I am taking the liberty of sending you this respectful greeting.

No great political action has brought us hither, but the fact that German ships of war are again calling at French harbors is symptomatic, and will certainly be welcomed by you with satisfaction ; therefore I could not deny myself the pleasure of giving you this bit of information.

I am glad, gracious lady, to take this opportunity to express to you a son's gratitude for the true comradeship which you have given my father ; I know how precious it has been to him and how thankfully he has accepted it.

With the request that you present my sincerest regards to your husband, I am

Yours most respectfully and faithfully

Moritz von Egidy, Lieutenant at Sea

EVENTS AND MEETINGS

What a comforting expression you have found for your loss and ours in those words, " The consciousness that an Egidy was here " ;[1] truly and with all my heart I thank you for those words; they are worth infinitely more to me than many, many words, dear and well meant though they might be, because — this may sound far enough from altruistic, but nevertheless is not to remain unspoken — because they animate a thought which lay in my mind but which I had not yet found any expression for. I do not know whether you know this immediate feeling of thankfulness which comes over one in such a case, and which I should like to make you understand.

All the more I am sorry to be obliged to tell you that you have been misinformed about father's funeral, particularly because the information is so entirely contrary to father's spirit. There is a lack of recognition of the courageous, magnanimous act of the priest, Court Chaplain Rogge, who appears in a wholly false light, from the fact that he is only mentioned on the occasion when, in accordance with the ritual of our Church (in which father was still a member in spite of everything), he pronounced the blessing.

Yes, indeed, it was a courageous act for a royal Prussian court chaplain, who, perhaps, the very next day preached before the Emperor in the Potsdam Garrison church, to say such words as you will find in the February number of *Versöhnung*, and the impression of this fine act of his on the assembly was quite extraordinary, as was openly acknowledged by men who, perhaps for the first time in dozens of years, were listening again to a minister, and who had come there in the secret apprehension of having their feelings of love for my father hurt in some way.

Yes, the long way to the grave; but still it infused such a firm,

[1] The passage from my eulogy here referred to ran thus:

The consciousness that an Egidy was here was such a comforting, strengthening, joyous consciousness. We had him; this possession was like the possession of a check book. If ever assistance, consolation, support were required in a spiritual campaign, in an ethical dilemma, all one had to do was to produce the check book; Egidy was certain to honor it instantly. Always the right word, the unhesitating opinion, nobility pure of dross. Even if there were heard on all sides: " The world is bad, every one thinks only of himself, there is no improvement, there are no clear notions of duty, no straight paths of virtue," we could always smile calmly and say to ourselves, " That is not true; there is an Egidy here."

steadfast trust into our hearts as I escorted my splendid mother along; our eyes were constantly attracted by the dazzling white heron plume on the fur hussar cap as it nodded in front of us, keeping time to the step of the bearers; the white plume, pointing upward, seemed to us a symbol in the falling shadows of the evening. You know his motto: " Forward ! upward ! "

Especially interesting to me was the news on page 61 about the resolution of the organized English workingmen; for you see on the very evening before I got the book I had quite a long discussion with the professor who lectures for us on history here at the Academy. He asserts that, in consequence of the English election law, the predominant power in parliament will more and more pass over to the side of the masses, i.e. the workingmen; and herein, he says, lies the chief danger for peace, for the instinct of the masses is always directed to war, especially in England, where the people's heads are turned by their imperialistic notions, joined with an ever more and more pronounced national conceit. A more striking answer to this assertion than the so-called resolution I can scarcely imagine.

Have I already told you, Baroness, that I presented "Marmaduke" (in English text) to a French officer, with the dedication *Un souvenir [de] nos idées qui se rencontraient,* — and that, too, after a speech on the *Alliance franco-allemande,* which was made in the presence of French army and navy officers, officials, and merchants, at four o'clock in the morning, if you please, in our wardroom, on the *Seeadler,* and not long before Fashoda, when the Russian friendship was still very warm. The affair is noteworthy, for the reason that the Frenchman is usually, in a large company, quite extraordinarily careful and reserved. Moreover, the speech was made by a French physician who was on the expedition with Marchand when lack of support from his reserve stations compelled him to return. It was known quite accurately in Madagascar at that time, April, 1898, that a French expedition must have arrived at the Nile or would soon arrive there, and every day the news of it was expected.

Remember me kindly to your husband, and I kiss your hand as

Your very devoted

Moritz von Egidy

LVII

BEFORE THE HAGUE

STEAD told me that the Emperor Nicholas, in
speaking to him of his circular, had said:

"Have I had a single letter, or has a single person
ever represented to me that I exaggerate the danger?
Not one! they all agree that I have spoken the truth.
'But,' they ask me, 'what do you propose as a preven-
tive?' As if it were my affair and mine alone to pre-
scribe a remedy for a disease from which all the nations
are suffering!"

Even on the peoples' side there was not that enthusiasm which the author of the rescript might have expected. "How diminish the burdens that rest so heavily
on the shoulders of the people?" he cries to his fellow-
rulers, and he begs them to seek some means to avoid

the evil that threatens the whole world. And what is the answer to it? The masses to whom the Emperor specially appealed remained indifferent. Although the threat of war between France and England seemed to be dispelled, the preparations were continued unabated on both sides. The German Emperor, on his return from his journey to Jerusalem, immediately insisted on increasing his army by twenty-six thousand men.

In St. Petersburg a feeling of deep discouragement prevailed. By the beginning of December the disappointment was so great that the authorities almost decided to give up the project and call instead a conference of ambassadors in that capital.

But the world had, after all, not remained so indifferent. In England mass meetings were held in behalf of the projected Conference. William T. Stead proposed the scheme of an international peace crusade. The peace societies of the Continent gave a mighty response; thus, for example, in Austria our Union provided for participation in that action by means of assemblies and public demonstrations, and for many weeks in succession the " International Peace Crusade " formed a standing rubric in the *Neue Freie Presse* and the *Neues Wiener Tagblatt*. In the same way the peace workers were bestirring themselves in other countries.

By this means, as well as through the influence of a few resolute members of the Russian government, the hope of success was again awakened in St. Petersburg, and the half-formed determination to substitute a simple gathering of ambassadors in place of the Conference was dropped; on the sixteenth of January a second circular was dispatched by Count Muravieff, once more inviting the governments to participate in the Conference as planned, and "suggesting" a programme of eight points:

1. An agreement not to increase, during a fixed period, the present strength of the armed military and naval forces, nor the budgets pertaining thereto, and a preliminary examination of the means by which a reduction might be effected in future in the forces and budgets above mentioned.

2. To prohibit the adoption, in the armies and fleets, of any new kind of firearms and explosives, or of any kinds of powder more powerful than those now in use either for rifles or cannon.

3. To restrict the use of the formidable explosives now existing, and to prohibit the throwing of projectiles or explosives of any kind from balloons or by similar means.

4. To prohibit the use, in naval warfare, of submarine torpedo boats or plungers, or other similar engines of destruction, and to adopt an agreement not to construct, in the future, vessels with rams.

5. To apply to naval warfare the definitions of the Geneva Convention of 1864 as amended by the additional articles of 1868.

6. To neutralize, in accordance with the same convention, ships and boats engaged in saving those in danger of drowning during or after an engagement.

7. To revise the declaration concerning the laws and customs of war which was elaborated in 1874 by the Conference of Brussels but has remained unratified to the present time.

8. To accept in principle the employment of the "good offices" of mediation and optional arbitration in cases lending themselves thereto, with the object of preventing armed conflicts between nations; and to come to an understanding with respect to the mode of applying these good offices, and to establish a uniform practice in using them.

It is understood that all questions concerning the political relations of states and the order of things established by treaties, and, in general, all questions which do not directly fall within the programme adopted by the cabinets, are to be absolutely excluded from the deliberations of the conference.

When the text of the second circular is compared with the first, it can be seen how much water had been poured into the fiery wine that was first offered to the world. In the first document there is no trace of points 3–7. Only in points 1 and 8 are the fundamental thoughts preserved. The other six points were evidently inserted as a result of the replies, recommendations, and opinions that Count Muravieff had gathered in his journey through Europe, and perhaps also from personal letters emanating from the various courts.

In the press, also, numerous utterances had declared that the only reasonable and positive result which could be attained by the Conference was to be found in modifying the regulations of war and in the domain of the Red Cross. Here even those who were not opponents of war and militarism would be able and willing to coöperate. Out of diplomatic consideration for such persons the six points in question were inserted. The famous military surgeon Professor Esmarch, a brother-in-law of the German Empress, worked especially hard for the Red Cross at the Conference.

By this introduction of questions concerning military customs and the humanizing of war into the deliberations of the Peace Conference, a wedge (surely not

without purpose) was driven into it calculated to rob it
of its individual character. That was distinctly shown
in the Second Hague Conference, in 1907.

But I will not anticipate the historic evolution of
things. For the time being I will confine myself to the
year 1899, the last year of the departing century.

The conference was called; the date of its opening
was set. Points 1 and 8 of the programme contained
in essence everything that a complete revolution in
accordance with the opinions of the peace champions
could involve; and I remember that we — I mean my
husband and myself and all our colleagues — faced the
event, when it was announced, as one would face a
momentous crisis full of promise, or rather already
fulfilled. I was conscious of this historic phenomenon
not merely as something that was taking place in the
world without, but as my own inmost experience, as
altogether a phase of my personal destiny. And I
regarded it as " the one important thing."

The skeptics of that day shrugged their shoulders
at this notion, and even the wise ones of to-day would
largely smile at it. Certainly, they might say, universal
peace has not resulted from the Hague Conference;
on the contrary, horrible wars followed it, and since
it was called and repeated, the rivalry in increasing
armaments has gone on with accelerating strength.

It is hard to make headway against such naïve
arguments when they are based on succession of
events rather than on their connection and their

causes. There are minds on the chessboard of society which absolutely cannot see farther than from one square, from one move, to the next.

Assuredly, for the great majority the whole matter was something so novel, so unprecedented, so unexpected, and it was so unapproachable by familiar paths of thought and feeling, that the widespread misconception of it was quite natural. For the rest of us, who for years had been concentrating our labor, our thought, and our desires on this field, for us who had traced its origins and seen the bright-shining goal clearly outlined before us, for us it was just as natural to realize that the new epoch — the warless day, *l'ère sans violence*, as Egidy used to call it — had already come when the first steps toward its practical inauguration were taken so publicly.

In January, 1899, my husband and I went to Berlin to work there in behalf of the crusade, or at least to arrange for a meeting in behalf of the coming Conference. Our first call was on the Russian ambassador, Osten-Sacken. It was remarkable, but we found that he was no enthusiast for the affair inaugurated by his *auguste maître;* his wife also showed herself rather skeptical.

I addressed notes of invitation to the various leaders of political and scientific circles of Berlin to meet for a discussion. Many of the gentlemen responded to my call, and after a very interesting debate a committee was formed to take charge of public demonstrations

in favor of the Peace Conference. Unfortunately, my
diary of that period was not kept up, and I cannot
mention by name all those who responded to my invitation and suggestion, or who declined it. I remember
only that the deputies, Theodor Barth and Professor
Förster, — the latter also director of the observatory,
— were among the first group; that General du Verdy
wrote a very sympathetic letter, and that Bebel replied
with the following interesting note, which is still in
my possession:

Berlin, January 31, 1899
Dear Madam:

You had the kindness to invite me to call last Sunday. Unfortunately, I was unable to respond to your desire, because the letter did
not tell me where you were, and I was unable to learn until it was
too late.

Permit me herewith to add a few words regarding my position on
the question of the Russian Emperor's peace manifesto, since I may
take it for granted that I have to attribute to this matter the honor
of your letter.

The Social-Democratic party is sympathetically disposed toward
the thought that underlies the manifesto. Up to the present time it
has been the only party that has opposed the development of militarism in almost the same words as the Russian Emperor's; it has
been alone and consistent in upholding the idea of national brotherhood for the purpose of promoting the common interests of mankind.

The fact that now the sovereign of an empire like Russia, whose
policy hitherto has demanded militarism first of all and made it
necessary, should at this time appear as its opponent, is highly noteworthy, but cannot prevent us from looking upon the action with a
certain distrust until it is proved by corresponding deeds that this is
unjustified. The calling of the Conference, with the familiar programme lately published, is not as yet sufficient.

Moreover, there are at all events very important internal political

231

reasons that have incited the Russian government to undertake the advocacy of the imperial plan, which otherwise would scarcely have happened. Even an absolute autocrat is not supremely powerful.

·For the reason here briefly summarized, the Social-Democratic party is somewhat cool toward an agitation in behalf of the Emperor's manifesto; it cannot by a heart-and-soul participation in this agitation undertake the responsibility for what will be said and done towards the acceptance and glorification of the Emperor's manifesto. If representatives of the party should then wish to protest, this would only cause discord, which would be detrimental to the cause itself.

I believe, therefore, that it is in the interest of both sides to march in separate columns in this campaign, and to allow each tendency to advocate its special standpoint independently.

With great respect,

A. Bebel

While we were in Berlin a great service in honor of Egidy was held (January 29). It was inspiring and elevating.

The next day there was a public meeting called by the Berlin Peace Society, at which Dr. Hirsch, Schmidt-Cabanis the writer, and I made addresses.

In response to an invitation from the Countess Gurowska we went from Berlin for a fortnight's visit at Château Montboron in Nice. I was to speak both at Cannes and at Nice about the approaching conference. We were met at the railway station at Nice by our hostess's husband and General Türr. It was just at the time of the great carnival, and the two gentlemen took us to the city hall, where we had a fine view of the battle of flowers. The following day we were again invited to the city hall to witness the burning of Prince Carnival, a figure constructed of straw.

The reception rooms of the hall were crowded with distinguished guests, and among others I met Madame Juliette Adam. "You must come to-morrow to the Baroness's lecture," said a gentleman of our group to her. "To a lecture on peace? I?" cried the editor of *La Nouvelle Revue.* "Certainly not, I am for war." I was drawn into a discussion with her, in which I defended my side in a low voice, she hers in a wrathful tone well suited to the subject discussed.

The same evening I made the acquaintance of a very sympathetic Frenchman, M. Catusse, who had just been appointed consul general for France in Sweden. He proved to be a warm fellow-champion. Our conversation — as was the case with almost all conversations at that time — turned upon the *Affaire.* And then he told me the following: His wife kept a diary. On one page in it, during the year 1894, it was noted that an officer who had been sitting next her at a banquet, and who had followed the trial and had the day before been present at the degradation of Alfred Dreyfus, said to her after dinner, *Hier nous avons condamné un innocent* ("Yesterday we punished an innocent man").

My lecture, which I delivered under the chairmanship of General Türr, won me enthusiastic applause from a very large cosmopolitan audience. Many of the Russians who were present asked to be presented to me in order to express their appreciation; among others an elderly lady clad in deep mourning, who announced that she was the mother of Marie Bashkirtseff, that young genius who died so prematurely.

The next day I saw her in her own home, and found that it was a sort of memorial temple to the departed; on all the walls there was nothing but pictures painted by Marie Bashkirtseff, or representing Marie herself at all periods of her life and in the most varying phases, always full of beauty and charm. Neither could the sorrowful mother speak of anything else than of her famous daughter.

A few days later I gave a lecture in Cannes. Luncheon on the *Arche de Noé;* Italian singers on board; magnificent weather; guests Count Rochechouart, the mayor, the president of the Nautical Club, Türr, and another gentleman — I do not remember his name — with a brutal face. The table talk turns on Dreyfus.

" I do not admit," says Count Rochechouart, "that seven officers condemned a comrade without being certain of their position."

The Mayor: "Other people, not knowing the circumstances, have no right to express an opinion."

The Nautical President: "A dozen bullets ought to have been sent through his body."

Rochechouart: " I belong to only one league — it is impossible to be of another — Déroulède's."

The Brutal Man: "Obviously; I should like to see you being anything else."

So these are my fellow-banqueters before a lecture on peace!

234

BEFORE THE HAGUE

The lecture fell very flat. The hall was pretty empty. No enthusiasm. I have not often made such a miserable speech. After the lecture, which ended about four o'clock in the afternoon, we took a walk through the wonderful city of gardens.

In Nice we were rejoiced by a call which brought back sweet recollections of the beautiful days in the Caucasus. I read in the local newspaper that Prince Lucien Murat and his wife, born Princesse de Rohan, had come to make a visit to the Empress Eugénie in neighboring Cimièz. I immediately wrote a note to my former little German pupil to tell him that we were near at hand. The next day the young couple came to see us. One cloud only darkened the delight of the reunion, namely, the tragic death of Prince Achille Murat, Lucien's father. The incident was not mentioned.

On our return to Harmannsdorf our days were filled with preparations for the journey to The Hague; I wrote numerous articles and sent letters to all points of the compass. I had buried myself in Bloch's great work and had written him about it. In reply I received the following letter:

Warsaw, April 8, 1899

My dear Baroness:

Heartiest thanks for your kind lines. The service ascribed to me is, however, only the result of the movement against war which has been going on, and in which you personally, gracious Baroness, have taken such an important part; and I must bear witness that your personal talent, in my opinion, has accomplished more than all technical arguments can possibly accomplish.

Unfortunately I could not write you sooner because I had an unusual task to finish. Unfortunately, also, I am still so very busy that I can only send a sketch in place of the desired programme.

In my opinion it would be best for an agitation to be made, to the end that the Conference *in pleno*, or that single states, should inaugurate an investigation as to the possibility of carrying through a great war.

At this moment the governments are not humble enough, public opinion is not as yet ripe enough, to be able to obtain results from the Conference. It would be much more practical if the sessions could be postponed until autumn, so as to let the separate states have time for arranging investigations and preparing public opinion.

I will at all events endeavor to meet you so as to talk the matter over more in detail. I shall be in London about the fourteenth, at Hotel Cecil, and shall be at the Grand Hôtel in Paris toward the eighteenth, and there I expect to remain about a fortnight.

I will do my best to promote matters in the direction indicated.

It is impossible for me to predict to-day whether I shall be able to get to Scheveningen. At any rate I shall take the liberty of writing you in regard to this, and one of the principal motives of my desire to be there would be to have the opportunity of becoming better acquainted with you.

With genuine loyalty and respect

J. Bloch

I also asked Prince Scipione Borghese to come to The Hague, as I had just been informed that he had come out in favor of the peace cause. He wrote back:

My dear Madam: Felice Scovolo, Lago di Garda, April 20, 1899

Your pleasant letter, which I am very late in answering, has excited our desires more than you would believe possible. To spend some time with you and *un groupe du high-life pacifique*, closely following the work of this Conference, which is without contradiction one of the culminating facts of the history of our century, seems to us a delicious dream.

236

BEFORE THE HAGUE

Unhappily your interesting invitation will preserve all the beauty of a dream, which is always somewhat melancholy because of its unreality. The marriage of my youngest sister to Count Hoyos, which is to be celebrated toward the end of May in the depths of Hungary, calls us in that direction, and up to that time I am kept here by the carrying out of a social and agrarian transformation in which I am enormously interested and which keeps me at its beck and call.

As for the Conference, the idea of which is in itself so beautiful and its convocation such a great victory, I hope that the good will of certain governments may compensate for the ill will of so many others, and that the whole thing will not remain in the realm of ideas but will give us some practical fruits. . . .

You will find in our two Italian delegates, Count Nigra and Count Zanini, two charming men who are personally very well disposed.

Sincerely yours
Scipione Borghese

I received from Paris the subjoined letter, from one who was quite unknown to me. It was the first step of an animated intercourse both epistolary and personal, — I may say of a faithful friendship and collaboration which has not yet ceased to ally me with the author, the most successful peace worker in France.

Paris, April 10, 1899

My dear Madam:

Since I have abandoned diplomacy to enter Parliament, I have begun to publish in the *Revue des deux mondes* a series of studies on the precarious state of Europe and on the necessity imposed on all civilized states of uniting in behalf of progress and of war on evil. These studies, the first dated April 1, 1896, the second July 19, 1897, will shortly be brought to a close by a third part, in which international arbitration and relative disarmament are brought forward as the conclusion.

My nomination as one of the French delegates to The Hague will prevent me from finishing this long work, though at the same time permitting me to make it more united. I perceive, in fact, that I still require many indispensable data not found in books. Perhaps I might obtain them by addressing myself to your kindness of heart, since you allow none of the manifestations of public opinion regarding universal peace to escape you.

This is the question that preoccupies me: Is popular sentiment in Austria-Hungary generally and personally hostile to war? No one can know that, but still one may have an impression. What is yours?

If in each country in the world a like opinion, not in the clouds but well thought out, could be obtained, with what force it could and should weigh on the governments and consequently on their delegates at the Conference.

Please accept, madam, the very respectful admiration of a French-man who, without knowing you, is devoted to you.

D'Estournelles de Constant

In my reply to this letter I brought up the hindrances which, through the apathetic and sometimes hostile opinions of influential persons and of the masses, were blocking the work of the Conference. From this point of view I pleaded for a continuity of the international conferences; for, while I expected everything from the development of the movement as already started, certainly not much was to be expected from this first session, made up as it was of at least as many doubters and opponents as adherents. Thereupon Baron d'Estournelles wrote me a long letter, from which I translate the following passage:

I am completely in accord with you, gracious lady, only I am somewhat more optimistic than you are with regard to the results of the Conference. I believe, and the more I think it over the more I believe, that the Conference cannot help doing some good — more than is expected of it. The members will feel the revelation of the living world, the wishes of humanity, and the nearness of the terrible dangers that threaten Europe.

None of the governments represented at The Hague will be willing to expose themselves to the unpopularity, the dissatisfaction, the ridicule, of the people, which would be evoked by a failure or a wretched, disappointing result.

Therefore, voluntarily or involuntarily, some good will be accomplished, and, once on this path, it must be pursued to the end. It will be impossible, it will be dangerous, to hold back.

The pamphlet entitled " Perpetual Peace," by the Munich professor Von Stengel, came out. In this all the arguments of the opponents, all the glorification of war and of armaments, that have ever been brought against the notion of peace are summed up, and there is added out-and-out derision of the approaching conference daydream. And the author of this pamphlet had been nominated by the German government as its representative at the Hague Conference! This aroused great consternation in our circles, and the German peace associations protested publicly.

From Austria, Lammasch, professor of international law, and Count Welsersheimb, attached to the diplomatic service, were appointed as delegates. The latter, hitherto a stranger to me, made me a call in order to secure facts relating to the peace movement.

On the eleventh of May I received a telegram from Bloch. The desire to form a committee, consisting of political economists, military men, and politicians, which should institute and publish investigations concerning the presumable results of a future war between the great powers, characterized the aim of Bloch's plans and action. He telegraphed:

Shall reach The Hague the sixteenth. Hope to find room at your hotel. In case Conference at the beginning fails to institute serious investigation, plan to form a committee which shall undertake this work. I have letters from Prussian generals which show that the idea is already ripe. I am ready to guarantee the expenses. It would be very desirable, using Vienna as a rendezvous, to secure a number of names of political economists and statisticians, and, if possible, of military men. I think that, for execution of the plan, reporters on special divisions of my work, or independent workers, should be nominated, who subsequently should be coördinated through a central committee. Any other method, however, equally acceptable.

Bloch.

The two grand masters of the movement, Hodgson Pratt and Élie Ducommun, sent me the following letters before my departure for The Hague:

Madame la Baronne: St. Germain-en-Laye [without date]

I see from the newspapers that you are, as is most fitting, at The Hague. You are a witness of one of the greatest events of modern times, and I venture to write a few lines to congratulate you on the fact that you have been able to contribute to the bringing about of this great event. All changes in human affairs are in these days due to the all-powerful influence of *public opinion;* and you have possessed special gifts and opportunities of contributing to the formation of that great power of opinion. The very fact of your being *a woman,* and of your being a member of the aristocracy in an essentially aristocratic and military nation, has powerfully attracted attention in Continental Europe by your writings and speeches. You have been able to speak and write with a special and personal experience not possessed by the majority of the advocates of international unity and concord. To this work you have brought the great gifts of eloquence and sincere enthusiasm. God has blessed your efforts in enabling you to see at least some of the results of your devoted and unselfish work.

BEFORE THE HAGUE

In such a moment it is alike a pleasure and a duty to give expression to the feelings which, as a humble brother during many years, I entertained in regard to your great services with all my heart.

I hoped to have said this to you *viva voce* at Bern a few weeks ago, and was much disappointed at not seeing you there. I regretted that the members of the commission did not see their way to the appointment of two or three experts in the question of arbitration tribunals, and so forth, such as Mr. La Fontaine, and others.

But doubtless there are delegates who will do all that is necessary, and influence their colleagues by their knowledge and earnestness. It is a profound source of satisfaction to know that Sir Julian Pauncefote is taking part in the proceedings; no better man in our cause could have been sent.

I desire to be heartily remembered to the Baron von Suttner; and remain with profound esteem,

Yours truly

Hodgson Pratt

Bern, May 10, 1899

My dear Madam and dear Colleague:

You have caused me great joy in addressing to me your two letters, which I consider as the private diary of an apostle of peace, and which we shall preserve with particular care because there will be found in them, in time to come, precious information. Many of our friends to whom I have communicated your impressions have got from reading them a confidence and a courage which they to some degree lacked. Continue, I beg of you, to keep me informed in this way.

The editing of the bimonthly correspondence will naturally demand the greatest prudence, and I shall find it difficult to make selections from the reports of the press; your *renseignements intimes* will help me out of this difficult pass.

You cannot believe how many inquiries for information I receive to which I am obliged to reply immediately, carefully guarding my replies. It is a good sign, for it means that everywhere people are beginning to interest themselves in the questions that figure in the programme of The Hague; but the bad side of the medal is that, as I am obliged to remain at my post, ready at any given moment to radiate from the center to the extremities whatever it may become necessary to communicate to the groups of peace at a given moment, I cannot bring to you at The Hague the support of my presence and my efforts. Each to his place! You fit admirably in yours, and that is the main thing.

Bon courage!

Every good wish to M. de Suttner, I beg of you, and to the other devoted peace workers who may inquire for me occasionally.

> Your devoted and affectionate colleague
>
> Élie Ducommun

The founder of the Red Cross, Henri Dunant, gave me the following directions for the way we are traveling. Proof is shown therein that Henri Dunant desired from the Conference not the promotion of the work which he had established, but rather the establishment of a great new work, international justice. No longer was " Red Cross" his rallying cry, but " White Banners."

My dear Baroness :   May 16, 1899

Permit me, madam, to insist very strongly on what I consider a capital point, namely, the extreme importance of seeing the Congress pass an official, diplomatic resolution on the subject of a *Permanent Diplomatic Commission on Mediation*. In my letter of the twelfth I called it a " Permanent Bureau on Mediation"; now the word "Commission" is more suitable, and, too, it must not be confounded with the permanent International Bureau of Peace at Bern, which is a voluntary work and has no diplomatic mission — that is to say, in the eyes of diplomacy it does not count.

All our efforts ought to be concentrated on this special point, without concerning ourselves with the rest. And for this, personal dealings on your part with the delegates are necessary. But in my opinion it is important to go no farther. Let them discuss the first seven articles of the official Russian programme as much as they please, and let us not meddle with it; do not dispute with them on this subject, for it would weaken the authority of your words. But, as to Article 8 of the said programme, stand firm on the necessity, the urgency, the opportuneness, and even the courtesy toward his Majesty the Tsar, of a formal diplomatic decision of the Hague Conference, in a "resolution" to be made obligatory by the subsequent official ratification of all civilized governments. Hint to the delegates that it would be desirable that this resolution relative to Article 8 should be distinct from all the others relative to the first seven articles.

Whatever be the instructions of their respective governments, the delegates can always telegraph or write their governments on this special point, either before or at the moment of the discussion of Article 8, to ask for special instructions relative to it. This was done during the Geneva Congress of 1864, and many governments wired their delegates authorization to sign the protocol of the convention. With much more reason they could authorize the signature of a "special resolution relative to Article 8."

To attain these ends, it is important to talk the delegates over, to win them one by one, to astonish them by the moderation of our desires and the definiteness of what we wish. You alone, madam, are capable of doing this. The opportunity is unique; but let us keep within bounds. If this resolution is passed, everything is won. The future will develop all that we can desire; but let us not lose ourselves in details.

I was at Brussels in 1874, when Prince Gortchakoff cheated me out of my congress in favor of prisoners of war (under preparation for two years) by supplanting it with a congress on the "usages of war," swallowing up the prisoners and even the Geneva Convention! I suffered terribly at that time, for there was no result, and here for twenty-five years those deliberations taken in secret congress have remained a dead letter!

You know that Article 8 runs thus:

The acceptance, in principle, of the use of good offices, mediation, and voluntary arbitration, in cases adapted to such means, with the object of preventing armed conflicts between nations; an agreement as to the mode of applying these means; and the adoption of a uniform practice in using them.

I am, my dear Baroness, most respectfully yours

H. Dunant

243

P.S. At some moment during the Congress — which will last a long time — could you not see the young Queen in order to explain all this to her?

1. Article 8 must be made the subject of a special "resolution" by the Hague Congress (a separate protocol).

2. And on the subject of this special resolution the Congress should try to find a diplomatic method of acting which shall permit Holland to play the part which the Swiss Federal Council plays for the Geneva Convention. It is a fine rôle.

Affairs do not proceed promptly in diplomacy. The Swiss Federal Council convoked the governments by a diplomatic invitation dated June 6, 1864. But the recommendation signed by France went to the same states a few days later in June.

Mr. Drouyn de Lhuys, Minister of Foreign Affairs in Paris, and I had arranged that on April 22, 1864; and from that time the Swiss Federal Council at Bern has had all the protocols in its possession. Only last year it received notices of assent to the Geneva Convention from the Transvaal, the Republic of Uruguay, Nicaragua, and Honduras; and that has been pending since 1864. Holland should play for the "resolution" resulting from Article 8 of the programme of the Congress the same rôle as the Swiss Federal Council does for the Convention. For this purpose the delegates taken individually must be persuaded to separate the protocols; one protocol for the first seven articles of the programme (or any other way, as they please) and an entirely separate and independent protocol for the "resolution" proceeding from Article 8.

And now, with minds keyed high, and with joyous hearts, we got ready to go to The Hague.

LVIII

THE FIRST PEACE CONFERENCE AT THE HAGUE

My Hague diary · Arrival · First interview · Stead's interviews with the Tsar and with Bülow · Our call on the Austrian delegation · Divine service in the Russian chapel · Opening session · Johann von Bloch · Party at Beaufort's · Yang-Yü and his wife · Baron d'Estournelles · Léon Bourgeois · We give a dinner · Richet's call · Luncheon with Frau Moscheles · Andrew D. White · Extract from Staal's opening speech · Call on our ambassador's wife · Count Costantino Nigra · Reception at court · Lord Aberdeen · Sir Julian Pauncefote · Bloch plans a series of lectures · Plenary assembly of May 25 · The Russian, English, and American motions

IN 1900 I published a comprehensive book[1] in which I gathered together all the events of my sojourn at The Hague, all the reports regarding the proceedings, the text of the most important speeches, and the accurate statement of the various conventions. Those who may wish to have a detailed account of the character, the course of events, and the direct results of that historic assemblage I would refer to that publication. Here I shall merely introduce my personal recollections; I shall copy in their original form extracts from my private journal which I used and elaborated for that book, of course excluding everything that was too confidential and therefore uninteresting.

[1] *Die Haager Friedenskonferenz, Tagebuchblätter,* Dresden und Leipzig, E. Pierson. 2d edition, 1901. Price 2 marks.

At the same time I shall introduce minutes of the proceedings and observations on world politics, for, if I am to give the history of my life conscientiously, these things require much space. They were not applied as accidental embroidery, but have been woven into the very fabric of my existence. Whatever has taken place either in behalf of the cause of peace or in opposition to it, anywhere in the world, — and especially what occurred in those days at The Hague, where the Conference was called together in the name of that cause, — was not a mere experience from without, it was an essential part of my life.

May 16. Arrival at The Hague. The city steeped in the magic of spring. Radiant sunshine. Lilac perfumes in the cool air. Our rooms in the hotel all ready. Nine o'clock in the evening. We are still sitting in the dining-room. The correspondent of the *Neues Wiener Tagblatt* is announced. Receive him and he takes his place at our table. He begins the interview with great liveliness:

" Have just been having a talk with the representative of a first-class power. There seems to be no great doubt as to the prospective outcome, — amplification of the Geneva Convention — "

" If nothing more than that should be accomplished, it would be an outrageous trick played on the hopes of the nations, and also a disappointment for the Tsar, whose wishes for an arbitral tribunal — "

The correspondent laughingly interrupted me:

"We spoke about this also. Now that is simply childish. The states would not comply with a decision which did not please them."

" Such a case has never once occurred."

" For the reason that, up to the present time, arbitration has settled only trivialities; but when vital questions are concerned — "

Forever and ever the time-worn arguments. I heard it come in its regular sequence, "the vital question," although no one knows exactly what he means by it. What, indeed, can these "vital" concerns be that are best promoted by killing off men by the hundred thousand?

May 17. Stead arrived. Directly from St. Petersburg, where he had an audience with Nicholas II, lasting an hour and a half, and spoke quite candidly about Finland. The Tsar also empowered him to speak on the same theme — in favor of Finnish liberties — the next day in a public assembly.

Stead also stopped over in Berlin on his way hither, and had a conversation with Bülow, bringing up among other things the case of Professor Stengel and his anti-peace pamphlet. Herr von Bülow at first denied that the professor had written the brochure, and was quite hot about it.

" It is not true," he declared, "it is pure invention."

" That cannot well be said, for the pamphlet is in its third edition. . . . "

"It was a simple lecture," the minister now opined, "delivered in a gathering of friends, and issued by the publisher behind the author's back."

That is scarcely thinkable either; but this much is clear, — the pamphlet, if not its author, is disavowed. The appointment had been made, it was claimed, without any knowledge of the lecture. And if that were the case, Herr von Stengel should have declined the appointment. Any one who has publicly called an endeavor a daydream does not proceed to take part in the dreaming. Suppose then the intention or the orders were to oppose it! But even if these orders were not directly given, still it is melancholy that an opponent of the cause should be sent as a delegate.

The Grelixes have arrived too. Felix Moscheles tells of the campaign of agitation which he and Stead have undertaken all through the English cities. He was one of the deputation that communicated the results of the crusade to the Russian ambassador, who had already been appointed to head the Russian delegation. Herr von Staal said to Moscheles: "The Conference is admirably prepared for by these public demonstrations of the people's desire for peace. If I may be pardoned for using the vulgar phrase, *Vous avez mis du foin dans nos bottes.*"[1]

In the afternoon a round of calls. When our carriage draws up before the Hotel Paulez, Count Welsersheimb

[1] This might be translated, "You have furnished us straw for our bricks."
— TRANSLATOR.

248

comes out and invites us up to his drawing-room, saying that the whole Austrian delegation is assembled there. In fact, the little room is filled with our fellow-countrymen, among them Herr von Merey, head of a division in the Ministry of Foreign Affairs, — slender, aristocratic, agreeable; Viktor von Khuepach zu Ried, lieutenant colonel on the general staff; Count Soltys, commander; Professor Lammasch, abrupt but at the same time polite; Count Zichy, not a delegate but Austrian ambassador at Munich. The conversation turns naturally on the Conference. I have the impression that those present are filled with lively interest regarding this phenomenon "Conference," but an interest mingled with astonishment and skepticism, with an amazed and curious excitement, such as the marvels of nature seen for the first time are wont to arouse.

May 18. The eighteenth of May, 1899! This is an epoch-making date in the history of the world. As I write it down I am deeply impressed with this conviction. It is the first time, since history began to be written, that the representatives of the governments come together to find a means for "securing a permanent, genuine peace" for the world. Whether or not this means will be found in the Conference that is to be opened to-day has nothing to do with the magnitude of the event. In the endeavor lies the new direction!

May 19. This is the way yesterday went: In the morning, divine service in the Russian chapel in

celebration of the Tsar's birthday. My Own and I
were invited. The place is small and scarcely a hundred people were present, the men in gala uniform, the
ladies in semi-informal dress. The high mass begins.
The congregation, all standing, reverent and devout,
follow it. It seemed to me as if it were my part not
to pray *for* Nicholas II, but to address *to* him the
petition: "O thou brave of heart, remain firm! Let
not the ingratitude and the spite and the imbecility of
the world penetrate to thee to disturb and paralyze;
even if an attempt is made to belittle and misinterpret
and even block thy work, remain firm!"

The priest holds out the cross to be kissed: the
mass is over. Now greetings and introductions are
exchanged. I make the acquaintance of Minister
Beaufort's wife.

Drive to the opening session of the Conference. Brilliant sunshine. Numerous carriages proceed through
the shaded avenues to the "House in the Wood," as
if in a festive parade in the Prater or the Bois. At
the grated gate a military guard of honor makes the
customary salutes. I am the only woman permitted
to be present.

What I experienced here was like the fulfillment of a
lofty ambitious dream. "Peace Conference!" For ten
long years the words and the idea have been laughed
to scorn; its advocates, feeble private persons, are regarded as "Utopians" (the favorite polite circumlocu-
tion for "crazy fellows"); and now, at the summons of

the most powerful of the war lords, the representatives of all the sovereigns are gathering, and their assembly bears that very name, " Peace Conference."

From the opening address of Minister Beaufort:

By his initiative the Emperor of Russia has desired to fulfill the wish expressed by his predecessor, Alexander I, that all the rulers of Europe should come to an understanding together, so as to live like brethren and to support one another mutually in their necessities.

It seems to me that Nicholas II desired more than that; the question does not affect so much the necessities of all rulers as those of all nations. The armaments are burdensome to the nations, not to the rulers. The so-called dynastic interest lies more in military pomp and the prestige of warlike power.

And Beaufort again:

The object of the Conference is to seek for means to put a limit to incessant armaments and alleviate the heavy distress that weighs on the nations. The day of the assembling of this Conference will be one of the most notable in the history of the closing century.

After Beaufort's speech Ambassador Staal is chosen president of the Conference. Then follow the other nominations; the whole piece of business lasts only half an hour, — it was intended to be merely a formal opening ceremony. The first session is appointed for the twentieth, and at the same time it is announced that journalists will not be admitted to the deliberations. (Alas!)

May 19. Bloch arrived. We greet each other like old friends. A man of sixty, with short-cropped, grizzly beard, a bright, kindly expression, unconstrained, elegant manners, a thoroughly natural, simple mode of speech. I inquire of him as to the reception of his book by the Tsar. Bloch tells us the story, and the delegates and journalists in the drawing-room listen with interest:

Yes, the Tsar has studied the work thoroughly. When he received me in audience, the maps and tables from the book lay spread out on the tables, and he had me carefully explain all the figures and diagrams. I explained until I was tired out, but Nicholas II did not grow weary. He kept asking new questions or throwing in observations which testified to his deep appreciation and interest. " So *this* is the way the next war would develop," he said; "*those* would be the results, would they ? "

The Ministry of War, to which a copy had to be submitted, furnished the Emperor with a report and voted to authorize its publication. In justifying its report it said: " Such a comprehensive and technical book will not be much read; it is therefore far less dangerous than the Suttner novel, *Die Waffen nieder*. Inasmuch as the censor passed the latter, Bloch's ' War of the Future ' may *a fortiori* be admitted."

In the evening a party at Beaufort's. Like all parties in court or diplomatic circles, and yet so entirely different. Something new has come into the world, namely, the official treatment of the theme "Universal Peace," and that necessarily — being indeed the *raison d'être* of this reception — introduces the topic for general discussion.

A question which very commonly serves to start the conversation is this: What do you expect from the Conference? This question was quite frequently put to me, or else this: Are you not happy to see your hopes so realized?

"Yes, very happy," I could answer truthfully enough; "I had not once hoped to see so much and that so speedily done." To the first question I had to reply that I expected from this Conference only that it would be a beginning, a first step, a foundation stone laid.

I am becoming acquainted with the majority of the participants, even with the delegate from China and his wife. He is at the same time ambassador to the court of Russia.

"In St. Petersburg I heard you much talked about," said Yang-Yü to me, through his interpreter, Lu Tseng-Tsiang; "Count Muravieff told me about his talk with you."

The Chinese delegate's young wife wears her native costume, including an embroidered silk robe, a tiny cap on her head, and paper flowers on each side of her temples. She is a pretty young woman, yet quite of the type which you see on Chinese porcelain; at the same time she is so heavily rouged that her face resembles a changeless enameled mask. She is very friendly and shakes hands vigorously with all who are presented to her. She is accompanied by her son, a lad of twelve or thirteen, who speaks English and French and interprets for her.

Meet many of the old friends, Descamps, Beernaert, Rahusen, and others.

A stranger approaches me: "Baroness, I am happy to meet you again." It is Baron d'Estournelles. We have not met before, but our preceding correspondence

253

justifies the word "revoir." He is a genial man, with fine head, dark mustache, and diplomatic manners; we have a heart-to-heart conversation. His speech sparkles with witty observations, but a profound earnestness inspires him for the Cause.

At my request he introduces to me his chief, Léon Bourgeois. The former French Prime Minister is the youngest head of a delegation, and when seen among all the white-haired ambassadors, veterans in diplomacy, such as Staal, Münster, Nigra, and Pauncefote, he with his black head resembles (as Stead says) a starling among sea gulls.

M. Bourgeois tells me about Frédéric Passy, whom he has lately seen and talked with. Our *doyen* would gladly have come to The Hague, but he had to give it up on account of an eye trouble. He submitted to an operation in the hope that he might be able to come to the city of the Conference with restored eyesight; but Bourgeois says that the operation, although it was successful, has not been attended by so prompt a recovery as had been expected.

May 20. Again a round of calls. The drive through the streets of The Hague is exactly like going through a park. Not only in the *bosch*, where the *huis* put at the service of the Conference stands, but everywhere are gigantic old trees; everywhere are green grass-plots; and everywhere, in this May time so rich in flowers, are heard the lovely carols of the birds. Almost every house has a garden, and houses for rent are not to be seen; every house, built in the style of a villa or a small château, is the home of only one family. Of course this is true only of the aristocratic quarter, which surrounds the royal palace and leads from the squares where the best hotels, like Vieux Doelen and others, are situated, down to Scheveningen.

Our drawing-room is always full of callers, and from early in the morning with interviewers; to-day, among others, the editors of the *Frankfurter Zeitung*, the *Écho de Paris*, and *Black and White*.

From Paris comes the news that the operation on Frédéric Passy has had such unfavorable consequences that not only is he suffering intolerable pain but even his life is in danger. Great consternation in our whole circle. Of all the living champions of peace Frédéric Passy is without question the most loved and honored by all who know him and his work.

At the first plenary session to-day Herr von Staal is to define in his address the goal and direction which his imperial master wishes the Conference to take. How regrettable that the press is excluded! The president's speech would be telegraphed this very day to all the newspapers in the world.

May 21. Whitsunday. Dr. Trueblood from Boston arrived. He tells us that he knows for a certainty that the United States government has committed to its delegates a thoroughly formulated plan for a court of arbitration.

A sculptor from Berlin, Löher is his name, shows

us the model of a peace memorial which he would like to exhibit at the Paris Exposition of 1900. Thus in new regions, in forms more and more varied, the new ideal is cherished.

At the same time, to be sure, how deeply rooted, how mighty is the old ideal still, that of war, — everywhere prevalent, even among those attending this Conference; just read Professor Stengel's pamphlet! . . . And the fearful thing is, ideas progress slowly, while events march swiftly. If a case like that at Fashoda, if the controversy in the Transvaal, suddenly precipitates a conflict while the Conference is still in session, how it would disturb its theoretical labors!

We give a small dinner. Our guests are Okolic-zany, the Austrian ambassador at The Hague, Count Welsersheimb, Baron d'Estournelles, Count Gurko, and Councilor von Bloch. It was a satisfaction to me to hear Baron d'Estournelles talk with my countrymen about the hopes and views with which the members of the French delegation are inspired. A satisfaction for this reason, that I had been compelled to hear many Austrians, not here but in Vienna, ask, " How can the Conference succeed? Even though we are sincere lovers of peace, the French, who know no other thought than revenge, and who are represented at the Conference only out of politeness to the Tsar, will assuredly make every endeavor to prevent any results, even if they do not purposely conjure up a conflict!"

If by chance Herr von Okoliczany and Count Wel-sersheimb had this notion of their French colleagues in the Conference, they have certainly this evening been set right.

My guests also listen with lively interest to Bloch's remarks and elucidations. Of course all know about his great book, have read criticisms of it, and have had a chance to turn the leaves of the six volumes as they lie on my drawing-room table; and so they give the most eager attention to what the author himself relates regarding the establishment of his work and its results. In this exposition Bloch speaks so calmly, modestly, and to the point! It is felt that his convic-tion rests on scrupulously investigated facts; he is conscious in his own mind that he has gathered the simple truth and given it out in its full scope.

D'Estournelles announces a visitor. To-morrow Charles Richet is coming to The Hague as D'Estour-nelles's guest. This very day Richet's latest book had reached me, — a succinct history of the peace move-ment. The French savant, editor of the *Revue scienti-fique*, is with us heart and soul; he and Frédéric Passy are members of the board of directors of the French Peace Society. It is therefore a twofold pleasure to hear that the representative of France here at The Hague is a friend of his; more than a friend, an ad-mirer. *C'est un grand cœur, une belle intelligence;* such is D'Estournelles's judgment on Charles Richet.

May 22. Another "meeting again" (*Wiedersehen*)

with an old acquaintance whom I had never seen; Charles Richet calls on us and brings us greetings from our poor Passy. He has hopes that he will get well, but none that he will come to The Hague. Richet proves to be a great enthusiast in our cause. I wanted to keep him for luncheon, but he and D'Estournelles are invited to the French ambassador's.

In the meantime we had an invitation to a luncheon given by Frau Grete Moscheles to Andrew D. White, head of the American delegation and ambassador to Berlin.

The information which Dr. White gave us filled us all with the keenest satisfaction: "I am guilty of no indiscretion," he said at dessert, "if I tell you that at the first session of the arbitration committee we shall bring forward a complete plan for an international tribunal, — and this at the command of the United States government. I cannot as yet give the details, but the fact itself will, and should, be no secret."

May 23. In spite of closed doors, Staal's opening address is already known. An English paper has printed it. I extract the specially significant passages:

The name "Peace Conference," which has been conferred on our meeting by the instinct of the nations, anticipating the decisions of the governments, designates correctly the object of our endeavors; the "Peace Conference" cannot be unfaithful to the mission intrusted to it; it must bring forth a tangible result such as the whole world confidently expects from it.

. . . Let me be permitted to say that diplomacy, following a general process of development, is no longer what it formerly was, — an art in which personal cleverness plays the chief rôle, — but is on the point of becoming a science with definite rules for the settlement of international difficulties. This is to-day the ideal aim which it must keep before its eyes, and it will unquestionably be a great advance if there is a successful attempt made here to settle some of those rules.

Therefore we must take special pains to generalize and to codify the application of the principles of arbitration as well as of mediation and friendly offices. These ideas, so to speak, form the very kernel of our task, the common aim of our endeavors, that is to say the solution of international controversies by peaceful means.

. . . The nations cherish a burning desire for peace, and we are responsible to mankind and to the governments that have empowered us with their authority, we are responsible to ourselves, to do a profitable work in establishing methods of employing some of the means for securing peace. In the front rank of these means stand arbitration and mediation.

Charles Richet and his son breakfast with us. One thing Richet said makes a deep impression on me: " On all sides we are compelled to hear it said that the time has not yet come to carry out our ideals. This may be so, but certainly the present is the time to prepare for it."

In the afternoon a call on Frau von Okoliczany. This lady — born Princess Lobanof — has the reputation of having been a dazzling beauty. She is still beautiful. Figure, shoulders, arms of statuesque harmony of lines. The white cashmere tea gown in which she received us has loose sleeves which leave her fair, round arms free. Hands have their individual physiognomies, as is well known; Frau von Okoliczany's beautiful hands accompany her vivacious conversation with what might be called vivacious pantomime, and the motions of her arms are eloquent.

A caller comes in,—Count Costantino Nigra. Can it be possible that this slender, tall man, with his thick, wavy hair still blond, with his regular features showing scarcely any marks of age, is already seventy years old? Of course the conversation turns on the Conference and its objects. Count Nigra gives the impression of being thoroughly imbued with the solemnity of the task, and of being hopeful of its results.

Of course it is his duty, not only from a diplomatic point of view but almost from that of propriety, to speak in this way. One would hardly dare to take part in official, nay more, secret, deliberations, and then make light of them in a drawing-room conversation. Only to Baron von Stengel did it happen to be sent to a Conference the object of which he had shortly before characterized as "a daydream." . . . But apart from diplomatic punctiliousness, you are instinctively aware when any one speaks frankly and from conviction, and I get the impression that Count Nigra is going to work earnestly and zealously for the cause.

May 24   D'après les ordres de
                    Sa Majesté *la Reine*
          Le Maréchal de la Cour a l'honneur d'inviter
    Monsieur le Baron, Madame la Baronne Berthe Suttner
      née Comtesse Kinsky, et Mademoiselle de Suttner [1]
                à une Soirée au Palais
            Mercredi le 24 Mai à 9½ heures
                       en Gala

[1] My niece Maria Louise was with us at The Hague.

THE FIRST PEACE CONFERENCE

One court function is like another: the long line of carriages which drive in à *la file* through the palace gates; the broad, covered steps adorned with flowers, where the liveried lackeys stand on either side and with dumb show indicate the way; the lofty, gilded drawing-rooms with polished parqueted floors; the numberless uniforms and gala court costumes of the men, the trailing light robes of the ladies, who are adorned with diamonds, flowers, and heron plumes; the atmosphere full of excitement and expectation.

The first halls through which we pass are rather empty; we are shown by the master of ceremonies through a vast, half-filled room, and farther still into a salon which is quite densely crowded. Here people are standing almost tête-à-tête. Nods of recognition and greetings are exchanged; there is lively conversation. Some one remarks that it is different at the English court. There the appearance of the Queen is awaited in religious silence.

A half hour elapses. In the adjoining drawing-room the guests take their places round the center, which is left vacant. These are the diplomats and their wives, for whom their majesties will hold court. The Chinaman and his wife again make the most striking appearance in this circle. They are in silken robes with rich embroidery of flowers, but Mrs. Yang wears for the adornment of her head only the usual paper flowers hanging down over her temples.

"Leurs Majestés les Reines!"

A lane is made in the circle and in come Queen Wilhelmina and Queen Emma surrounded by their courtiers. Both are in white. A white veil flows down from the Queen mother's diadem. The girl Queen wears the broad band of the Order of Catherine, which this day was conferred upon her by Herr von Staal in the name of the Tsar.

The circle is completed. The Queen stands for a moment before each lady and gentleman, bows, speaks a few words, bows again, and passes on.

After this diplomatic court is over, the other presentations are made. Frau von Okoliczany leads me up to her Majesty and calls me by name.

A brief conversation in French ensues. The young Queen, graciously smiling, asks me, just as she probably asks most of the others, if this is the first time I have ever visited The Hague and how I like it. I include in my reply the observation that my sojourn in Holland is made particularly happy by the greatness of the cause that brought me there. The gracious little sovereign nods at that but says nothing.

I was presented also to Queen Emma by our ambassador's wife.

After the two royal women have spoken with all present, the whole company withdraws into a third salon, an enormous room, probably the ballroom, where a long table, covered with flowers, fruits, cold dishes, tea, and other liquid refreshments, stands along one side, while near the other are little round tables at which the guests may sit. An orchestra in the gallery plays various concert pieces. As I listened I was surprised to hear the intermezzo from *Cavalleria Rusticana.*

But not much attention is given to the music. Ear and eye and mind are occupied with other things. Did I begin by saying that this court function was like all others? That was wrong. This is a court function such as has never been seen before since courts began, — a court function which only a year ago, if prophesied, would have been laughed to scorn as the wildest freak of the imagination.

" Baroness, the Minister of War desires to be presented to you."

Then again, — " Gracious lady, permit me to introduce myself; my name is Kramer, Secretary in the Ministry of War, and I am eager to tell you that the ideal for which you stand in your novel I have been cherishing in silence for two and thirty years, and now I am heartily rejoiced to see its accomplishment drawing nearer."

I had a long conversation with Lu Tseng-Tsiang, Secretary of the Chinese Embassy in St. Petersburg.

" For us Chinese especially," he remarked, " the attainment of the object set by the Conference would be most highly desirable, for we are particularly threatened by the most serious dangers of the European policy of force."

Herr von Staal talks with me and Herr von Descamps about Johann von Bloch and his book. " C'est un homme remarquable," he observes. " He wants to prove that peace is no longer a Utopia, but that, in the present state of arms and armies, it is Utopia for civilized nations to wage war. And," adds the Russian diplomat, " he may be right."

May 25. A card is brought me, announcing the Earl of Aberdeen. I have been for some time in correspondence with Lady Isabel Aberdeen, who is to preside at the forthcoming Congress of Women in London.

The earl, formerly Governor of Canada, — still a young man of tall, slender figure, with a short, black beard, — brings me greetings from his wife. He tells me that he has been taking an active part in the great campaign of meetings organized by Stead, and has spoken at the gatherings. Charles Richet joins us, also a few German newspaper correspondents, who hitherto have heard and written only things derogatory to the cause of peace; they lay stress especially on the principle that the only guaranty for peace lies in the thorough armament of Germany, since all the other nations are hungry for war. It was a great satisfaction to me that they could hear the Frenchman and the Englishman defend the cause in perfect unanimity and with the most powerful arguments. At the same time, these two men are no "obscure cranks," but one of them is among the highest dignitaries of the British Empire and the other is one of the most distinguished savants of the University of Paris.

In the afternoon, at the reception at the Russian

THE FIRST PEACE CONFERENCE

Embassy, we meet Sir Julian Pauncefote. He is seventy-one years old, but of robust physique; his head and beard are already white, his beard cut in Austrian style with the chin shaven; figure tall and slender; expression of face friendly and noble. Just as services rendered on the battlefield justify promotion to a superior command in a campaign of war, so distinguished deeds in behalf of peace give a suitable title to appointment as a delegate to this Conference. Sir Julian in his diplomatic career has to his credit two great victories in the campaign of peace.

He was ambassador in Washington when Cleveland's message on the Venezuela question startled the world, and everywhere the tidings flew that war between the United States and England was unavoidable. If a Chamberlain had been in his place at that post, possibly matters might have gone to hostilities. Sir Julian was able to conduct affairs in such a calm and conciliatory tone that the matter was submitted to the court of arbitration which, at this very moment, under the chairmanship of Professor von Martens, is deliberating on it in Paris. Secondly, Sir Julian is the man who, together with the United States Secretary of State Olney, on the eleventh of January, 1899, signed the famous arbitration treaty between America and Great Britain — the first treaty of the sort that was ever drawn up. He is not responsible for the fact that the ratification which had to ensue failed by three votes of the requisite two-thirds majority.

Just as Dr. White had told us a few days before of the plan of the Americans, so now Sir Julian assures us that his delegation, too, will come out with a definite proposal in the third committee (that on arbitration). He cherishes the strongest hopes of a positive result. I bring the conversation to the stillborn Anglo-American treaty. He replies that the matter will certainly be taken up again. "What does not succeed on the first throw, my dear Baroness, succeeds on the second or the third."

In the evening a party at the house of the Queen's head chamberlain. Again make the acquaintance of many great people, among them distinguished "foreigners." The German delegation is the only one from which no one does me the honor of greeting me. Count Münster treats me as if I were a rattlebrain. When Professor Stengel spoke in his pamphlet of the "comical persons" of the peace movement, from whose grotesque behavior and ideas he could not sufficiently warn people, he evidently included me in the number.

May 26. Bloch has conceived the idea of having a series of lectures to which the public shall be invited. No other place, no other opportunity, is so well suited for representing the "Utopia of War." The documentary and statistic-bolstered facts and conclusions which these lectures will contain must be of especial interest, he says, to the military delegates. My Own and I are assisting him in his arrangements, going round with him in search of halls, giving orders, and the like.

THE FIRST PEACE CONFERENCE

A visit from the correspondent of the *Frankfurter Zeitung*. He has just come from Herr von Stengel, who assured the reporter that he had protested only against the excrescences of the peace movement (well, yes, the comical persons),— that, nevertheless, as a delegate he should do his best to help the cause along. Very good!

The correspondents of *Figaro* and of the *Écho de Paris* interview me. Mr. Leveson-Gower, Secretary of the British Embassy, in behalf of the *North American Review* asks me to furnish an article on the movement for the July number.

At three o'clock, in Hotel Vieux Doelen, on business. Meet Stead there.

" At last I see you," I cried. " I always expect news from you, as you are on such intimate terms with the delegates. . . ."

" And you shall have it. More important and better news to-day than you could have hoped. Here is a copy of the report which I have just sent to the English newspapers. Read it and rejoice with me. The Conference has done a wonderfully fine stroke of work."

Here is an extract from the report :

PLENARY MEETING OF MAY 25

On the Order of the Day the subject of the third committee is "Peaceable Adjustment of International Controversies."

Herr von Staal introduces the Russian proposals as a basis for the deliberations. It is a document consisting of eighteen articles bearing the title, "Elements for the Elaboration of a Convention to

267

be concluded between the Powers taking Part in the Conference."
These elements are (1) Good offices and mediation, (2) International
arbitration, (3) International commissions of inquiry.

Before the discussion of the articles begins, Sir Julian Pauncefote
rises in the name of his government and moves that a supplementary
article be added to the Russian plan, namely, the organization of a
permanent court of arbitration. In a brief but very impressive speech
the English delegate advocates this motion. He refers to the arguments which are contained in his colleague Descamps's "Address to
the Governments."[1]

The words and the positive action of the chief of the English delegates evidently cause a great sensation. As he ends his speech, a
solemn silence reigns. Many of the members look at one another in
sheer astonishment — many of them, perhaps, for the first time
appreciate that serious matters are to be treated, brought forward by
practical statesmen acting with sincerity.

Still greater is the surprise when Herr von Staal declares that the
Russian government also has in readiness a plan, in twenty-six articles,
for the establishment of a permanent court of arbitration.

Next comes Dr. White with the American proposition. In the
introduction it says: " The proposition shows the earnest desire of
the President of the United States that a permanent international
tribunal be established for the adjustment, by means of arbitration,
of the controversies between nations, and shows the readiness of the
President to assist in its establishment." How radical this proposal
was in its intentions can be seen in the third and fourth articles.

" Article III. The tribunal is to be permanent, and ready at any
moment to undertake all cases that are submitted.

" Article IV. All controversies of every kind[2] shall be subject to
decision by mutual agreement, and every case submitted must be
accompanied by a pledge to abide by the decision of the tribunal."

[1] He refers to the letter, the composition of which, as decreed by the
Interparliamentary Conference of 1894, was intrusted to Chevalier Descamps
and H. La Fontaine, and which, at the direction of the Interparliamentary
Congress of 1895, was sent to all the governments in the name of the Union.
[2] Nothing of the later limitations of "vital interests" and "honor of the
nations." (Observation of 1908.)

Indeed a fine stroke of work! So here at the very beginning are positive, concrete plans in the name of four governments, proposed for discussion and settlement. What a pity that such initiatives have not come also from Austria, Germany, and France!

What a pity, too, that the reports of this session, together with the exact texts of the propositions, are not instantly telegraphed into all the four quarters of the world and published and discussed in all the newspapers, so that some understanding of the great interests here involved may begin to dawn upon the world, and it may be a witness and a judge as to the way and manner, how and by whom, these interests are here represented!

LIX

THE FIRST PEACE CONFERENCE AT THE
HAGUE (*continued*)

J. Novikof · Reception at the Baroness Grovestins's · Dr. Holls · Utterances of the nationalistic press · Excursion to Scheveningen · We give a small dinner · Threatening letter to Herr von Staal · At Ten Kate's · Reports from Descamps · Beernaert on the Geneva Convention · Letter from Levysohn · Results in the matter of mediation · New acquaintances · First of Bloch's evening lectures: subject, "The Development of Firearms" · Stead publishes a daily chronicle on the Conference · Young Vasily's album · Removal to Scheveningen · Baron Pirquet brings a letter from the Interparliamentary Union of Brussels ⁻ Bloch's second lecture: subject, "Mobilization" · My birthday · Dinner at Okoliczany's · Lieutenant Pichon · Letters from aëronauts · Discussion on the permanent tribunal · President Kruger and Sir Alfred Milner · An amusing incident · Bloch's third lecture: subject, "Naval Warfare" · A conversation with Léon Bourgeois · His call to Paris · False reports and denials · What Emperor Nicholas said to Stead · Rumor of the blocking of the arbitration business · Bloch's final lecture: subject, "The War of the Future"

MAY 28. Novikof arrived. What kind of a man do you think is the author of sociological-philosophical works of seven hundred royal-octavo pages each, with such titles as *Les luttes entre sociétés humaines et leurs phases successives, La théorie organique des sociétés,* and the like? I have read these books and this is the idea of the man which I had in my mind: White bearded, with spectacles, in externalities a trifle neglectful of appearances, — for if a person sticks all day long poring over learned books and carries round socialistic problems in his head, he can scarcely be expected to bother himself with the petty vanities of the toilet; I imagined him very earnest but free from pedantry, — for his style is fresh and sparkling, — and probably a bit gloomy, for if one looks so searchingly into the motive powers of the world, has been busied so incessantly with the phenomena of wretchedness and suffering, a mood of melancholy might well ' be expected.

And the actual Novikof? An elegant man of the world, the jolliest of companions, with far too youthful an appearance for his forty-nine years; full of wit and *entrain* in his conversation. I believe these characteristics, charming as they are, injure him to a certain extent. Any one who has not read his books would not suspect what a man he is, would not take up the reading of them with that feeling of awe with which one should bury one's self in scientific works.

In the forenoon a reception at the house of the Baroness Grovestins. Almost all the delegates are present. On the stairs I meet Count Münster and his daughter. In the drawing-room the family of the Chinese delegate forms the center of a numerous group. Madame Yang wears the selfsame coiffure as at the court, the same paper flowers down her temples, and though it is daytime she is painted like a mask, just as if she were under a chandelier. And yet there is a touch of lovableness in her pretty little face. Her gestures when she extends her hand are something like a wooden doll's; but then she shakes the hand of the other person so heartily that it seems to mean, " For life, old comrade! " Her son of twelve and her little daughter of eight, both also in Chinese costume, accompany her, and they bear the brunt of the conversation, for they speak both English and French.

These children will not be brought up as pure, unadulterated Chinese. Behind their wall lies henceforth for them a piece of the world, — a world, moreover, in which all nations are joined to treat together in the name of universal peace; this idea will remain all their lives bound up with the recollection of the sweetmeats which Fräulein von Grovestins, with pretty speeches, offers them on a Delft plate. Gradually all Chinese walls — there are others than that one which bounds the Middle Kingdom — will fall. We already see them tottering.

Make new acquaintances, among them Dr. Holls, the second American delegate.[1] He sits down with me on a small corner sofa. We talk German together. He is by profession a lawyer in New York; comes from a German-American family; has a tall, thick-set, angular figure, and his eyebrows are outlined high on his forehead like circumflex accents. He confirms the news

---

[1] The delegates for the United States of America were Añdrew D. White, United States ambassador at Berlin ; Seth Low, president of Columbia University; Stanford Newell, envoy extraordinary and minister plenipotentiary at The Hague; Captain Alfred T. Mahan, United States Navy ; William Crozier, captain of artillery ; Frederick W. Holls, lawyer, of New York, secretary to the delegation. Mr. Holls died in 1903. — TRANSLATOR.

that I have heard from Stead. He informs me that public interest in the Conference is nowhere else so keen as in his own country. Cablegrams are received every day; resolutions and letters of sympathy come from all the states and from the most diverse circles. Each one of these messages is gratefully acknowledged, and they not only are instrumental in strengthening the American delegates but also make a strong impression on the representatives of other countries, who cannot fail to see in this interest displayed by the Republic of the West a significant sign of the times. I express my regret that this information does not immediately make the round of the European press.

"Yes," assents Holls, "the exclusion of journalists was a great mistake. The majority of the European states are represented here by diplomats who see in mystery and secrecy the factors of successful diplomacy. We Americans and a few others were opposed to it — but the majority decided. Now it may result that the representatives of the great newspapers will feel insulted and go away — a few have already done so. Their editors will retaliate by belittling or ignoring the Conference."

May 29. By way of exception, no party. Spend the evening at home with a group of friends, — Fried, the Grelix couple, the painter Ten Kate, and Novikof. We get a scornful satisfaction in reading aloud a package of extracts from the German nationalistic press.

As the various *Neueste Nachrichten* and the various

Lokalanzeiger in Berlin, Leipzig, Dresden, Munich, and elsewhere comment on the Conference, we find unqualified such expressions as "The disgusting drama at The Hague," "The Conference of Absurdities," "The noxious nuisance now under way, which must arouse righteous indignation in all right-thinking men and genuine Germans," "For the development of universal history the comedy at The Hague will signify about as much as a visit from 'Charley's Aunt' would signify in the life of a single individual."

And even *Vorwärts* (*et tu, Brute !*) — which is not nationalistic but scouts the Conference because it was called together by an autocrat and is composed of aristocrats and bourgeois — even *Vorwärts* writes: "How long will the augurs restrain themselves before they burst out into Homeric laughter and separate amid the laughter of the world ? "

Give heed, ye contemporaries! If ye fail to take seriously such a serious work of beneficence, and to remind those who are engaged in it — even though there be among them men of contrary opinion — of the seriousness of their task, to hold them responsible for its accomplishment, to take them at their word, — take care, I say, lest ye yourselves have to repent not amid the laughter but amid the tears of the world!

May 30. Excursion to Scheveningen. From the city, which lies in the midst of a garden, you drive a couple of miles through avenues lined all the way with trees, like a park, down to the seashore. Along the

way, to right and left, are multitudes of villas behind
flowering gardens. In Scheveningen itself, along the
shore, multitudes of hotels. Everything as yet is
deserted. A cold, salty wind blows from the North
Sea, which under a gray sky rolls in gray billows.
The wicker chairs are not yet brought down on the
beach and the bathing machines are not in their accustomed places. On the broad terrace of the Kurhaus,
around the silent music pavilion, already stand countless rows of tables and chairs, but all unoccupied. On
the sea no ships or boats are to be seen; the bathing
season does not seem to be open yet even for the
sea gulls.

Only a few carriages and pedestrians enliven the
beach and the streets. Scheveningen is indeed for all
the residents of The Hague, and now specially for the
members of the Conference, a general goal for promenading. We exchange greetings with many acquaintances. Our fellow-countryman, Count Welsersheimb,
has come down on his bicycle, and chats with us as he
wheels for some distance beside our carriage. Herr
von Okoliczany, accompanied by his slender daughter,
rides by. The Chinese flag is seen waving over the
Hotel Oranje; Yang-Yü, with his family, is the only
delegate who has already left The Hague and taken
up his residence at Scheveningen.

All those dikes, those structures! How painstaking
and courageous the Dutch people have been in rescuing their land from the waters! *Those* are battles

worthy of men — against the weight and the wrath of the elements. Should the dike-building against the wrath of our fellow-men be alone unaccomplishable?

We gave a small dinner, the party consisting of Rahusen, president of the Chamber; Von Khuepach, the Austrian military delegate; the second Russian delegate, Vasily[1]; Novikof, Bloch, and we three, — a small circle at a round table, the most advantageous arrangement for general and animated conversation. When the coffee was brought, we were joined by the correspondent of the *Neue Freie Presse*, Dr. Frischauer, whom I had invited, but who was prevented from coming sooner.

After dinner a soirée at the Karnebeeks'. Frau von Staal tells me, in the course of a conversation, how her husband is besieged every day with addresses, memoranda, pamphlets, and deputations from all parts of the world.

"And I suppose with numberless letters also, many of them right crazy ones?"

"Oh, yes, even with threatening letters! Anonymous warnings that there is a plan on foot to assassinate him."

"Why! that is horrible! How does Herr von Staal take that?"

"He smiles at it!"

[1] The Russian delegates were Von Staal, ambassador at London; Martens, of the Ministry of Foreign Affairs; Vasily, also of the Foreign Department; and five technical delegates. — TRANSLATOR.

The artist Ten Kate to-day gives us a jolly dinner at the hotel Twe Steeden, where ·he lives during his sojourn at The Hague — his own home is the estate Epé. His lovely wife does the honors. Among the guests are Mesdames von Waszklewicz and Selenka, Herr von Bloch, Novikof, Dr. Trueblood, and A. H. Fried, — in short, a little Peace Congress ·in itself; and it is still more a Peace Congress when after dinner the door opens and in comes the Chevalier Descamps.

"Excuse the intrusion," he exclaims; my rooms are situated above this dining-room. Your jolly voices reached me up there, and when I asked who were celebrating a wedding downstairs I learned who were here, and so I come, uninvited, but as the bringer of good tidings; we had a splendid session to-day."

He is surrounded and interrogated. He tells us the third committee has been that very afternoon wrestling with the question of the arbitration tribunal, and indeed, as Descamps assures us, in a very satisfactory manner. The plan broached in the well-known " memorandum to the governments " has been taken as a basis of the new scheme; and the firm intention of the majority of the members of the committee to bring the matter to a positive result was manifested in that session. Descamps himself has been intrusted with the report on the project. So the matter is certainly in good hands.

A call from Beernaert and his wife. He tells me with satisfaction the result of the session from which he has just come. The second committee, of which he is chairman, has voted to recommend the Brussels Treaty (an extension of the Geneva Convention of 1864).

" It delights me that you are delighted," I replied, "but I tell you frankly that the question of the humanization of war — especially in a Peace Congress — cannot interest me. The business concerns the codification of peace. Saint George rode forth to kill the dragon, not merely to trim its claws. Or, as Frédéric Passy says, *On n'humanise pas le carnage, on le condamne, parce qu'on s'humanise*" ("Carnage is not humanized, it is condemned because men grow more human").

" *Vous êtes une intransigeante*—an irreconcilable," he remarks with a smile, and consoles me with the simultaneous progress of the Conference on the arbitration question, of which I know he is the steadfast promoter.

I received the following letter from the editor of the *Berliner Tageblatt*, to whom I had expressed my regret and astonishment that no correspondence from the Conference was to be found in a paper of such wide circulation:

My dear Baroness: Berlin, May 31, 1899

Your kind letter of yesterday's date compels me to inform you that, in the first place, we are not unrepresented at the Hague Congress, so that we are informed of everything necessary and worth knowing; and, in the second place, that, in view of the hostile treatment the members of the Congress have seen fit to accord the press, I consider it unbecoming to degrade journalism by dancing attendance on the various statesmen.

THE FIRST PEACE CONFERENCE

Since the gentlemen, nevertheless, can only by the aid of publicity show any proof of their industry and their good behavior, — a proof which they must have to show to their superiors, — I quietly wait until things come to me, and communicate to my readers only what is worth their knowing.

If such a man as Mr. Stead complains that nothing is told him, you will easily comprehend that men who are not accustomed to be received by the Tsar feel somewhat cool toward the actions of diplomacy.

All this will not prevent me from joyously recognizing even the slightest advance toward better things made during the deliberations of the Congress, but I consider my paper and my readers too good to snap up the crumbs that may fall from the news table of the Congress.

I trust that you will be able to appreciate this attitude of an independent and liberal newspaper, and that you will not, after this statement, find anything strange in our position.

With the expression of the most especial consideration I have the honor of remaining

Yours most sincerely

Dr. Artur Levysohn

An unwarranted standpoint. Events of the day have to be communicated by the press in accordance with their significance and entirely apart from the sensibilities of the journalists. Consideration for the public must turn the scale.

To-day the bathing season and the Kurhaus at Scheveningen were opened. Herr von Bloch invited us to a dinner at the Kurhaus. Among those present were the journalists, Dillon and Dr. Frischauer. He tells us, from information communicated to him by Professor Martens, that the principle of mediation has been incorporated into the text of the Convention;

279

especially the duty of neutral states to offer "good offices" at the threat of war or after the outbreak of hostilities, and this henceforth shall never be regarded as an "unfriendly act." Count Nigra is to be thanked for this last paragraph.

June 2. Dr. Frischauer takes his departure. He comes to say good-by to us, and authorizes me to send to the *Neue Freie Presse* in the form of telegrams and letters everything interesting that may happen.

In the evening the usual Friday reception at the Beauforts'. Make several new acquaintances; among them Turkhan Pasha. In his elegant external appearance he reminds me of Rudolf Hoyos; he has been for many years Minister of Foreign Affairs, and bears the title of Vizier. He enjoyed the dubious fortune of having been military governor of the island of Crete. He speaks the purest French, is courteous and gracious, but a slightly satirical tone dominates his conversation.

I also meet Noury Bey, the second Turkish delegate, a man at least forty years of age, with very delicate features and reddish beard; he is inspector in the Ministry of Public Works. Last year he was sent as delegate from Turkey to the anti-anarchist Congress at Rome. Both the Ottoman dignitaries give me the impression of not regarding the success of the business here as especially likely or desirable.

Chedomille Myatovic, former Servian Minister of Foreign Affairs and now Minister Plenipotentiary at

London, is on the other hand an enthusiastic adherent of the ends proposed by the Conference.

Augustin d'Ornellos Vasconsellos, the delegate from Portugal, tells me that he has translated Goethe's *Faust* into his vernacular.

I meet De Mier, Mexican ambassador in Paris. Except the United States and Mexico, no American country is represented here. .

June 3. The evening of Bloch's lecture. The public invited. Almost all the delegates present. Many journalists, Dutch and foreign. Subject, "The Development of Firearms." Behind the lecturer's desk a white background for the stereopticon pictures. Bloch speaks with great naturalness and simplicity; never seeks oratorical effects. It is evident that he does not care to "deliver an address," but only to say what he has to say. He wants to show a picture of the war of the future. And where would he find a more suitable public than the audience assembled here, — diplomats and military men who would be called upon to deliberate over some such war or to wage it, but are now called upon to avoid it?

The historic development of firearms, from the first flintlock down to the latest models, is displayed before the audience by means of pictures and charts. The projectile of the new infantry weapon sweeps away everything that it encounters, within a range of six hundred meters. But still greater improvements beckon. In all armies experiments are being made

with rifles of smaller caliber. It is calculated that
if in the Franco-Prussian War the present-day guns
had been used, the losses would have been at least
four times as great; if the newest models had been
used, the losses would have been thirteen times as
great. To be sure, such a transformation in the armies
of the *Dreibund* and of the *Zweibund* would cost four
billion francs.

(Now, in view of such a fine result — just consider,
thirteen times more dead and maimed than with the
primitive musket — four billions would not indeed be
too much, and this sum is easily raised by somewhat
increasing the living expenses of the laboring people!)

That parenthesis is mine, not Bloch's. His lecture
is quite objective; he makes no bitter attacks; he ad-
duces figures and data; the drawing of conclusions he
leaves to the reason and the conscience of his hearers.

The lecture is interrupted by a half hour's recess.
In an adjoining hall, tables are loaded with all kinds of
refreshments, which are passed round. Bloch is host,
and the lecture halls are transformed into drawing-
rooms, where greetings are exchanged, new acquaintances are made, and impressions of the lecture are
compared.

June 5. The editor of the *Dagblad* has granted
Stead the first pages of his paper for the publication
of a daily chronicle of the Conference. To-day the first
number appeared. Excellently prepared. Will be of
great use. A splendid man, this Stead. First his nine

months' campaign in writing and speaking, and now this labor !

A seventeen-year-old son of Vasily's calls on me. He brings an album, on the cover of which appears in relief the word " Pax," and he is getting all the members of the Conference and the friends of peace who are here to write their names in it. How many high military officers will immortalize themselves in the Pax album ! And the impression made on this youth will certainly never be effaced. In what an entirely different way the generation that will succeed us will approach the idea of universal peace — they who will have been witnesses of this idea rising up and forcing its way into offi- cial circles and into the foreground of contemporary history. In our youth such a thing was either quite unknown or made a matter of ridicule. If this boy who is making a collection of contemporary auto- graphs under the rubric " Pax " shall sometime obtain office and honors, perhaps have to speak a weighty word in the political questions of the future, then he will think very differently from our grizzled politicians about the cause of national justice, and if at that day a new official Peace Congress should be called, in which he and his like should have to give their votes, then the proceedings would be attended by many less doubts and difficulties than can possibly be the case with the present Conference, the first of its kind.

June 6. We move down to Scheveningen to the Hotel Kurhaus. It does not take us long to get settled.

At the end of two hours our corner drawing-room looks as cozy as if it had been occupied for two years — thanks to the kindness of the manager, Herr Goldbeck, who permits us to arrange everything in our rooms just as we please. The prettiest furniture of the as yet rather empty hotel is put entirely at our service. Great studio windows occupy nearly all of two walls. One, opposite the door, frames a picture of the sea; at the other the red silken shades are pulled down and cause the whole room to be bathed in a ruddy glow. Flowers in vases, in jardinières, and in pots; splendid baskets of fruit, pineapples, melons, grapes, — the last a delicate attention of Herr von Bloch's; books, pamphlets, maps, newspapers.

At yesterday's session M. Descamps reported on the work of the committee. Léon Bourgeois presided. How pleasant that now Stead's chronicle contains all these details of the sessions and the authentic texts of the articles proposed. Now one can follow the course of events quite accurately. An agreement has been reached regarding several articles of the Russian proposal concerning good offices and mediation.

Only there stands in the articles the fatal clause, "If circumstances permit." Here is clearly seen the result of compromise, which is generally contained in the text of resolutions of such committees, composed of advocates and opponents of any cause. Only under the condition of a rider which robs the main article of its universal validity will those of the other party give up their opposition. The back door is saved, and that is the main thing with them.

Arrival of Baron Pirquet. He has been in Brussels, where the council of the Interparliamentary Union held a session in order to lay out a programme for the Conference that is to take place in August at Christiania; and he brings a letter from the Union to the colleagues that are attending the Hague Congress.

Pirquet breaks the news to me that my cousin Christian Kinsky, in whose house we had spent so many pleasant hours, had died suddenly a few days before.

In the evening Bloch's second lecture. He depicts the difficulties that would attend the mobilization of the modern millionfold armies. After the first fortnight of a war of the future a tenth part of the armies — not counting the wounded — would be in the hospitals. He also cites a statement made by General Haeseler: " If the improvement of firearms continues, there will not be enough survivors to bury the dead."

This lecture, like the first, was interrupted by a recess for conversation and refreshments. We talked with Léon Bourgeois about events in Paris. There, it seems, a band of young men of title (Boni de Castellane and others) attacked the President's hat with their canes. Bourgeois grants that this is disgusting; " but," he adds, " it is no more dangerous than the foam on the seashore."

June 7. At yesterday's session the deliberations of the first committee (on the laws of war, weapons, etc.)

had the floor. Concerning this I make no entry in my diary. The securing and organizing of peace have nothing to do with the regulation of war, nothing at all — quite the contrary! It is desired — that is, it is desired by many — that the opposition between the two ends be abolished; they desire that the one be substituted in place of the other! They are driving in the wedge that shall split the work of peace.

Imagine a congress convened for the enfranchisement of slaves; would a convention then be necessary in regard to the treatment of the negroes, concerning, for instance, the number of blows that might be meted out to them when they should show themselves lazy in the work of the sugar plantations?

Or in the movement against torture as a means of securing justice, would the agreement that the oil to be dropped into the victim's ears should be heated only to thirty degrees instead of up to the boiling point have been a stage on the way to the goal, or rather a tarrying on that other way which was to be abandoned?

June 9. My Own waked me with a kiss and a warm " I thank thee! "

" What for? "

" That thou wert born! "

Yes, quite right, — it is my birthday. That does not interest me, but what is going to be born here, — national justice; that takes my whole mind captive. Yesterday was devoted to the work of the third committee on Article X of the proposal for a court of arbitration, — namely, the article that shall determine the cases in which appeal to the court of arbitration is to be obligatory, cases which "do not touch either vital interests or the honor of states." There again the back door, or rather a barn door, for the entrance of war. He has good defenders here, the brutal fellow!"

Great dinner at the residence of our ambassador, Okoliczany. My neighbors are the Russian chargé d'affaires and M. Pichon, assistant secretary of the French Delegation, — a young lieutenant with a saucy little mustache. But he has understanding, and sympathy for our cause, and is a great admirer of D'Estournelles. He acknowledges that the world is progressing, and that a coming civilization will have no more room for war; only he defends the colonial policy of war. He himself has been in the Sudan.

June 10. It is hard for me to keep up with my correspondence. I have never before in the course of a whole year received so many letters, telegrams, and voluminous writings as now, while I am here at The Hague. They announce schemes, proposals, infallible methods for securing peace. And all of this I am expected to make comprehensible to the delegates! Inventors of airships and flying machines send me their plans and prospectuses. By the conquest of the atmosphere the boundaries with their customhouses and fortifications must needs disappear, opine these aëronautical letter writers.

Or is it true that the ministers of war are hurrying to build air fleets? and to form flying regiments of uhlans? All new inventions are invariably employed by the war authorities. And yet I am firmly persuaded that every technical improvement, especially all means of easier communication, ultimately lead to universal peace.

Yesterday the arbitration committee took up Article XIII of the Russian plan, calling for immediate consideration of the question of a permanent tribunal, and that, too, of a tribunal not merely *in posse* but *in esse.*

While they are here treating theoretically about arbitration, it is said that the matter is to be put to a practical test once again. President Kruger has proposed to Sir Alfred Milner that certain differences of opinion should be submitted to arbitration. Sir Alfred objected that such an action would put in question England's sovereignty.

June 11. At the Grovestins's Sunday reception something amusing happened to me. A Spanish lady, Señora Perez, asked me what I thought of peace. I must have made a dubious face, for she anticipated my answer, saying, " Do not decide, I beg of you, until you have read a book entitled *Die Waffen nieder.* Have you heard of it ? "

" Oh, yes, until I am sick of it."

"Oh, no, no; first read it, and then express your opinion. The author is said to be at The Hague."

" The author is sitting next you."

THE FIRST PEACE CONFERENCE

As so often happens, Señora Perez had missed my name when we were introduced.

Bloch gives a small dinner at the Hotel Royal. After dinner we drive to his third lecture. Subject, "Naval Warfare." The fate of wars is decided not at sea but on land. Between two evenly matched fleets there will be no decisive victory, but mutual destruction of the fleets. The impossibility of protecting marine commerce in times of war. Comparison of the expenses for the fleet with the value of commerce; the pretended protection costs a hundred times more than the worth of what is protected.

Count Nigra sits near me. Bloch's deductions greatly interest him. We speak of the results to be expected.

"The world finds it hard to understand," said Nigra, "how momentous are the foundations here being laid for the building of the future; nor does it understand that the calling of the Conference is in itself an event of supreme importance."

During the intermission an alarming rumor circulates, to the effect that in the debate about the court of arbitration the "dead point" was reached, — a decisive opposition on the part of one of the great powers.

June 12. During the morning our quiet excursion in celebration of our twenty-third wedding anniversary. In the evening a few guests at dinner, — Bihourd, the French ambassador at The Hague, Captain Shein, of the Russian navy, Léon Bourgeois, Bloch, and Theodor Herzl.

I hardly ever had a more interesting table companion than Bourgeois. What made our conversation so particularly enjoyable was our complete agreement in matters concerning peace. The former — and perhaps the future, who knows? — French Premier is enthusiastic for the objects of the Conference. The task which he has to fulfill here seems to him far more productive and important than the formation of a cabinet. In Paris a ministerial crisis is at hand and Bourgeois will probably be recalled; but he firmly intends to return so as to bring to an end to the best of his ability the work here, " which promises to be useful to the world and at the same time to his fatherland."

We talk among other things of the French national press. I regret the hectoring tone, especially in that portion of the press which the people at large read.

" That is not so bad," he replies. " Nowhere else do the people — especially the workingmen — read the newspapers so much as with us; but they have no faith in them. The French laborer buys a newspaper, reads it, chatters about it, but does n't pin his faith to it. His mind is open, awake, and he is thirsty for everything that is free and upright. Race hatred disgusts him. I know what is thought in the workingmen's circles, for I myself come from them."

I ask him about the "dead point" in the arbitration question.

" I cannot say anything just now," is his reply, "but be assured — nothing will be left untried."

We conclude the evening in the great music hall, where a concert arranged by Manager Goldbeck is given in honor of the delegates. Bourgeois is obliged to depart before the other guests; he must go back to the city, he explains apologetically.

After a while Count Nigra comes up to me: "Do you know the news? The French ministry fell some hours ago. M. Bourgeois has just been summoned to Paris by telegraph."

June 13. The *Neues Wiener Tagblatt* prints a dispatch from The Hague: "The negotiations regarding the court of arbitration, as we learn by telegraph from Brussels, have completely gone to pieces."

I send a line to Chevalier Descamps, requesting him, if the above-mentioned news is false, to write a denial and let me send it immediately to the paper. Descamps himself comes to bring me the answer. The news is false, and he allows me to make the desired correction. At the same time he begs me to write this very day to Émile Arnaud, asking him if he will not cease attacking in the *Indépendance belge* the projected system of a permanent bureau and pleading for permanent treaties instead; one at a distance cannot judge what at the moment is to be attained, and what an obstacle it is in the way of the workers here if what has been secured with difficulty meets with the opposition of its own friends.

June 14. Up to the present time the question of armaments has been considered in the Conference only from one side, namely, to the end that agreements may be reached as to renouncing further perfection of weapons. Yet the idea was regarded as impracticable. In spite of a very eloquent plea of General den Beer Poortugael, who proposed that all the armies should retain the present type of arms, the committee came to the conclusion that it would be impossible to carry out such a regulation. Nothing as yet has been said about Emperor Nicholas's own proposition as to limitation of armaments. The debates steer clear of this question so far. A favorable result would be all the more desirable, since lately Admiral Goschen declared in the House of Commons that the projected increase of the British fleet would be immediately stopped if at the Hague Conference a limitation of armaments should be determined upon.

Stead tells me what Emperor Nicholas said to him four weeks ago:

" Why are they always talking about disarmament? I never used the expression; it does not appear in the rescript. I know only too well that immediate disarmament is excluded. It is, indeed, difficult to speak of the diminution of armaments. Surely the most practical step, and the first that should be taken, would be an attempt to come to an agreement to refrain from increasing armaments for a term of years. After four or five years we should learn to trust one another and to keep our word. By this means we should secure a basis for a proposal to reduce the armaments."

THE FIRST PEACE CONFERENCE

These words lead to the conclusion that the Russian delegates will offer in the Conference a motion for stopping the increase of armaments.

Meantime the rumor grows more and more prevalent that the question of a court of arbitration has come to a pause, owing to the declarations of the German delegates that the principle of arbitration is directly contrary to the principle of state sovereignty, which Germany in no circumstances will renounce.

I receive from Berlin the telegraphic query, " How about Zorn's[1] speech ? "

I send the telegram to the professor named, who is staying also at the Kurhaus, and receive for answer, " I know nothing about a speech by Zorn."

Stead, in his to-day's chronicle, contradicts the alarming rumors and writes:

Whatever may be the attitude which the German government may ultimately assume, nothing could be more correct than the attitude of the German delegates. They are working with their colleagues in what we hope will prove a great establishment for assuring universal peace, and it is to be greatly regretted that their coöperation has been so misrepresented during the last few days.

In the evening Bloch's last lecture. Subject, " The War of the Future from the Economic Standpoint." Almost all the delegates, also President Staal, present. I learn that some Russian military members of the Conference were very indignant over Bloch's lectures, and demanded his arrest.

[1] Professor Zorn of the Law Faculty in the University of Bonn, scientific delegate to the Peace Congress. — TRANSLATOR.

LX

THE FIRST PEACE CONFERENCE AT THE
HAGUE (*concluded*)

JUNE 15. In the afternoon a reception given by
Monsieur and Madame d'Estournelles. The whole
Congress comes and goes. Dr. White is buried
in a conversation with Count Münster. Then he
comes to me.

" If you can bring any pressure to bear on influential persons, Baroness, do it now. Every possible
measure must be employed to clear away the difficulties that are springing up. . . . The most important
question before our Congress — that of a court of
arbitration — has reached a turning point; that is
what I was talking with Count Münster about."

I promised to go to one of my friends staying at
The Hague, and in high favor with the German Emperor's uncle, the Grand Duke of Baden, and urge him
to apply to the prince in these critical circumstances.

THE FIRST PEACE CONFERENCE

Our host introduced me to Professor Zorn. First of all I thank him for his denial in regard to "Zorn's speech," of which he still knows absolutely nothing.

"In fact, no such speech was ever made," replied the professor. "I took part in the discussion, but I made no speech and made no such remarks as many newspapers attributed to me."

The conversation turns on the Bloch lectures.

"Pure fallacies," said the professor. "Military men think that a war of the future will be less bloody than those of the past."

"Less bloody! with these weapons, with this tenfold faster firing per minute —"

"All the fewer missiles will hit —"

"Oh, no, the war of the future cannot be palliated; what the future needs is peace."

"That is found only in heaven!"

In the evening a great party at the Okoliczanys'. A new person makes her appearance, — Madame Ratazzi, Türr's sister-in-law, born Bonaparte Wyse. I saw this woman thirty years ago at Homburg, the greatest beauty I ever met. And now? Alas! how miserable to look on *des ans l'irréparable outrage* (the irreparable ravages of the years).

Long conversation with our host. He holds the opinion that, sooner or later, even without any conference, Europe must arrive at the formation of a union; the ceaseless expense for armaments, necessitated by lack of unity, the constant rivalries of commerce, the

policy of protection, — all this, unless a change ensues, exposes Europe to the danger of being ruined
by America. A peace alliance uniting our part of
the world is a necessity. This is the same thesis as
our Minister of Foreign Affairs, Count Goluchowski,
advanced in a noteworthy *exposé* before the Congress
was called together.

General den Beer Poortugael joins me. I express
my admiration of his latest speech. He assures me
that the limitation of armaments must be striven for,
not only because the nations expect this result from
the Conference, but also because it is the only way to
escape the threatened catastrophe. Remarkable words
from the lips of a general !

June 16. In the evening a reception at Beaufort's.
I make the acquaintance of Professor Martens. He
arrived to-day from Paris, where he is acting as president in the Venezuela arbitration tribunal. He will
attend only one session and then return immediately
to Paris. Speaking of the condition of things here, he
tells me that, even though many of the powers should
hesitate or delay to sign the convention, this would do
no harm, because the protocols will be left open, even
for the powers that are not represented here.

Another exotic acquaintance, Mirza Rhiza Khan,
the delegate from Persia.[1] He is forty-five years old,

---

[1] Persia was represented at the First Peace Conference at The Hague by
Aide-de-camp General Mirza Rhiza Khan (Arfa-ud-Dovleh), ambassador at
St. Petersburg and Stockholm, and Mirza Samad Khan (Montazis-Sultanah),
counselor of legation. — TRANSLATOR.

has Oriental features, a thick black mustache, and sparkling eyes; his white uniform is decorated with numberless orders; on his cap is the Persian lion. In 1889 he accompanied the former shah, Nasr-ed-Din, as his adjutant general on his tour through Europe. Now he is ambassador to St. Petersburg. He was educated in Constantinople and Tiflis, and tells us of the Princess Tamara of Georgia, whom he knows very well; she is now at the Caucasian baths of Botjom.

June 17. An artistic festival arranged by the government in honor of the Conference, comprising living pictures, musical productions, and national dances. Make the acquaintance of Baron von Stengel. He is very stiff and repelling. We exchange only a few words — something about "loyal opposition" and "there must needs be different views"; a few indifferent observations about the performances of the evening and we soon separate.

A Dutch army physician introduces himself to me. He had read my novel while in Borneo. The sufferings that he had witnessed there in the practice of his calling exceed all belief. He had been mortally unhappy, and so the book had made a double impression on him, and had awakened in him a longing for the accomplishment of everything which the Conference at The Hague has in view.

June 18. I receive from the daughter-in-law of Professor Lüdwig Buchner, who had died not long ago, the following letter in reply to a letter of condolence:

RECORDS OF AN EVENTFUL LIFE

My dear Baroness,   Darmstadt, June 17, 1899

A year of the loftiest triumph! May all that are to follow be as rich in success! This is what all your most faithful admirers desire with glowing enthusiasm.

Your kind sympathy called forth by the departure of our beloved father has been a great comfort to us. Many mourn for him with us. He, the faithful champion of the truth, will be survived by his works. Happy as his life was, his death was no less enviable. Even in the midst of his fullest creative powers he glided without a sound, without a sigh, from gentle slumber into the Unknown. Many times, when tormented by his trying cough, weary from sleepless nights, he spoke of his approaching end; and so it found him with the calm of a true philosopher. Everything had been put in readiness with the greatest care for this event. He was enabled to pass away calmly; a rich life lay behind him. He had employed his great intellectual gifts wholly for the good of his fellow-men. The kindness and fidelity of his heart were rewarded by the purest joys of a sweet family life. He knew that his loving, self-sacrificing wife was surrounded by a grateful band of children, in whose happiness the deeply bereaved woman will find her best consolation. We all console one another, in our deep sorrow for the irremediable gap in our family circle, by thoughts of the beautiful, happy life which he was permitted to enjoy so long.

For the ninth of June I wish you with my whole heart happiness and health, and I hope that you may retain all your joyous powers of creation, which have allowed you in the past to overcome so many difficulties. In such a victorious career your inspiration will never be paralyzed, and you will march forward on the road to that victory which is to secure the happiness of mankind!

With the deepest respect

Your wholly devoted

Marie Büchner

The debates on the arbitration tribunal have come to a pause; they will not be resumed until fresh instructions have been received. Dr. Holls and Professor Zorn have gone to Hannover, where the German Emperor is at present sojourning. Mr. White intrusted to Dr. Holls a long letter to Bülow.

In the course of the afternoon we receive many callers, including Frau von Okoliczany and her daughter, Mevrouw Smeth, and Mirza Rhiza Khan. The Persian delegate tells me that he has been endeavoring to introduce the Latin alphabet into Persia, but that it has met with great opposition, especially among the priests, who declare that it is a sin to make use of any other letters than those in which the Koran is written.

Baron and Baroness d'Estournelles also call on me to-day. We talk about Professor Zorn. D'Estournelles assures me that this German delegate is striving with all his might to bring the matter of the arbitration tribunal to a favorable conclusion: *Il pense comme vous et moi.*

Now I doubt that. I will go as far as to believe, as Stead states also in the *Dagblad*, that Professor Zorn is determined that the matter of the arbitration tribunal shall not be shipwrecked; but that he is as radical in his views as D'Estournelles or as I — he himself would repudiate the idea!

June 19. Trip to Amsterdam with a large party. We drove three times around the whole city and hurried through the museums, allowing the pictures by Van Dyck and Franz Hals and Rubens to flash before our eyes. Only before Rembrandt's great painting,

"The Night Watch," which we had recently seen presented as a living picture, we remained for half an hour in contemplation. At your very first entrance into the suite of galleries it shines upon you from the farthest background. You would think that the sun was shining on it; but its brilliancy comes from its colors.

In the museum is a splendid case filled with Indian treasures, consisting of rings and chains and all sorts of jewels taken as loot from conquered rajahs; therefore simply freebooters' booty. Mankind does not look upon it as such.

We visit also the diamond-polishing works. A whole house filled with workmen. On every floor a different phase of the transformation which this precious form of carbon goes through before it becomes an ornament. On the top floor, reached by a very narrow wooden staircase, sit the most skillful of the laborers, who give the last finish to the stones. They allow the foreign visitors to look; they explain the processes. The trouble seems too great! What effort and what patience to make this dull, hard substance glitter with a hundred facets!

The manager shows us on a velvet ground the models in crystal of all the largest and most famous diamonds that are in the possession of the various crowned heads, — the Kohinoor and others. I did not heed the names attached to these little globules of glass representing millions in value.

"Since so many diamonds have been mined in the Transvaal," said one of the polishers, "we can scarcely keep up with our work; and yet there are thousands of us diamond cutters in Amsterdam."

"Just see!" remarked Herr von Bloch to us, "just see how the world hangs together! Suppose war should break out in the Transvaal, the consequences would be that here in Amsterdam thousands of working-men's families would suffer from want!"

We had dinner — all excursions culminate in eating — at a restaurant from which there was a view of a canal full of life and movement. It was a beautiful, lively picture from the open window near which I sat. On the other side of the canal are old houses, truly Dutch in appearance, and a church with a very lofty belfry. Boats and scows were moving up and down heavily laden with flowers, — mainly tulips, roses, and lilies. Suddenly the bells in the tower began to ring; the tones kept interweaving, and for ten minutes a melodious, silver-clear chime of bells continued to play.

Not until late at night did we return to The Hague. At the waiting room of the railway station we meet Dr. Holls. He has just come back from Germany, whither he had gone accompanied by Professor Zorn, with a mission to smooth out at the main source the difficulties that had arisen in the matter of the arbitration tribunal.

"Any news? Any news?" we ask in the greatest excitement.

"I cannot tell you anything yet," replied Dr. Holls. "Only I will mention the title of one of Shakespeare's plays, 'All's well that ends well.'"[1]

June 21. Léon Bourgeois, who had only just come from Paris, is recalled again by Loubet and commissioned to form a cabinet. Will he be able, will he be willing, to renounce the task of being prime minister? I have it from his own lips that this is his purpose; he is going to do his very utmost to return to The Hague in order to see the business of the arbitration tribunal through to the end.

To-day I went with the painter Ten Kate to the photographer. A sculptor, a friend of his, wants to chisel my bust, and for this purpose I must be taken *en face* and *en profil*, in three-quarters profile and from behind, wrapped statuesquely in some soft, flowing white material, with my hair arranged in Grecian style and with a palm branch as an ornament for the breast. The process lasted several hours.

I was posed and pulled into shape. Then the photographer, whose name is Wollrabe, goes to his camera, looks in, shakes his head, and hobbles back to me — he has a wooden leg — to pull my left shoulder a little toward the right, to lift my chin, and to twitch my draperies down; and in this he has the critical and practical aid of Master Ten Kate. "There, now it's all right" (*So, jetzt ist es jutt*). Hop, hop, hop to the

---

[1] For an account of the outcome of this critical situation see Andrew D. White's "Autobiography."

camera. Again a shaking of the head and hop, hop, hop back to me again. After a little tugging, — "There, now it's all right." And so half a dozen times for each exposure. And all the while I must preserve the earnest physiognomy of a statue, in spite of the great temptation to laugh at the forest-goblin-like, to-and-fro stumping of the so-hard-to-be-satisfied Wollrabe, who, by the way, has wonderfully beautiful pictures in his studio, among them the best extant portrait of the young queen.

One ought to be, indeed, especially young and beautiful to be painted and chiseled. And not only the hop, hop, hop of my photographer with his funny bird name — "Wool-raven" — strikes me as comical, but also his white-draped model, adorned with the vegetable of peace — but I must not laugh!

June 23. The article proposed in the programme for "an agreement concerning the use of certain weapons and forbidding new purchases and inventions" has been decided in the negative. Stead, speaking with me regarding this matter, says:

"Do not for a moment imagine that this is a bad thing. Rudyard Kipling wrote me at the beginning of the peace crusade, 'War will last until some inventive genius furnishes a machine which will annihilate fifty per cent of the combatants as soon as they face one another.' Therefore I think that the Conference, while it has decisively rejected a whole series of proposals — even those that came from the Tsar — in the line of prohibiting the improvement of cannon and other weapons, has been acting in behalf of peace and not of war."

"I think so too," I reply; "only that is not their reason for doing as they have. The military men who have voted the measure down have done so for the special purpose of promoting militarism."

To-day the Congress is considering a weighty point, Section 1 of Muravieff's second circular:

An understanding not to increase for a fixed period the present effective of the armed military and naval forces, and, at the same time, not to increase the budgets pertaining thereto.

This is the question that is of greatest importance for the champions of peace, for it touches the evil of armed peace.

This condition — according to Türr, *la peur armée* — has this basis: the presupposition on which the relations of nations are established is that the neighbor has the morals of a bandit and the conscience of a pirate!

Bad news from London, — the House of Commons has granted four million pounds for purposes of war.

Under date of June 27 I confided to my diary the text of the whole "armament" debate, which took place on the twenty-third and twenty-sixth of the month. Here I will introduce only the most notable passages. This is sufficient to bring out the attitude of the various governments toward this question.

THE FIRST PEACE CONFERENCE

FIRST SESSION, JUNE 23. HERR BEERNAERT, CHAIRMAN

We have now reached the serious problem which the Russian government placed first of all, so worded that it instantly aroused the attention of the world.

This time it is not the nations, but a mighty monarch, who believes that the enormous burdens that are the result of the armed peace in which Europe has been existing since 1871 are calculated " to paralyze public welfare at its sources, and that their constant increase involves an oppressive load which the nations will have ever greater and greater difficulty in enduring."

Count Muravieff's circular has stated the problem in a little more condensed form as follows: " What are the means by which a limit might be set to the increase of armaments? Could the nations pledge themselves against an increase or even in favor of a reduction? "

I hope that our honored president, his Excellency von Staal, who has asked for the floor, will give us an explicit explanation of these points.

Herr von Staal said:

. . . " The question before us — limitation of the military budget and of the military establishment — deserves a thorough investigation, all the more from the fact (let me repeat it) that this constitutes the chief purpose of our assemblage, namely, to lighten as far as possible the terrible burden which oppresses the nations and checks their material as well as their moral development.

" Do I need to say that there is no question here of Utopian and chimerical measures? It does not mean that we shall proceed to disarmament. What we desire is a limitation, a period of quiescence, in the constantly accelerating race of armaments and expenditures.

" We make this proposition in the conviction that if an agreement is reached, a gradual reduction will take place. Immovability does not belong to the domain of history, and if we succeed in preserving a certain stability for a few years, it may be taken for granted that the advantageous tendency toward diminution of military expenditures will be confirmed and developed. The movement would perfectly correspond to the ideas which inspire the Russian rescript.

"But we have not yet got that far. At the present moment the question before us is only for a cessation, for a fixed period of years, in the increase of the military budgets and of the contingents."

General den Beer Poortugael:

"Gentlemen: Here we find ourselves facing the chief object of Muravieff's circular. It is truly worth while for us to concentrate our powers to the highest endeavor. We must regard the great interests of the nations, so intimately bound up with his recommendation, and I believe that I am not going too far when I say that the question must be treated with a certain reverence.

"The armies and military budgets that have been steadily growing larger and larger for the last quarter of a century have now attained gigantic, terrifying, dangerous dimensions. Four millions of men under arms and army budgets of five billions of francs a year! Is that not terrible?

"Truly, this increase of armies, of fleets, of budgets, of debts, seems to have been brought out of a Pandora's box, the gift of a wicked fairy who desires the misfortune of Europe. War is sure to arise from this method of foresight, which is meant to safeguard peace. The increase of contingents and of expenses will be the real cause of war.

. . . "To the states which, through our military organizations, are bound together like mountain climbers in the Alps by a rope, the Tsar has said, 'Let us make a common endeavor, let us pause on this path which leads to the abyss, else we are lost.'

"A halt, then! Fellow-delegates, it is our duty to use our utmost endeavors. It will be worth while. Let us call a halt!"

This speech, spoken in an impassioned voice, aroused amazement. Many could not refrain from applause; others could hardly help shaking their heads. Some one is said to have remarked, "Bebel, out and out!"

Now the Russian motion was submitted.

THE PROGRAMME

Colonel von Schilinsky's remarks:

. . . "It may be asked, gentlemen, whether the nations represented at the Conference will be perfectly satisfied if we bring them the arbitration tribunal and laws for seasons of war, but nothing for seasons of peace, — this armed peace, which bears so heavily upon them that often the statement is heard that an open war would be better than this concealed war of armaments, this perpetual rivalry where every nation exhibits greater armies in time of peace than it ever did before during the greatest wars.

. . . " Moreover, this continued increase of military power fails to attain its object, for the relative strength of the various countries remains the same. If any government increases its troops, forms new battalions, its neighbor follows its example without delay, so as to preserve the proportions; the neighbor's neighbor does the same, and so it goes on without end. The effective increases, but the proportions remain about the same.

. . . " Moreover, we are proposing nothing new. The limitation of contingents and of the budget has long been customary in many countries. For example, there is the *Septennat* in Germany. This means that the total number of the troops in time of peace is fixed for seven — now five — years. In Russia also the war budget is established on a five years' basis. So it is a question of well-known measures which have been used for a long time, which alarm no one, and which bring about good results; it is a question of applying these regulations for even a shorter time, if you please. The only novelty about it is the resolution, the courage to state that it is time to call a halt.

And Russia moves that we call a halt."

After Colonel von Schilinsky had spoken, Captain Sheïn made a similar proposal for the navy. All this perfectly corresponds with what Emperor Nicholas said to Stead, and also with the utterances that Muravieff had made in my presence.

The truth is, the Russian government, in the presence of the whole world, in behalf of the welfare of all nations, has officially proposed to the other governments that they should come to an agreement henceforth not to increase armaments. At the same time, it has clearly opened up the prospect of a subsequent reduction. The accompanying proposals for a permanent tribunal, the arbitration code, and the propositions regarding mediation as well, — all this shows that, whatever the decisions of the Conference may be, the promoters have done their part honorably.

Session of June 26. The Commission assembles again. Léon Bourgeois has arrived. Colonel von Schwarzhoff is opposing the Russian motion. He takes sides also against General den Beer Poortugael; he cannot, he says, accept these ideas, and is unwilling that his silence should be construed as assent. The German people is not oppressed by the weight of taxes; it is not on the sheer edge of the abyss; it is not hastening to ruin, — quite the contrary. As regards the universal duty to bear arms, the German does not regard it as a heavy burden but as a sacred and patriotic duty, to the fulfillment of which he owes his existence, his prosperity, and his future. Then he speaks of the difficulties which beset the plan of limiting armaments, and explains that it would meet with insuperable technical obstacles.

The German delegate's speech is regarded by the others as a clear proof that Germany is going to vote against the limitation motion.

Then Schilinsky, Den Beer Poortugael, and Dr. Stancioff of Bulgaria speak once more in defense of the motion.

The chairman proposes the nomination of a committee to study into the subject. For this committee the opponent, Colonel von Schwarzhoff, and the maker of the motion are chosen; also army and navy experts.

June 30. So, then, to-day, in the "House in the Wood," the fate of the proposal for limitation of armaments was decided.

Rejected. Referred for further consideration to the cabinets of the great powers. A resolution made by Léon Bourgeois and adopted by the Conference saved the principle.

Last soirée at Minister Beaufort's.

Sir Julian Pauncefote comes and sits by me. Of course I lead the conversation to the Conference again and ask him how long it will probably continue.

"At least a fortnight," Sir Julian opines. "I can assure you," he adds, "the Conference is doing a great work, and other conferences will follow. To be sure, the limitation clause was voted down, yet with the general declaration that it must be taken up later. But, on the other hand, the permanent tribunal has become a fact, and for this result Professor Zorn is to be specially praised for his endeavors."

Turkhan Pasha escorts me to the refreshment table. There Herr Beernaert hands me an ice. He has recently arrived from Brussels, where the disturbances have fortunately come to an end. The obstruction of the socialists in the Chamber consisted in their always starting the Marseillaise whenever any one began to speak.

"Things are now all right again," says the minister, "*ils ont mis bas les armes*. But here I understand some things are not all right. 'Limitation' is buried; the military experts declared it was out of the question."

"Buried? At all events, the flowers are saved. Bildt[1] spoke wonderfully, beautifully; and a motion by Bourgeois was voted and assures a resurrection. The coffin is not nailed up; the boards are loose. . . ."

"Such questions," I added, "should not be treated from the technical but from a quite different standpoint. If the military men alone are to be allowed to decide about disarmament —"

"Surely," says Herr Beernaert, finishing my sentence. "It is as if cobblers should deliberate on how men could give up wearing footgear!"

July 1. Now I know the report concerning yesterday's limitation session. Servia first declared its adhesion; then Greece its dissent. Hereupon the report of the commission on studies was read—a very laconic report:

1. That it would be very difficult, even for a space of only five years, to fix the number of the troops without simultaneously regulating other elements of defense.

2. That it would be no less difficult to regulate the elements of this defense by means of an international convention, since the defense is organized in each country from very different points of view.

Consequently the committee regrets its inability to accept the proposal made in the name of the Russian government.

[1] Baron von Bildt, ambassador from Sweden and Norway to the court of Italy. He was the only delegate plenipotentiary from Scandinavia; but Sweden and Norway each sent two technical delegates. — TRANSLATOR.

THE FIRST PEACE CONFERENCE

The committee recommends that the subject of the subsequent decision be intrusted to the respective governments.

Such is the text of the military commission's report; and so the matter was simply set aside. The execution of the proposal offers difficulties, "consequently" it cannot be accepted! This "consequently," however, is not satisfactory. The motive adduced for setting aside a project of such wide scope is not sufficient. There is more to be said about it than that it is difficult to carry out. It must also be clear whether it is not desirable, beneficent, nay, more, essential. And if this conclusion is reached, then if it is to be rejected, there must be a better reason than its difficulty; its impossibility must be shown.

But the matter before us cannot be impossible in principle; certainly not in the form just presented. And it must not be rejected, but rather postponed for future realization. This was the feeling of a large part of the Conference; and two other delegates — the Swede Baron Bildt and the Frenchman Léon Bourgeois — give expression to this feeling in fiery extempore speeches.

From Baron Bildt's speech (" It is not enough "):

. . . Now, at the conclusion of our labors, we shall realize that we have faced one of the most important problems of the century, and that we have accomplished very little. We have no right to cherish illusions. If the transactions of the Conference come to public knowledge, then, in spite of all that has been done for arbitration, the Red Cross, and the rest, a loud cry will be raised, "It is not enough!"

And the majority of us, in our own consciences, will justify that outcry, "It is not enough!" To be sure, our consciences will tell us, for our consolation, that we have done our duty, because we have been faithful to the instructions that have been given us. But I venture to say that our duty is not yet completed, and that we still have something left to do. That is, to investigate with the greatest frankness and truth and to report to our governments what defects are to be found in the preparation or execution of the great work, and with steadfastness, with obstinacy, to seek the means to do better and to do more. Now let these means be found in new conferences, in direct negotiations, or simply in the policy of a good example. This is the duty which is left for us to fulfill.

This speech made a sensation. The applause had not died down when the head of the French delegation took the floor.

From Léon Bourgeois's speech ("Our task is higher"):

I have listened with great delight to Baron Bildt's eloquent words. They correspond not only to my personal feelings and those of my colleagues of the French delegation,[1] but also, I am sure, to the unanimous feelings of the Conference. I join in the appeal which Baron Bildt has made. I believe that (to express his ideas still more explicitly) our commission has something further to do.

I have carefully read the text of the conclusion reached by the technical committee. This text shows the difficulties which at the present moment attend the limitation of armament. This investigation was also the mandate of the committee. But our commission is under obligation to regard the problem before us from a universal and higher standpoint.

. . . Colonel von Schwarzhoff tells us that Germany easily bears the burdens of its military organization, and that in spite of these burdens it can point to a great economical development.

[1] These were M. Georges Bihourd, ambassador at The Hague, Baron d'Estournelles de Constant, and three technical delegates — General Mounier, Rear Admiral Péphau, and Professor Louis Renault of the Law Faculty and legal adviser to the Ministry of Foreign Affairs. — TRANSLATOR.

THE FIRST PEACE CONFERENCE

I come from a country which also bears cheerfully the obligations of national defense, and we hope next year, when the Exposition will be held, to show the world that our products and our economical development stand on a high level. But the colonel will grant me that in his country as well as in mine, if a share of the considerable resources now spent for military purposes were devoted to the service of productive activity, the total of prosperity would be developed at a much more rapid rate.

Moreover, we have here not only to take into account how *our* country endures the burdens of the armed peace. Our task is higher, — we are called upon to consider the joint situation of all the nations.

After futher considerations, Bourgeois proposes that the question be referred to the governments for further discussion at the next Conference. But, that the position of the present Conference may be brought to a definite expression, he offers the following amendment to the report:

The commission takes the view that the limitation of the military burdens resting on the world would be in the highest degree desirable for the improvement of the moral and material condition of mankind.

This resolution was adopted.

I immediately translated the text of both speeches and dispatched it to the *Neue Freie Presse.*

July 2. Yesterday a ball at the Staals'. When we arrive, at ten o'clock, the drawing-rooms are already almost full. All the lower rooms of the Vieux Doelen — the peristyle, salons, dining-room, and other apartments — have been engaged for this function and are richly decorated. The walls of the ballroom are adorned with greenery from which gleam white lilies. Nothing but white flowers everywhere, the symbols of peace. There is a flood of electric light from the chandeliers. The orchestra is hidden behind a hedge of palms. Softly lighted corridors lead to smaller adjoining rooms, in which the guests find nooks for confidential conversation. The doors leading from the ballroom to the terrace stand open, and a broad flight of steps leads down into the lighted garden.

All the delegates are present except Admiral Fisher,[1] whose absence is all the more to be regretted because he is one of the jolliest of the dancers.

Baron Bildt presents his son to me, a young man of twenty-two, just arrived from Upsala, where he is studying at the University.

"I was on the point of devoting myself to a military career," the young Swede told me in the course of our conversation. "And do you know, gracious lady, what kept me from it? The reading of your book. And to-day, in this company, I am doubly glad that I chose another profession. Perhaps later it will be permitted me to labor for the great cause that brought my father to The Hague."

"I see; a new ambition is awaking, in a new field! Remain faithful to this impulse, and may you sometime by means of it become a judge in the International Arbitration Court or Swedish Minister of Peace!"

"Oh, how glad I should be!"

---

[1] Sir John A. Fisher, Vice Admiral, technical delegate from Great Britain. — TRANSLATOR.

THE FIRST PEACE CONFERENCE

Andrew D. White urges me, in case I have the opportunity, to oppose those pessimistic prejudices which have gone abroad regarding the Conference, and which render more difficult the possibility of further work and the assembling of new conferences. He expresses the opinion that the Emperor of Russia has one good means at his command, — simply to introduce into his country the shipwrecked "limitation" or even the reduction of the military effective. He is the autocrat — his will decides. And the policy of such an example would be most effective.

Well, indeed, the manifesto, the summoning of the Conference, the motions laid before it, which implied the pledge that he would do what he proposed, — all these things were indeed examples. But those who are eagerly bent on the preservation of the entire military system have not been constrained to follow in the same track. How can any one venture, after all, in a matter requiring common agreement, to take the lead alone?

A Russian tells me that in his own country there is also a strong military party which holds the Tsar's plans in deep disfavor, so that, even in his immediate proximity, opposition and differences of opinion are strongly felt. It would require iron energy to hold out against them. Alas, the cruel are apt to be iron. . . .

We give an afternoon reception. Among those present are Herr and Frau Berends and their daughter; Dr. White and his wife, who has just arrived;

Monsieur and Madame Descamps; our countrymen, Count Welsersheimb, Lieutenant Colonel von Khuepach, and Professor Lammasch; my young Russian officer whom I met at yesterday's ball, and young Bildt; Dr. Holls; Bourgeois; the Persian ambassador; Bonnefon; Vasily and his son; Pompili; Schmidt auf Altenstadt, editor of the *Dagblad;* Herr von Raffaelovitch and his daughter; and Minister Beernaert.

Beernaert goes to-morrow to Brussels. They have had a ministerial crisis there too.

"I am going to play the rôle of Bourgeois at Brussels," he said with a laugh.

"Then," rejoined the other, "play it to the end and come back."

To-day I noted a deep remark uttered by Léon Bourgeois. The talk turned on the great progressive ideas which permeate the world so slowly, altogether too slowly, because the daily happenings, the problems and sensations of the moment, claim everybody's entire attention. *L'actualité, c'est l'ennemi*, said he.

The Swedish envoy's son again took his oath to me that he would remain true to the ideal of peace and work for it according to his ability.

The conversation reverted to that session in which Colonel Schwarzhoff delivered his speech against the proposition of limitation. The gentlemen remarked that he had spoken with great *mordant.* Now the German equivalent for that word is not *beissend* ("biting") but *schneidig* ("keen"). In either case it is an adjective

316

expressing admiration. Now, it seems to me, sharp
teeth and polished sonority are very valuable things
in their place, but are they specially suited for the
Peace Conference?

At dinner we are in Oriental company, — with
Noury Bey and Mirza Rhiza Khan. Were it not for
the fez, one might take Noury Bey for a Frenchman.
He takes the point of view of the Turkish patriotic
party, faithful to the Sultan, not that of the Young
Turks. The persecution of the Armenians has been
necessary, he says; they are revolutionists, rebels, con-
spirators. In short, they are wicked lambs; the wolf
is in the right!

We were regretting the failure of the project for
restricting armaments or talking of something similar,
I do not remember exactly what.

" But that is a thing," remarked Noury Bey to my
husband, "which you, as an Austrian patriot, ought to
approve of."

"We friends of peace do not recognize this contradiction," replied my husband; "what one must regret
as a man, one cannot be glad of as a patriot. And
indeed it is a mistake to believe that what will not
benefit mankind will be useful to one's own country.
In any case, the interest of humanity, absolute right,
always stands higher than the special advantages of
any one country."

"Splendid!" cried Noury Bey in amazement, but
not without irony. "People with such views ought

to be appointed judges in the coming international tribunal."

July 4. To-day, in connection with the American holiday, an excursion to Delft in commemoration of Grotius. In the early morning a severe storm is raging and rain is beating on the window panes. We countermand our order for a carriage and stay at home.

It is a melancholy, gloomy day. The windows rattle and tremble; an ice-cold wind forces itself in. Gray are the rolling clouds and the foaming angry sea. Lamentation, brawling, and menace commingle in the roar of wind and waves.

The beach is deserted. As far as the eye can see there is not a living creature. The bath houses and covered chairs and booths are all moved off — or have the billows carried them away? The high, foam-capped breakers tumble over one another and come nearer and nearer, and are already dashing over the terrace wall. Perhaps the whole terrace may be destroyed, as it was a few years ago. And all the time this tumultuous lamentation! How can one feel cheerful?

Truly, there is reason enough for melancholy. This Conference, which should show sorrow-laden, danger-threatened mankind a way to get finally rid of the sorrow and the dangers which arise not from the elements but from their own selves, — how its work has met with misunderstanding and resistance both in the world outside and in its own midst! Nowhere enthusiastic aid — nay, not even eager curiosity, and not once a warm word from those who hold the power in their hands. Cold, cold are all the hearts—cold as the draft that penetrates through the rattling windows. I am chilled to the bone!

In the evening a festival in the concert room in honor of the American delegates. The decorations are star-spangled banners; there is a rendering of American songs. Dr. Holls tells me that the Grotius festival was a brilliant success, and useful words were spoken, especially by Ambassador White. He also informs me that the permanent Court of Arbitration is accepted. Only the paragraph about obligatory cases is omitted.

July 5. In reply to my note of regret, addressed to Andrew D. White, and explaining that our absence from the festival was caused by the weather, I receive the following reply:

House in the Wood, July 5, 1899

Dear Baroness von Suttner:

We were very sorry not to see you and the Baron at Delft, but we fully understood and appreciated the reason. We really did not expect more than a dozen or twenty people, and were greatly surprised to see so large a number present.

It was to me very inspiring and gave me new hopes as to the results of the Conference.

I beg you not to forget what I urged upon you at our last meeting. We are to accomplish here more than we dared hope when we came together, — far more; and the great thing is to prevent thoughtless, feather-brained enthusiasts from discrediting the work, since to do so is to discourage all future efforts of this sort.

We have paved the way for future conferences which will develop our work — unless the people at large are taught that nothing has been done in this way.

Please call me kindly to the remembrance of Baron von Suttner, and I remain, dear madam, most respectfully and truly yours,

Andrew D. White

July 6. At the last session an important article was added to the project of the arbitration tribunal. It was proposed by D'Estournelles, and is to the effect that the signatory powers, in case of a conflict threatening between two or more countries, shall consider it their duty to remind these powers that the Court of Arbitration stands open to them.

Servia and Roumania make a lively protest against the word "duty." Roumania, represented by Beldimann, moreover protests regularly, consistently, and forever.

After a persuasive speech by Léon Bourgeois, D'Estournelles's motion is adopted.

July 7. We take our departure. Ever so many friends accompany us to the railway station. The coach is filled with farewell bouquets. Good-by, thou lovely city of gardens! Will coming generations make pilgrimages to thee because the first International Court of Arbitration came into existence here? Enriched by the memories of lovely days and interesting people, and by uplifting impressions, I take my departure from thee, historic place. . . .

We were obliged, on account of private affairs, to leave before the close of the Conference, but I received from there every day papers, letters, and dispatches, which kept me informed of the progress and the *acte final* of the Conference.

I jot down here the most important of these records. On the seventh of July the session of the third committee (on peaceful adjustment of international controversies) adjourned until the seventeenth, that in the meantime further instructions might be received from the governments. Sir Julian Pauncefote makes a trip to London. The articles which principally give occasion for seeking further instructions are those that treat of the International Commission of Inquiry. The text up for debate runs:

> In cases of an international nature, involving neither honor nor vital interests, and arising from a difference of opinion on points of fact, the signatory powers recommend that the parties, having been unable to come to an agreement by the usual means of diplomacy, should, as far as circumstances allow, institute an international commission of inquiry, which shall clear away these differences by getting at the facts through an impartial and conscientious investigation.

What a bundle of limitations! "As far as circumstances allow," "neither honor nor vital interests." It can be seen with what timidity and circumspection these grewsome instruments called "jurisdiction," "process of inquiry"—that is, right and truth,—are taken hold of. Torpedoes, dumdum bullets, ekrasit, and lyddite—we are already used to such things, we are no longer afraid of them; but legal processes in international affairs,—those would be too dangerous for vital interests: at all events, for the interests of militarism. . . .

The origin of this formula "honor and vital interests of a nation" is well known. It has always been produced in the following form by the opponents of international arbitration: "Hitherto courts of arbitration have exercised their functions in small matters but not in important ones." What has hitherto been used as an argument is now to be incorporated in a treaty!

To some the limitations seem superfluous, to others the whole proposition seems too far-reaching and — being without precedent — too uncanny; hence the adjournment to wait for further instructions. Stead, in his chronicle in the *Dagblad*, calls attention to this and implores the committee to modify the article at the next reading.

On the nineteenth of July the committee assembles again. Herr Beldimann in an hour's speech attacks the Commission of Inquiry with all his energy. Roumania, he declares, will enter into no arrangement that shall have an obligatory character. Not for a moment will it permit the rights of its sovereign independence to be brought into question. (I love the Roumanians proud!) He moves the rejection of the whole proposition. Servia upholds the arguments of the previous speaker. Chevalier Descamps defends the motion, and he is followed in this by Herr Martens, who speaks with still greater energy. Objections like those expressed by the representative of Roumania ought not to prevent an arrangement which is calculated to assure universal peace and avoid conflicts.

In the afternoon comes the second meeting of the committee. The text of the controverted paragraph is somewhat altered. An additional clause reads:

The report of the International Commission of Inquiry is limited to a statement of facts, and has in no way the character of an arbitral decision. It leaves the powers that are in dispute entire freedom as to the weight to be given to this statement.

On the other hand, the phrase "honor and vital interests" is omitted. Roumania and Servia desire to wait for further instructions by wire.

July 20. The articles regarding mediation and good offices are accepted without objection. When the article on the Commission of Inquiry is reached, Beldimann declares that he has not yet received any reply from his government. A few delegates are indignant at the further procrastination, and it is finally decided to take up the article again in two days. Now, without further objections, the reading of the report is continued. When Article 27 is reached, — the one proposed by D'Estournelles, which lays an obligation upon the powers to remind parties in dispute that there is a Tribunal, — the interest of the session reaches its culminating point.

The representatives of Roumania and Servia set themselves in violent opposition to it. But Professor Zorn warmly advocates its acceptance. Dr. Holls declares that Article 27 is the crown of the whole work, and he decidedly protests against any change in its wording.

Count Nigra, kindled by the electricity of the atmosphere, springs up and apostrophizes the representatives of the Danube states: " We are here neither as great nor as small states; we are all alike sovereign — we act here as free and equal."

The sensation of the session was still to come. Never before had a more excited and more elevated feeling ruled in the "House in the Wood." Never before had the transactions aroused so much moral enthusiasm. So the moment was favorable when Léon Bourgeois took the floor, and in fiery words, in the name of France, supplemented the speech made by Professor Zorn. In one point he was obliged, he said, to oppose Count Nigra, — there are great and smaller powers. But the measure of greatness is not to be found in the area of their territory, nor in the effective of their troops, nor in the number of their inhabitants. The greatness of a power is to be measured by the greatness of its ideas and by the faithfulness with which it adheres to the principles on which the progress of mankind is based.

The orator spoke further in the same tenor, and all listened as if under a spell. When he ended, the storm of applause would not cease, and one delegate after another warmly pressed around the speaker to congratulate him.

And Article 27 was accepted.

July 22. Again the Commission of Inquiry. The question is asked whether the representatives of Roumania, Greece, and Servia have received the answers of their governments. Mr. Delyannis declares, in the name of Greece, that he has been instructed to accept the new form of the convention. Dr. Velkovitch,[1] in the name of Servia, makes a similar declaration. Now it is Roumania's turn. The president announces that he has just had a letter from Herr Beldimann, stating that his instructions have come to-day authorizing him to accept the new form, but only on condition that the eliminated clauses, "honor and interests of the nations" and "when circumstances allow," be restored. Otherwise Roumania cannot sign the convention.

Put to vote, the Beldimann ultimatum is accepted.

In the last plenary session, on July 28, Descamps's "Rapport final à la Conférence sur le règlement pacifique des conflits internationaux" is read.

The introduction to this document brings out thoughts and points of view which embrace the whole ideal of peace, — I might rather say the whole gospel of peace, — as, for example:

> Resolved to use every endeavor to bring about the peaceful solution of international conflicts; recognizing the solidarity which unites shoulder to shoulder all the civilized nations; desirous of extending the sovereignty of law and of strengthening the sentiment of international justice, etc., the undersigned [the names follow] have agreed upon the following provisions.

The first of the sixty-one paragraphs gives the gist of everything that is elaborated in the rest:

[1] Dr. Voïslaf Velkovitch, professor of law in the University of Belgrade; the other representatives of Servia were Miyatovitch, envoy at London and The Hague, and Colonel Maschin, envoy at Cetinje. — TRANSLATOR.

325

"With a view to obviating, as far as possible, recourse to force in the relations between states, the signatory powers agree to use their best efforts to insure the pacific settlement of international differences."

Early on July 29 the conventions were signed in the "House in the Wood," and the formal concluding session took place in the afternoon. The last word — it was uttered by D'Estournelles — was:

"May our Conference be a beginning, not a conclusion. May our countries, by inaugurating new assemblages such as this has been, continue to serve the cause of civilization and of peace!"

LXI

AFTER THE HAGUE CONFERENCE

A S soon as we returned to Harmannsdorf I set to work revising my diary from which have been taken, for this autobiography, most of the passages referring to the Conference. I sent the book to the publisher, and it appeared in 1900, but I cannot report any great awakening of interest thereby. The contemporary world is either indifferent or unfriendly in its attitude toward the Hague Conference.

We remained at home only a short time. After about three weeks we started forth again, this time for Norway. Invitations from the management of the Interparliamentary Conference which was to meet there from the first to the sixth of August had come to us, as well as to Herr von Bloch, requesting us to attend the deliberations and festivities as guests of honor. We did not require a second invitation. A journey to the Northland, what a holiday!

Again a wholly new part of the world opening before us. We reached Christiania on the evening of July 30. On the thirty-first the ship placed at the disposal of the interparliamentarians was to arrive. This ship was met by another, on which were the managers of the Conference as well as such of the deputies as had preferred to come by rail. John Lund invited us to accompany him on the trip.

There were many other guests besides us on board. We met many old friends and acquaintances, including Ullman (the president of the Storthing), Von Bar of the University of Göttingen, Marcoartu, Baron Pirquet, and others. It was two o'clock in the afternoon, the blue sky was cloudless, the fiord lay bathed in the brightest sunshine, and a cool breeze stirred the air. A military orchestra was on board, and to the strains of the Norwegian national hymn our steamer moved away. Streamers of the various colors of the fourteen countries represented at the Conference waved from the masts.

We made many new acquaintances. The wife of Blehr, afterwards minister but at that time ambassador in Stockholm, told me about the progress of the woman's movement already started in Norway; she said that they were not far from the attainment of suffrage. Every one, from the wives of statesmen down

328

to the peasant women, was taking an active part in political life.

I asked if it were true that Sweden and Norway were living like quarrelsome brethren.

" No," replied Frau Blehr, " the relationship is that of a marriage in which the man has everything, the wife nothing, to say; and, according to modern ideas, that can be no kind of a happy marriage. Norway, in this union, plays the part of the wife without authority, and what she wants is what to-day the woman with equal privileges demands in marriage — the right to her own personality."

We sailed past a small flotilla of war vessels which were in readiness to meet the ship of the interparliamentarians and give it convoy. A war flotilla to meet a ship of peace! This new method of showing honor surprised me. Lund told us that the committee had found some difficulty in overcoming the opposition of the conservatives, who regarded it as out of character that military honors should be paid to the champions of antimilitarism. Such parties are accustomed to take great stock in the notion of a quiet amalgamation of contrarieties. Soldiers and pacifists need not be antagonistic or endeavor to destroy one another, but may join in a higher unity, — an army fighting for assured legal protection.

Greetings and shouts were exchanged between our ship and the fleet, although this conduct was contrary to the stipulation that during the trip they should take no notice of each other. About five o'clock the vessels met. John Lund and other members of the Storthing were rowed over to the parliamentary vessel and boarded her to extend greetings.

The fortification of Oskarborg fired a salute. At the foot of the walls troops were drawn up and a loud hurrah, divided into three regular periods and nine times repeated, — that being the Northern cheer, — came across distinctly, and the flags were dipped in salutation. Beyond Oskarborg, as soon as the two parliamentary vessels arrived, the war ships took the lead and gave convoy up to the city of the Congress.

At nine o'clock in the evening, but still in clear daylight, we make our entry into Christiania. The quay along its whole extent is thronged with jubilant townspeople; people stream forth from all the side streets.

On the evening of the first of August there is a miscellaneous assemblage, with a concert in the Hans-Haugen, a public garden situated on a hill. We meet old acquaintances: Dr. Barth from Berlin, Dr. Harmening from Jena, Pierantoni from Rome, Senator Labiche from Paris, Count Albert Apponyi from Budapest, Gniewocz and Dr. Millanich from Vienna. Also many new delegates attending their first Inter-parliamentary Conference are presented to me; among them several members of the Center in the German Reichstag, Dr. Herold, and a few of the Young-Czech party from the Austrian parliament.

AFTER THE HAGUE CONFERENCE

A gigantic figure approaches me. I instantly recognize the characteristic head with the white lion's mane: oh, joy — it is Björnstjerne Björnson. He kisses my hand and we chat a few minutes; but soon a frail little woman in a white gown hurries up to him, with the words, " Father, they are looking for you. . . ."

Björnson introduces his daughter, Frau Ibsen.

A buffet was arranged for the assembled guests in a large hall. During the festival the papers arrive with news about the close of the Conference at The Hague. A passage from Beaufort's speech was most eagerly discussed. On account of technical difficulties the formula for a limitation of armaments adapted to the new conditions in all countries has not as yet been drawn up, but all are agreed on the principle that this formula must be sought and found. Here now is a task laid out for the Interparliamentary Union, namely, to develop further the work begun at The Hague.

At this writing — 1908 — however, that formula has not been found. Parliamentarians, with but few exceptions, when they are not in the Conference but in parliament, do nothing but consent, consent. The study of the problem was postponed from the first to the second and from the second to the third Hague Conference, and still it remains uninvestigated. Where there is no will, there is no way.

On the next day — to return to 1899 — came the formal opening in the Storthing. At the earlier Conferences scarcely more than sixty or eighty persons were present; this time there are more than three hundred. Germany, which hitherto has been represented by not more than two or three, sends forty to Christiania; France sends twenty-six, Austria fourteen. If this continues, special halls will have to be built for the " Interparliament " !

I noted the final sentence from Minister of State Steen's opening speech: " And so we shall be victorious — which will be a blessing to the defeated." That gives the criterion for what all noble champions of the future are to attain.

President Ullman makes a report on the Nobel foundation. The first distribution is to take place on the tenth of December, 1901. The interest accruing up to that time is to be employed as a capital fund for the creation of a Nobel Institute in Christiania, that is, a central school for the study and development of international law. From the annual income of the bequest (200,000 Swedish kroner) 50,000 kroner are to be reserved for the support of the Institute.

For the first time the United States of America is represented at an Interparliamentary Conference. Mr. Barrows reports that in his country there are many people who have never seen an officer and many officers who have never seen their regiment assembled. He believes that he is warranted — especially in view of the instructions and proposals intrusted to the delegates to the Hague Conference — in declaring that the jingo spirit, which was aroused by the last war with

Spain, and which is in such absolute opposition to the fundamental principles of the land of the star-spangled banner, will never get the upper hand.

So this was the first time that an American representative appeared in the arena of the Interparliamentary Union; but of late the New World is taking the first place in the universal peace movement. From that direction will come for the Old World the impulse, the example, — perhaps the necessity, — for the creation of United Europe.

Mr. Barrows was followed by Count Albert Apponyi. He informed the meeting that Koloman von Szell, the former leader of the Hungarian Interparliamentary group, had now become prime minister. Fiery, eloquent as always, flowed Apponyi's speech, and when he had finished, Björnson went up to him and pressed his hand.

In the evening a garden party at Minister of State Steen's. Here I met Ibsen. Long ago I had written him to get his views in regard to the peace cause. He then replied that his life was wholly devoted to the dramatic art and he had no views at all on the question at issue. I now wanted to ask if his presence was a sign of an awakened interest in the movement, but some one came between us and I had no other chance to resume the interrupted conversation.

The next afternoon we made the acquaintance of all the members of the French group present. M. Catusse, the recently accredited ambassador of France at

Stockholm, whom we had met before both at Nice and at The Hague, had invited all his French colleagues to take tea with him, and my husband and I were also asked. We found more than a dozen members of the Chamber and the Senate, among them the former premier, Cochery.

We spoke of Léon Bourgeois. He had left The Hague for Paris on account of the last cabinet crisis, and there he had informed several of the gentlemen that he should be unwilling to undertake the formation of a new cabinet, because he considered the work that he had to complete at The Hague more important.

Senator Labiche told us that the day before, when he was introduced to Björnson, the poet asked him point blank, *Êtes-vous Dreyfusard?*—for Björnson himself is.

The day and evening ended with an entertainment given by the city. A hundred and fifty carriages were in readiness and took the guests to the Frognersättern, a favorite place of resort, the road to which winds up continuously for five miles through thick forest trees, past all the red cottages of the peasantry, which give the characteristic physiognomy to "the land of the thousand homesteads," as the poet of the national hymn (Björnson) calls his native land. In the midst of the forest, on high land, you pass glittering lakes, and, wherever there is a wide prospect, fiord and city gleam in ever-varying beauty.

On the second and last day of the Conference the transactions occupied the whole time from nine o'clock until five. The principal subject on the programme was the Conference at The Hague. Stanhope reads a message brought from there by W. T. Stead and bearing the signatures of Beernaert, Rahusen, D'Estournelles, Descamps, and others. This message communicates to their colleagues assembled at Christiania the outcome of the arbitration question, — a result which, as soon as its importance is grasped, will be recognized as the crowning event of the nineteenth century. The conclusion of the message read:

"So this is the machine which the Hague Conference has created, and it is for you, representatives of the nations, and for the nations to provide it with steam."

A duty which — I repeat it with regret — neither the nations nor their representatives up to the present time have fulfilled.

It was voted that Paris should be the place for the next Conference, and the date, 1900.

The last evening was devoted to the parting banquet, given by the Storthing. Björnson arose as the first speaker. He spoke French. His somewhat singsong tone was not well suited to the French accent, but the emphasis and the enthusiasm of the address atoned for that. His theme was "The Truth." Björnson wants to see truth injected into politics — politics should become ethical. Of course every self-respecting "practical politician" will smile indulgently at that idea. After leaving the table, the guests, four hundred in number, scattered through the many adjoining rooms. Here appeared a troop of young people in neat black clothes and white caps — I took them for students, but they were artisans — and sang Norwegian and German part songs. Björnson addressed them and they themselves expressed words of thanks to all the men and women present who were working for peace, that most important of all advantages for the laboring man.

While we were drinking our coffee, I had at last a long talk with Björnson. I can forgive him for not calling upon me, for he has not a moment of rest. He is regarded as a universal counselor. Young poets bring him their manuscripts; young women aspirants to a theatrical career play their heroine rôles before him; and he is incapable of refusing any one. Speaking of the artisans who had just been singing, he told me that in his country this class took more interest than the higher strata of society, in intellectual things. " I was recognized by them," he said, " much earlier than by the so-called intelligent class."

" And is n't it true," I asked, "that the peasants here are very advanced? I hear that there are no illiterate among them."

" Oh, the peasants," cried Björnson, "they are the foundation of our kingdom; they are its pillars."

We made the return journey from Norway in Bloch's company, though indeed only as far as Berlin. There our paths diverged, Bloch going to Warsaw and we to Vienna and Harmannsdorf.

AFTER THE HAGUE CONFERENCE

Here sad news and joyous news awaited us.

My Aunt Büschel, seventy-nine years old, whom I
was in the habit of visiting every week at Eggenburg
near by, to talk with her about old times, about Elvira,
and about my mother, — had peacefully passed away
during our absence. She had a short illness, and was
cared for by my relatives. With her death the last
link that connected me with the days of my youth
was broken.

The joyous event was a betrothal. On the day after
our return the whole family from the neighboring
Stockern drove over to Harmannsdorf accompanied
by a young cousin, Baron Johann Baptist Moser. All
wore mysterious looks as they whispered together
and put on such strange expressions! When we were
gathered together at lunch, and dessert was served, my
brother-in-law Richard suddenly rose and, portentously
clearing his throat, said, —

"My dear friends, I hereby inform you that yesterday evening my dear daughter Margarete and my dear
nephew Moser became engaged."

Universal jubilation, and I myself felt the tears of
joy coming into my eyes, for I had long cherished the
desire that these dearly beloved young folks, who were
so admirably suited to each other, should strike up a
match, and so the news brought keen delight to me.

I had no lack of work to do. The interrupted Hague
diary had to be finished; likewise the reports for my
periodical. This, by the way, was to cease publication

at the end of the year and to be absorbed by the *Friedenswarte*, edited by A. H. Fried, whose regular collaborator I am up to the present time.

One day I received several copies of the *Budapester Tagblatt* containing an excellent article by Count Albert Apponyi, who gave in it a very favorable report regarding the Hague Conference, and made the suggestion for a press league, to be associated with the Interparliamentary Union. I thanked the count for sending me the papers and praised the idea. In answer I received the following letter:

My dear Baroness: Eberhard, August 28, 1899

In thanking you for your friendly letter I must observe that, though I certainly estimate at its full value the submission of my lucubrations to your very competent criticism, the thought of burdening you with several copies of the *Budapester Tagblatt* was entirely due to the editors of that paper. Had it been my doings it would have been inexcusably presumptuous.

It rejoices me that the thoughts that I wrote down meet with your approval. The optimism which I display is, however, rather a tactical maneuver than actual conviction. The great powers at The Hague were less than lukewarm, and I am not sure that their assent to The Hague conventions — especially in the case of Germany and Austria-Hungary — will be given. The rulers do not want the thing to succeed; they do not want war, indeed, but every institution in which they can detect any limitation of their absolute power (to do either good or ill) is instinctively repugnant to them.

Meantime, we in Hungary — where, after the beneficent parliamentary revolution of this winter, we are perhaps on the way to recuperation (but I repeat the word " perhaps ") — will do our best to bring our monarchy, through constitutional methods of pressure, into the right course. My position for this end has become somewhat

338

better, and I will certainly make the most of it. I shall also endeavor
to form the press league mentioned in my article. It is intended to
form a connecting link between the Interparliamentary Union and the
people. As for the rest, only a kind Providence can make anything
good out of such wretched material.

With sincere respect,

Your wholly devoted

Albert Apponyi

As I turn over the leaves of my diary for that time,
I find that three different objects filled my soul, each
with different moods. There was my great life interest,
my "one thing essential," which just now through the
Hague Conference had arrived at such a mighty stage
of development. It was almost as if the goal, which
only a few years before was so far away, had now come
so near and was so distinct that soon all would per-
force take note of it and therefore hasten to it. I saw
clearly what I myself had to do: it was to give as
many of my fellow-countrymen as possible a knowledge of the results of the Conference, and I devoted
myself diligently to this task, writing numerous newspaper articles and my book on the Hague Conference.

I must confess I could not take an unqualified joy
in doing this, for I had been a witness to the opposition, open and secret, which had been directed at The
Hague against the realization of the "warless age."
But all the more strenuous was the obligation to put
to the service of the cause all the new facts and supports which the present state of the movement afforded
its defenders.

Something else was rising full of threat on the horizon. The war party in England seemed to be getting the upper hand; the Outlander crisis in the Transvaal was growing more and more acute. What if it broke into war? That would discredit the peace work that had been begun and would decidedly put it back. Can it be that between the two forces of Might and Right, Might is again to carry the day?

Another object of my thought and anxiety was found in our domestic circumstances. The losses in the quarries, in the failure of crops, and in unfortunate speculations had increased to such an extent that it was now almost impossible to keep our beloved Harmannsdorf above water much longer. And what then? What a grief for the poor old mother, for the sisters, and also for My Own, if the home nest were to be sacrificed!

The third field of my feelings and moods lay within our married happiness. In this was my peculiar inalienable home, my refuge for all possible conditions of life, — something beyond Harmannsdorf and the Transvaal, beyond everything, come what might, — and so the leaves of my diary are full not only of political and domestic records of all kinds, but also of memoranda of our gay little jokes, our confidential, enjoyable walks, our uplifting reading, our hours of music together, and our evening games of chess. To us personally nothing could happen. We had each other, — that was everything.

The thought that we might be torn apart by the all-destroyer Death we put out of our minds. And yet at that time I was not very strong and I believe My Own felt some alarm about my condition. I had suddenly become so languid; it was hard for me to walk; after a few steps I became so dizzy that I could scarcely stand. My Own dragged me off to a physician; I say "dragged," because all my life long I have been strenuously opposed to medical treatment. This physician gave me an examination and asked me all manner of questions and ordered — what do you suppose?

I will give the details because it is an interesting case. In the first place I followed his directions, which also was contrary to my custom; up to that time the only use I had made of medicine was to throw it out of the window. What is more, the treatment helped me. In a short time I became as healthy as a fish in water. Well then, what was the doctor's prescription? Bicycling! I, a heavy woman of fifty-six, who had never mounted a wheel, was now to attempt this schoolgirl's sport! It was comical, but I did it. The prescription was tremendously tempting to me. It had always been my keen desire to enjoy this skimming away on the thin-legged iron steed, and I had regretted that I was born too early to experience this delight. Now it was imposed upon me as a duty to my health! I immediately bought a wheel, and one of the castle servants was appointed my instructor. He helped me to mount the thing and down I went. Up again, down again — twenty times in succession. That was my first lesson.

" Would it not be better to try a tricycle?" asked My Own solicitously, for .he gained no confidence at all from this début. But I would not hear to it. " The doctor has prescribed bicycling and bicycling it shall be."

With a persistence at which I myself am amazed I kept up my lessons; more and more infrequently the wheel wobbled, ever more and more rare were the trees against which I obstinately steered, and after a long course of instruction — I certainly am not going to confess how long — I attained such skill that I wheeled in great style through the avenues of the park and really made a very elegantly executed figure eight!

In doing this I felt perfectly well; the blood circulated with reinvigorated energy; dashing away on the wheel became to me a perfect delight; I had no more attacks of lassitude; I grew slenderer, and at the same time I had a feeling as if youth, youth were streaming through my veins!

Things in the Transvaal were going from bad to worse. People in England, worked upon through their passion, were demanding war. The London pacifists were putting forth their utmost endeavors to ward off the misfortune; they instituted meetings, they wrote to the papers; W. T. Stead established a new weekly, *War against War*,—all in vain. Any one who pleaded

for peace was repudiated, scouted as a "Little Englishman," if not even held up to scorn and derision as
a traitor. Managers of halls would no longer permit
the use of them for peace meetings, and if such gatherings were held they were broken up by turbulent
mobs. Assaults even were committed. At a public
meeting held by the Peace Association in Trafalgar
Square, the orators were not only overwhelmed with
insults but were attacked with projectiles. An open
jackknife was hurled at Felix Moscheles, narrowly
escaping his head.

In the meantime the second Dreyfus trial was held
at Rennes, and with the same military fanaticism and
partisanship as in the days when Esterhazy was glorified and Zola was persecuted with shouts of à l'eau !
à l'eau ! Now a furious anti-Dreyfusard even makes
an attempt upon the life of the defendant's lawyer,
Labori. The court-martial condemns Dreyfus to death
— but he is pardoned.

In Vienna a meeting is held at which Dr. Lueger
declares, "Dreyfus belongs to the Devil's Island and
all the Jews as well." This impelled my husband to
call a counter meeting of his Union. The combat
with popular frenzy and against national hatred is a
hard, apparently quite hopeless, task, only just begun.
Pain and indignation and a bitter sense of feebleness
take possession of the combatant; but still there is
nothing else for him to do — he must take up the
fight. And since absolutely nothing in this world is

lost, such protests certainly have their effect ultimately in their own way, even if they seem for the moment to be wasted.

In the German empire plans for a tremendous fleet are adopted. "Our future lies on the water,"—therefore enormous increase of armament on the sea. Exactly the opposite of what was at the foundation of the Hague Conference. Bloch writes me that Emperor William is said to have persuaded the Tsar that the peace cause—that is, in the form of an arbitration tribunal and the limitation of armaments (the German Emperor is surely in favor of preserving peace by the protection of the bayonet)—is directly contrary to dynastic interests.

The South African war breaks out. Our opponents cry scornfully, "So this is the result of the Hague Conference, is it?"

I had desired to publish in my monthly an expression of opinion regarding this misfortune from an English peace champion so highly regarded as Philip Stanhope, who I knew would be deeply grieved by it. He replied that it would not be in good taste to express his views in foreign periodicals while his country was involved in war. Now that the war is long finished there is no indiscretion in my reproducing his letter:

Padworth House, Reading, November 19, 1899

Dear Baroness von Suttner:

I have to thank you most sincerely for your letter. In times like these, when one finds one's self in a small minority, the encouragement

344

of friends is of great service, and no one is more authorized than yourself to speak upon such an issue, having for many years given your life to the service of the cause of peace.

Just now it is impossible to write anything for publication in a foreign journal. While we are in the throes of a great war it would be unseemly to do so, and I will therefore ask you to kindly excuse me in this regard for the present. I may, however, say to yourself as a friend what I could not publicly say about the situation.

I think the jingo feeling is subsiding in England. Now that the people are at last realizing what war means, there is less shouting and enthusiasm. I am told that even in the music halls this tendency is very marked. Of course patriotic songs will always command a large audience and excite natural patriotic emotions, but people are beginning to think and to ask themselves what the war is about, and whether warfare is the best way of really pacifying South Africa. I have great confidence in the ultimate good sense of my countrymen when the fever has passed away.

All the same, the path of idealists like ourselves is not made more easy by what has happened.

I hope Baron von Suttner is well. Kindly remember me to him and allow me to subscribe myself as   Very sincerely yours

Philip Stanhope

I asked an expression of opinion from Count Nigra for the annual meeting of my Union. The ambassador replied with the following letter:

Rome, Grand Hotel, November 29, 1899

My dear Baroness:

You are quite right in seizing the occasion of the meeting of the Austrian peace society to ask a word of approbation and encouragement from those who worked for peace at the Conference at The Hague. That Conference has had to meet with two untoward accidents, — the Dreyfus affair and the conflict in the Transvaal. The first distracted public attention from our work; the other seems to contradict it. The coincidence is certainly very regrettable. But these are only passing incidents, while our work is destined to last as long as time lasts. The Conference is accused of not having produced immediate results. To tell the truth we enjoyed no illusion in this respect. We knew perfectly well that we had not been working to secure the peace of the world from one day to another. On the contrary, we had the consciousness of working for the future of humanity.

Moreover, is it true that the Conference had no immediate effect? I think that the mere fact that such a Conference was convoked by a powerful monarch, like the Emperor of Russia, that it was accepted by all the powers, and that it could meet and work for months with the purpose of making wars less frequent and less cruel for the nations, — that fact alone is already a great result. It proves at least that the ideas of peace and arbitration have entered into the consciousness of governments and of peoples.

Besides, as I have just said, we had in view not the fleeting moment but the future history of the world. The tree, the seed of which we have planted, is likely to grow but slowly, like everything else that is destined to increase and throw down deep roots. We shall not be able to repose in the shade of its branches, but those who follow us will gather its fruits. I have faith in our work for the future. The ideas that we have aroused in the minds of the governments and of the peoples cannot vanish like deceptive mirages. They have their *raisons d'être* in the universal consciousness. Like every human conception, they meet, in their application, with periods of arrested development and even, if one may thus express one's self, with passing eclipses. But nothing shall prevent their onward course. The end which we have set before ourselves is that of a forward march in constant progress. It is the law of history. Blind is he who does not see it.

So then, *sursum corda*, and let us remember that Christ blamed men of little faith. You can remind your assembly of this in order that it may be taken in elsewhere.

Accept, madam, my very sincere regards

Nigra

LXII

THE TURN OF THE CENTURY

NOW we began to write 1900. A new century. To be sure the ancient controversy raged a good deal as to whether the century began with the cipher or with the figure one; but I think that the number 1901 signifies that the first year of the twentieth century is finished, so that it begins with 1900, therefore it already is.[1] To be sure, time runs without figures into the Ocean of Eternity, but such turning points are always impressive.

Even the Tsar's rescript said, "This Conference should be, by the help of God, a happy presage for a

[1] There are a hundred cents to a dollar and a hundred years to a century. Ninety-nine cents do not make a dollar; nor does the year 1899 end the century. — TRANSLATOR.

century which is about to open." Our age, however, allowed this significant epoch to pass by without "turning over a new leaf," without saying, "Now we will dedicate the twentieth century by breaking with the old barbarism."

Barbarism was happily rescued by its admirers, and an immeasurably horrible and pitiful war, with lurid-glaring jingoism in its train, raged as a portentous presage marking the transition from the old century to the new.

All the pacifists were troubled and indignant over this turn of affairs; but none was disheartened. It is well known that the line of progress often runs back a little in order later to advance with accelerated rapidity; and the results already achieved, the unexpected new victories in the domain of the peace cause, were already in our hands. That certainly was not going backwards. In the work of the pioneers also there was no moment of inaction; the protests against the continuation of the South African war, the reminder to the powers that mediation was open to them, the articles, the petitions, — all these things were zealously attended to by our Bern Bureau, by Stead in his *Weekly*, by the Unions in their meetings. Even though no direct result was attained, still the principle was unviolated, the standpoint was held, the banner was kept aloft.

Our friends had organized an international demonstration in the form of an address to the powers,

signed by public societies and distinguished individuals of all nations. The names of those who were included were both numerous and imposing; but I will
here call attention only to the answer of one great
man who refused to join with us. I had sent out a
great many invitations, among others one to Henryk
Sienkiewicz. He sent me a long reply, in which he
declined to sign the petition because he held the
opinion that there were much worse and more press-
ing sufferings to be relieved than those of the Boers;
for instance, the sufferings of the Poles persecuted by
" Hakatism." He believed that the English would
never be able — even though they might be victorious
in the Transvaal — to attempt to denationalize the
people there and deprive them of all freedom. So we
might much better work for people nearer at home;
such was the conclusion of Sienkiewicz's letter:

Ah, madam, before taking up with Africa, interest yourself in Europe. A gigantic humanitarian work is within your reach. Endeavor
to make the spirit of the German nation ennoble the present *régime*,
and see to it that it does not become debased by false statesmanship.

England gave birth to a great minister who spent his life in defending the rights of oppressed Ireland; can you show me another
in all Europe? Leave the English spirit in peace, for it will of itself
attain the end that you propose, and work for causes nearer home.
Elevate political morality, ennoble the consciences of the mighty;
may the clouds of injustice and of treason against human right vanish away! May a breath of humanity freshen the air poisoned by
Hakatist currents! Carry the good tidings to your neighbors, bring
them words of love, endeavor to instill the Kingdom of Christ into
their souls. You have a noble heart, a good and unshaken will!

349

I replied in a few lines in which I informed him that I desired to reply to him in an open letter. Thereupon Sienkiewicz wrote back:

My dear Baroness: Warsaw, March 7, 1900

I allowed a Cracow newspaper to publish the letter which I sent in reply to yours, for in circumstances so important the greatest publicity cannot fail to be advantageous to the ideas which you, madam, defend with such commendable warmth.

The news that you wish to reply in an open letter causes me real joy. I believe that the more light we carry into these gloomy vaults the more we drive out of them the creatures that exist only in the darkness.

With assurances of my highest regard

Henryk Sienkiewicz

Our correspondence was accordingly published in French and Polish newspapers. The text of my reply is not within my reach; I only know that I pointed out that one should never say to any one who is undertaking something useful and helpful, " Better do this than that." If " this " as well as " that " is directed to the same end — freedom, and suppression of injustice and suffering — then do both; but better than that which is nearer in space is the universal; for if the general principle is saved, it can be applied to other and local cases.

All this political correspondence did not prevent me from exchanging letters with my own intimate friends. Even with our friends in the Caucasus, in spite of years of separation, intercourse was not broken off.

THE TURN OF THE CENTURY

The following letter from the Prince of Mingrelia, which I find in my letter-file for 1900, is a witness of that fact:

St. Petersburg, March 24 (April 6), 1900

My dear Baroness:

How much I should like to see you and chat with you! At St. Petersburg all your writings are translated and your individuality interests the public.

It is clear that the sympathies of all are aroused by your beautiful ideas. Nevertheless a strange thing is happening: every one is in favor of peace, and along with that all the powers are arming. International laws are easily read, but the application of them is pretty difficult. One must be resigned and confess that the system of Brennus is always the order of the day.[1] The English are doing in the Transvaal what others are doing elsewhere. Did not these very Boers who are pillaged now, first pillage the native Africans? In this world each has his turn. 'T is the great immutable law. "He who takes the sword shall perish by the sword." When one is a philosopher, injustice seems the rule, justice the exception.

Salomé will be in Paris in May, I think. I expect to take a trip in August. At all events I will keep you informed of my deeds and actions. I am going to send you my photograph very soon.

Please give my love to your husband, and think of me always as

Your very devoted

Niko

Count Apponyi was still at work on his press project. He wrote me regarding it:

Budapest, March 27, 1900

Dear Madam:

Yesterday something took place here which, with God's help, may prove of incalculable importance for the peace movement. That is, we have taken the first step toward the establishment of an international peace union of the press, and the Hungarian group, made up

[1] Brennus, leader of the Senonian Gauls, who took Rome in 390 B.C. Being offered a thousand pounds of gold as a ransom for the Capitol, he took it and went home. — TRANSLATOR.

351

of almost all the newspapers of the capital, is already formed. The proposed press union, for which we have elaborated a provisional charter, is to be organized in every degree parallel with the Interparliamentary Union, and is to be in constant touch with it. The idea originated with the Hungarian Interparliamentary Group, which, as a *Conseil interparlementaire* will make the motion at the Paris Conference, as indeed it has already done at the Brussels meeting, that all the national groups shall endeavor to help form the press groups, and that our Interparliamentary Bureau shall serve these groups as a center until there shall be so many of them that the independent international organization of the press can come into existence.

I have got the matter under way through correspondence; have written Descamps, Labiche, Rahusen, Dr. Hirsch, Stanhope, Pierantoni, and Pirquet. Pirquet is already at work on it; I have not yet had any answer from the others.

The importance of the plan scarcely requires argument. But I am taking the liberty of inclosing an extract from the address which I gave before the press club here and which clearly outlines my idea. It is hardly to be expected that the scheme will be everywhere so enthusiastically and unanimously adopted as it has been here, where an exceptional intimacy exists between parliament and press. But influential newspapers will everywhere be enlisted, and what we need is the systematic labors of these unpartisan journals.

What advantage is it if, for example, the *Neue Freie Presse* publishes to-day an article from your pen, Baroness, or one by Councilor Bloch, but on the other six days of the week speaks of the peace movement — if at all — in a scornful tone? Such sporadic articles of individual persons, no matter how distinguished, are put down as special labors, and any possible influence that they might have on the reader is immediately rendered nugatory. Only the constant logical attitude of the editorial boards renders the action of the press effectual. Now then, imagine the press organized and conducted for one purpose throughout the whole civilized world and brought into tactical partnership with the parliamentary activity; then that steam power which the Hague peace machinery needs to put it into action would be supplied. This seems to us practically much more important than to discover new articles which might be added to the Hague Convention.

After all this I hardly need to ask your benevolent furtherance of our scheme, for I do not believe that anything could impart more power to the peace movement than the success of this plan.

With greatest respect, I am

Your wholly devoted

Albert Apponyi

Undeterred by the South African war, the Interparliamentary Union held its Conference, and the Peace Unions likewise assembled for their annual Congress. Both organizations met in Paris, where the World's Exposition was being held. I got a letter from the French Senate inviting us to attend the Conference as guests. Various circumstances prevented us from accepting this invitation.

The Conference was opened with impressive words by the president of the Senate, M. Fallières, now President of the Republic. The sensation of the Conference was the bearing and eloquence of Count Apponyi. He outlined his plan for a press union to be allied with the Interparliamentary Bureau, and in fact the foundation for such a union was actually laid. Unfortunately the matter did not materialize and was not generally adopted. Success will come with the next attempt.

The political bitterness which at that time divided the French into two camps, under the still convulsing excitement of the " Affair," was a very unfavorable circumstance for the holding of an Interparliamentary

Conference. The following letter from Count Apponyi refers to this:

My dear Baroness:
Weidlingau, August 8, 1900

I should like to add to the accompanying text of my speech just a few remarks on the Paris Interparliamentary Conference.

We were very sorry indeed that you were not there, but you may well congratulate yourself that you were not. It was the gloomiest meeting, the most disappointing of all our hopes, of any that I ever attended. The French were for the most part absent: *Si M. un tel en est, je n'en suis pas;* so the word goes. It was an unfortunate idea to lay the scene of our endeavors in the France of to-day, where everything is regarded from the visual angle of a party quarrel so accentuated that it has almost reached the point of civil war.

Everything that is not in accord with the present régime, — more accurately, with the left wing of the present régime, — was on strike, Deschanel, president of the chamber, included; the press was partly indifferent, partly hostile. I am afraid that this Conference will have a bad reactionary influence on men's minds everywhere. The German group seemed to me infected by the French unsteadiness; it was numerously represented, but evaporated almost completely toward the end.

Perhaps I see things in too dark colors, but truly I have no personal reasons for doing so; my efforts were received in the friendliest spirit, and my group, numerously represented, made the most delightful picture. I can guarantee the soundness of this group.

But I do not give up the cause in France; as far as it was permitted me by the brevity of the time and the general flight of those concerned, I tried to get into touch with the absent parliamentary circles, and I shall certainly be able to strengthen these relations and perhaps serve as a neutral connecting link in the interest of our cause. No Frenchman is capable of uniting two of his fellow-countrymen who are not wholly unanimous in their views, even though it concerns an object highly regarded by both; not even our very sympathetic friend D'Estournelles, who is in great favor in all camps, at least socially. And without France nothing can be accomplished.

THE TURN OF THE CENTURY

If you ask the question, Who is to blame for this? I can only reply, All. But who is most to blame? That would be a long chapter, and I will not go into it, although I have a definite answer ready. I hope you will not lay this pessimistic statement of the case up against me; but we must see clearly, not so as to be discouraged, but so as to act in a suitable manner. With great respect

Your wholly devoted
Albert Apponyi

Our friend Dr. Clark, a Scotchman, who has never missed a Peace Congress and has always distinguished himself by his clever speeches characterized by a certain dry humor, had just been made the object of bitter attacks by the British press. He sent me the following explanation of the circumstances:

Ardnahane Cove, Dunbartonshire, September 11, 1900
Dear Madam von Suttner:

I have received your letter, for which I thank you very heartily. These are indeed evil days for the cause with which we are associated, though I cannot but think that the events of the last year must have led many to the contemplation of the awful waste of life and suffering caused by the present system of settling international disputes by force of arms, and will induce them to work for the day when arbitration shall take the place of war with its horrible human sacrifice.

You mention the letters written to President Kruger and General Joubert by me on the 29th of September of last year, which have lately been published by Mr. Chamberlain and copied by the continental press. It is quite true that there has been a great deal of misrepresentation on that subject. For some months before the war began there had been a small party in this country who had been working to bring about a peaceable settlement. I had some correspondence with President Kruger and General Joubert, in which I had advised them to make such concessions to the British government that the calamity of war might be averted, since the prosperity of

355

RECORDS OF AN EVENTFUL LIFE

South Africa must depend on the good faith and friendly feeling between the two white races. The published letters, to which you refer, are the last portion of this correspondence, and were written less than a fortnight before the war began. In my letter to President Kruger I gave him the result of an interview which I had with Mr. Chamberlain, in which I endeavored to induce him to accede to the repeated request which the Transvaal government had made that matters at issue should be settled by arbitration, and to consent that a permanent arbitration tribunal should be formed to which all present and future disputes should at once be submitted. I told him that the Transvaal government were willing to submit the differences pending between the two governments to a court of arbitration, consisting of the four chief justices of South Africa, and to accept the Lord Chief Justice of England as umpire in the event of the two colonial and two republican chief justices not being able to agree, — a suggestion which, as you will have seen, the colonial secretary was not able to accept.

The force of misrepresentation and calumny which the peace party here have had to endure from the virulent and unscrupulous jingo press can be estimated by the manner in which they have misrepresented my warning to President Kruger. I knew, as every one who knew anything of the geography of South Africa must have known, that the obvious line of action for the Boers to adopt would be that of seizing the passes, and I warned President Kruger that to do so would alienate the sympathy of many of their supporters in this country and on the continent of Europe. My words were deliberately misconstrued, and it was asserted that I urged the Boers to seize the passes. Nothing further from the truth can be imagined.

But, in spite of the difficulties with which we have had to contend, there is, undoubtedly, a large minority here who are firmly convinced that the war is an unjust one, and who regard the settlement by annexation as another wrong against which they will continue to protest. We shall go on working by all constitutional means for the restoration of the independence of the two republics, believing that by these means only can peace and prosperity exist once more in South Africa. We believe that we are working in a just cause, and shall hope in the not too distant future that we may be able to appeal to the justice of

356

this people, who will then have recognized the folly and wickedness for which they have been made responsible.

We do not doubt the future. We are sure that it is with us. It is true that the middle classes and the moderate liberals have abandoned their old watchword of " Peace, retrenchment, and reform," but the radicals and socialists are standing firmly by these principles. I send you a copy of the socialist paper *Justice*, which expressed fairly the attitude of the democratic party. I have, as you know, opposed the growth of socialism, which I formerly believed to be inimical to freedom and progress, but I am considerably modifying my views. The power for evil of the lawless and conscienceless capitalism which is now rampant is so great, and entails such unlimited moral and physical degeneracy, that I am convinced some form of collective action is a necessity to put an end to its baneful influence.

The history of this miserable war determines us to stand more determinedly by the principle of the substitution of arbitration for war. It becomes clearer and clearer that no permanent settlement can be based on war, and that, as between individuals, so between nations, magnanimity is not only morally desirable, *but it is the best policy*.

I am taking a yachting holiday in Scotland, but we may be overtaken by a general election here at any time.

Thanking you again for your letter, believe me to remain

Yours faithfully

G. B. Clark

But in this Transvaal affair I must also let the *altera pars* have its say. The English nation, so vilified on the Continent because of the Boer War, was not as a whole (as many liked to assert) led into this campaign merely by the passion for gain and through love of warfare. Noble motives — as is usually the case in every war — animated the majority. The desire is to " give freedom," to make wrong into right, to serve the fatherland; life itself is sacrificed. The object and aim may be praiseworthy; only it is unfortunate that the method is so unholy and vicious. I received the following letter from the sister of the Minister of Cape Colony:

Stockton, April 18, 1900

Madam:

Because of the high honor in which I bear you and the deep sympathy with which I read *Die Waffen nieder*, I send you this letter, written by a Cape Dutch woman, sister of Mr. Schreiner, Prime Minister of Cape Colony. I do not know if you are well enough acquainted with Cape politics to be aware of the full significance of the fact that he came into office as leader of the Afrikander Bond.

That his sister should write as she does about this war should surely come as a startling revelation to many people on the Continent who are so sorely misjudging my beloved country.

She will answer for you as to the motives of those Cape Dutch who are holding by the Union Jack. For those of my own country I, living in the heart of England, daily in touch with the lower, middle, and upper middle classes, affirm to you, as before God, that no wish for conquest and no lust for gold weighs anything at all with us.

We are giving the lives of our best beloved — giving them by thousands — to right wrong, to destroy oppression of our fellow-subjects, both white and black, to put an end to a very unjust and most corrupt form of government. Also to prevent our Colony of the Cape, Natal, Rhodesia, and Bechuanaland, conquered by our blood and treasure at various times, from being wrested from us.

This is the simple truth. We should like high-minded people abroad to know and recognize that truth. But if it may not be, we can only still repeat the old battle cry of our forefathers, " May God defend the right ! "

Pardon an insignificant old Englishwoman for venturing to address you. It is only because of the immense sympathy with your noble-hearted efforts to stop wars, ambitious and unjust, that I have done so. England loves peace also, and her united millions who now with one heart and soul are carrying out this war (and madam, the very peasants are naming their children after our generals) would never allow war to be made on our European neighbors. There is not the slightest wish or expectation of such a thing among us. Foreign journals which assert the contrary and thereby try to fan the flames of war are guilty of a European crime.

I am, madam, faithfully yours
Emily Axbell

The year 1900 brought, besides the struggle so obstinately contested in South Africa, still other warlike events into the world, notably the troubles in China. First the Boxer uprising, the assassination of the German ambassador Ketteler, then the expedition for rescue and revenge sent by the combined European powers.

I can still remember vividly with what feelings we followed the successive phases of these events. First the tidings of alarm, then the full horror of it. Then the Emperor William's " Pardon-will-not-be-granted " speech — " Never in a thousand years shall a Chinaman venture to look askance at a German!" Great Heavens! in a thousand years it is to be hoped that no man will any longer inspire other men with fear. . . . Then the anxious question every day, "Are the legations still safe?" Then the joy that something corresponding to our ideal had been spontaneously developed: an international protective army for the rescue of the oppressed European brotherhood-in-arms, — a precursor of European unity. Then again the sorrow at the behavior of this army. Not only protection but also revenge, cruelty, and looting!

359

The description of the outrages committed there by Europeans on noncombatants, even on the innocent, made one's blood run cold. The thing itself — a united force of French, Russian, and other troops under the command of a German general — belonged to the new methods that are to come; but the execution still showed the old spirit.

Even before things had reached their worst in China, the Chinese ambassador in St. Petersburg, Yang-Yü, whom we met at The Hague, wrote the following letter in reply to one which my husband had addressed to him in this emergency:

Imperial Chinese Embassy

My dear Baron: St. Petersburg, August 4 (17), 1900

The melancholy events now happening in my country often make me think of the friends of peace and those whom I had the honor of knowing at The Hague.

Your letter of the eighth instant has deeply touched me, and I am persuaded that, in spite of the fact that you are, as you say, a negligible quantity, you will finally triumph and rule. The light will shine from this negligible quantity, and a spark will suffice to kindle forever this pharos of peace. May the sword and the cannon of which you speak soon be beaten into plowshares.

So, then, it is a sacred duty for you to defend this noble cause without ever yielding to discouragement, with absolute firmness, resolution, and conviction, and without ever ceasing to make your voice heard !

I should be most happy if by my opinion and my personal impressions I could contribute in some way to the humanitarian work in which you are engaged. During journeys which I have taken, both as an envoy and as an investigator, I have visited the United States of America, Peru and other states of South America, Austria-Hungary,

360

THE TURN OF THE CENTURY

Germany, England, Spain, France, Holland, Japan, and Russia; everywhere I went I studied the customs of the people, and I have been particularly interested in the army, in commerce, and in agriculture, all of which I have found most perfectly administered. I took note of what differentiates these countries from ours and what benefits they have to confer upon my country. But what should I say? This incessant rivalry and this jealousy manifested among all nations somewhat detract from this perfection. If I have one desire to formulate, it is to see all countries rise superior to these sentiments and live always in a good understanding; this would assure them a lasting peace.

The conflict existing at present between China and the foreign powers comes in large part from mutual misunderstandings. I am firmly convinced that neither China nor any of these powers desires to break these pleasant relationships. Things have been pushed to this point, owing to the heedlessness of Chinese functionaries and military parties blinded by ambition. It is more than time to do away with these misunderstandings, and to reëstablish the old relations; otherwise, not only will China be brought to the greatest distress, but, moreover, international quarrels may result, and this would certainly not be in the interest of humanity as a whole. I hope that the governments of none of the countries will lose sight of the opportunity of putting an end to this state of things.

The first cause that prepared and brought about the present conflict is due to the sworn hatred of the people against the Christians. Assuredly the end pursued by the missionaries, of doing good to others, is very praiseworthy. But, as a general thing, right-thinking Chinese would not for anything in the world abandon the religion that comes down to them from their ancestors, for the sake of embracing one that is wholly foreign to them; the result is that the new converts are unfortunately in large measure dishonest people who hide behind the shelter of the Church to give themselves up to their evil passions, such as bringing lawsuits with impunity, and molesting and robbing their fellow-countrymen. The feelings of the people, which were at first merely wrath and indignation, and do not date from yesterday, have been changed into an implacable hatred, the fury of which it is impossible any longer to restrain. The Chinese no more desire to be

361

converted to Christianity than the Europeans would wish to embrace the maxims of Confucius.

My personal opinion is that commercial relations between China and the foreign powers may be developed to any desired extent; but as for the question of religion, it would be more prudent to allow each to respect his own as he understands it; this would be calculated to preserve the future from all conflict. I do not know whether the foreign governments will at last recognize the whole importance of the question and renounce it definitely.

In the belief that I have answered all your questions, I beg leave to assure you that I shall always be charmed to be useful and agreeable to you.   Yours with most sincere esteem

Yang-Yü, Chinese Minister

And a little later a second letter came from the same source:

Imperial Chinese Embassy

My dear Baron: St. Petersburg, September 10 (23), 1900

Sincere thanks for your kind letter, as well as for the newspaper clippings, which have greatly interested me.

I hasten to send you and the Baroness my best wishes for a good journey and a happy sojourn in Paris. I likewise hope that you will have a brilliant success in the noble assembly of the ninth Peace Congress. Once again you are going to spread the light and to plead for that peace cause which ought to be dear to every human heart. Therefore I should be greatly delighted to learn that all your endeavors toward this end have fully succeeded.

Yours with most sincere esteem

Yang-Yü, Chinese Minister

In the late summer we went to Paris to attend the Peace Congress that was to be held there, and to see the Exposition.

Johann von Bloch, who was living with his family at the Hotel Westminster, had invited us to stay at

362

the same hotel as his guests. Now I made the acquaintance of our friend's wife and daughters. Frau von
Bloch looked like her eldest daughter's sister, so similar and so young. This daughter is the wife of Herr
von Koszielski, formerly so well liked at the Berlin
court. He was known popularly as "Admiralski."
Bloch had good reason to be proud of his family. It
would be difficult to imagine a bouquet of prettier,
wittier, or more elegant women than the four that
formed his *entourage*.

The Congress was opened by Minister Millerand.
Frédéric Passy was honorary president; Professor
Charles Richet presided.

Madame Séverine was a new apparition. I had often
read, in the French papers, articles by this talented
woman, and had admired the brilliancy of her style,
and especially the greatness of her heart; for almost
always, when she wrote her chronicles, there was some
distress to reveal and to alleviate, some past wrong to
right, ideas of freedom and gentleness to defend. Now
I made her personal acquaintance and heard her speak.
One who has never listened to Madame Séverine's
extempore speeches has no notion to what a height
of passion and poetry eloquence can rise. Madame
Séverine is also interesting outwardly. She was then
forty-three years old, but her hair was already perfectly
white — the result of the tragedies of life which she
had passed through. She had dark, flashing eyes,
vivacious play of expression, and a neat figure. Toward

the close of her fascinating speech she greeted me as *notre sœur d'Autriche*, and when she finished, — both of us standing on the platform, — in my emotion I threw my arms around her, and that elicited a storm of jubilation in the hall.

We made a flying visit to the Exposition under the guidance of Charles Richet. All expositions are alike. The things that especially remained in my memory were the Eiffel Tower, the *trottoir roulant*, the tiny corner in the pavilion in which our Bern Bureau and its literature were displayed, and the gigantic hall in which army and navy had heaped up their latest appliances for destruction.

Richet invited us also to a small dinner given for a few friends. D'Estournelles sat next me. We talked about the general lack of information on the part of the public regarding the Hague Conference, and he told me that he had delivered explanatory lectures on this subject in various cities in France.

" Oh, if you could only come to Vienna and give such a lecture ! "

" You need only to invite me," he replied; " I will render you any service that you may require of me."

I made him shake hands on it.

At Paris during that time I formed a new bond of friendship which has proved very valuable to me. An English lady, the daughter of a sea captain, earning her living in Paris by giving English lessons, had asked to be presented to me in the Congress hall.

I exchanged a few pleasant words with her and then turned to others. The following day she wrote me a letter. This was filled with such enthusiasm, with such devotion to my cause and my person, that I was captivated and asked the writer to come to see me. Miss Alice Williams — for that was her name — came immediately and brought me a bunch of roses. But more than flowers, she brought me a soul — a soul overflowing with the ideals that are precious to me. As the daughter of an English "sea-bear," and rather chauvinistically educated and inclined, she had been, so she told me, converted by reading *Die Waffen nieder*, and from that time forth had been a devoted adherent. In the course of years she has proved that such was the case. I am deeply indebted to her for her friendship, her wise suggestions, her energy, and her activity.

After our return to Harmannsdorf I devoted myself once more to literary occupations. I wrote the novel *Marthas Kinder*, the sequel to *Die Waffen nieder*. My Own also again resumed his labors and wrote on his novel *Im Zeichen des Trusts*. But in spite of this we did not neglect our work for the Unions and our journalistic writing. I took especial pains to make the newspaper public acquainted with the Hague business, which now threatened to be entirely forgotten in the excitement of Chinese and South African events.

But, in the meantime, the various conventions were ratified and the judges of the permanent tribunal were nominated. In accordance with the agreement, each country was to nominate four judges from among its most influential and distinguished men. The number of names thus selected furnishes a list from which, in case of a controversy which is referred to the Hague tribunal, the contending parties may each select two judges, not belonging to their own land; and these in their turn will choose a fifth to serve as president of the court.

The newspapers brought us the names of the nominees. Among those from Austria were Count Schönborn, and Lammasch; from Hungary, Count Apponyi; from France, Bourgeois and D'Estournelles. Of the Russian judges I found only the name of Professor von Martens. So I wrote to him both to congratulate him and also to ask him who were the three others named by the Russian government. I received the following letter in reply:

My dear Baroness: St. Petersburg, November 1 (14), 1900.

I hasten to offer you my sincere thanks for your congratulations on my nomination as a member of the Permanent Court of Arbitration at The Hague. The honor which you have been good enough to speak of so warmly is indeed the greatest that I have ever received, and I am proud of it; it is a genuine pleasure to receive your felicitations. Your eminent merits in the defense of the interests of peace and arbitration have given you, madam, an exceptional place among the partisans of this great idea. I thank you again from the bottom of my heart.

THE TURN OF THE CENTURY

You ask me, madam, who are my Russian colleagues in the Permanent Court. I am happy to be able to tell you that they are the leading jurists and statesmen of Russia. Here are their names:

1. His Excellency, the Secretary of State, Pobyedonostsef, Procurator of the Holy Synod. M. Pobyedonostsef's religious ideas and his great influence in the most exalted governmental spheres are known throughout Europe; but he is at the same time a great lawyer, an accomplished scientist, and a sincere friend of international arbitration.

2. His Excellency, the Secretary of State, De Frisch, who holds in the Council of the Russian Empire the office of president of the " Section of Laws." He is a Russian statesman of very great influence in all legislative questions, and is one of the highest dignitaries of the empire. He has been president of the Grand Commission to elaborate the new criminal code of Russia.

3. His Excellency, the Secretary of State, Muravieff, present Minister of Justice for the Russian Empire. He is a statesman endowed with the greatest talents, and a very eminent lawyer. The late Count Muravieff was his cousin.

Finally, the last — is your humble servant. His Majesty the Emperor, by his nomination, in the month of May, of these Russian members of the Permanent Court of Arbitration, has certainly tried to prove once more what deep sympathy he feels for this creation of the Peace Conference, and his utmost desire to give this court the greatest possible *éclat* and the most serious importance. Such certainly is the opinion that at present obtains in high governmental spheres.

You would infinitely oblige me if you would send me three copies of your article on the Permanent Court and its members. Do you suppose you could possibly publish the article in the *Neue Freie Presse*, which is read in Russia? Madame de Martens wishes to be remembered, and I beg you to accept the assurance of my highest regard.   Martens

I received other letters from the newly appointed delegates, thanking me for my congratulations; but I will cite only the one from Count Schönborn:

Vienna, January 11, 1901

Dear Baroness:

Will you accept my heartiest and humblest thanks for the thoroughly kind letter of the eighth which reached me yesterday, and which I should have instantly answered had not an unusually long session of the Court of Administration occupied my time. Please accept at the same time my warmest thanks for your kindness in sending me the highly interesting publication, as well as your congratulations.

I am so deeply impressed by the importance of the duty imposed upon the Hague Court of Arbitration that I was at first dubious about accepting the nomination, and not until after some explanations were made which pacified my scruples did I dare accept the complimentary mandate.

We, that is to say the Arbitration Tribunal, shall not have much to attend to at first, probably, but I confidently hope that a good vital germ has been planted, and that later, if the institution proves its value in several apparently unimportant cases, the number of its adherents and the number and importance of the contentions submitted to it will increase.

With the expression of especial respect, I am

Yours sincerely

Friedrich Schönborn

I sent my congratulations, together with a copy of my Hague diary, to two German gentlemen nominated to the same dignity. One of them did not reply at all; the other sent me three marks!

The beginning of the year 1901 still brought no cessation of the Boer War. Such a mighty power opposed to such a small one, and yet the decision was so long delayed!

Many of Bloch's predictions regarding modern warfare were justified, — for instance, the advantage held

368

by those who were on the defensive, the long, indeci-
sive continuation of battles, the enormously increased
sacrifices of money and men, and many other things.
Bloch was at that time in London, where he was de-
livering lectures at the Navy Club before an audience
of admirals and generals. Moreover, he was busily
engaged with the preliminary arrangements for the
founding of his War and Peace Museum at Lucerne.

Mindful of the promise which I had obtained from
D'Estournelles, I wrote urging him to come to Vienna
and give a lecture on the Hague Conference. He
consented without hesitation. Count Apponyi, as soon
as he heard of his coming, invited him to take advantage of this opportunity to spend a few days with
him at his castle of Eberhard, and also to deliver a
lecture in Budapest. This invitation D'Estournelles
likewise accepted.

We put ourselves out to secure the attendance of
a select and influential audience for the lecture in
Vienna. I addressed myself to the then French ambassador, Marquis de Reverseaux, who gave me every
assistance in his power in behalf of his fellow-countryman, whom he so highly prized. He not only saw to
it that the members of his embassy should be present
at the lecture, but he also undertook to extend invitations to the whole diplomatic corps. We for our part
sent invitations to the ministers, to the principal officials at court, and to the leading politicians. We made
no attempt to arrange for a particularly democratic

assemblage, for in the first place the common people would not understand French, and in the second place we were particularly desirous that the political, court, and aristocratic circles, which are accustomed to look so superciliously cold upon the peace cause and the Hague Conference, should for once have a chance to hear an explanation of it from the lips of a man who was himself a diplomat and a politician and an aristocrat, and who had taken a prominent part in the work of the Hague Conference. I had also taken pains to get the directors of the Theresianum and the Oriental Academy to send us a number of their students, for the teaching offered would be particularly useful to just such young men, destined for political and diplomatic careers.

The affair went off brilliantly. D'Estournelles spoke splendidly, and the very numerous public, composed of just the elements that we desired, listened with great attention and approbation. It was a *succès*.

That evening — the lecture having occupied the time from four till six—we gave a small *souper intime* in honor of our foreign guest. Among those present were D'Estournelles's two Austrian colleagues of the Hague Court, Count Schönborn and Lammasch; also Barons Ernst von Plener and Peter Pirquet of the Austrian Interparliamentary Group.

This year we did not attend the Peace Congress, which was held at Glasgow. The following letter I received from the American delegate to the Hague Conference, Dr. Holls, who, as it appeared, had undertaken to make a journey through Europe on a peace mission. I had extended him an invitation to visit me in Vienna.

Claridge's Hotel, Brook Street, W.
July 26, 1901

My dear Madam:

Your friendly letter reached me here after many wanderings. I regret very sincerely not having seen you in Vienna, but my time there was exceedingly brief and almost wholly occupied with business.

As you have seen from the published interview, my journey to Russia was very satisfactory. But I do not believe that it would be advisable to publish anything further about it at present.

The miscomprehension of our work disturbs me very little; it must make its way by reason of its services. I should have been glad to discuss with you, more extensively than is possible by letter, the present phases of the question; but this year it is impossible. The thing to do now is to wait patiently. The plant is growing, and there is no object in disturbing its growth by too frequent investigation of how far it has already progressed. For that reason I regret even the holding of a Peace Congress this year.

General resolutions of condemnation are of very little value. The most we can do now is to make excrescences of militarism — for example, silly dueling — ridiculous.

With hearty respect, I remain
Yours sincerely
Dr. W. Holls

On the twelfth of June we celebrated our silver wedding; not by a great festival at home, with congratulations, deputations, and toasts, but, as usual, by an excursion into solitude. Sacred day! The retrospect upon five-and-twenty years of undisturbed comradeship! We had left Harmannsdorf two days before

— no one knew where we had gone — like a pair of fugitive lovers. The festal day we spent in a romantic forest region, hiding ourselves in the deepest depths of the woods and calling up reminiscence after reminiscence! A rich life lay behind us. And what might come in the future? How much farther should we wander together on the path that leads from the silver to the golden wedding? How fortunate that fate gives no answer to such questions!

I had written again to the sage of Yasnaya Polyana, and in reply received the following very characteristic lines:

Dear Baroness: August 28, 1901

I thank you for your good letter. It was very pleasant for me to know that you retain a kindly memory of me.

At the risk of being tiresome to you by repeating what I have many times said in my writings, and what I believe I have written to you, I cannot refrain from saying once again that the longer I live and the more I consider the question of war the more I am convinced that the sole solution of the question is for the citizens to refuse to be soldiers. As long as every man at the age of twenty or twenty-one abjures his religion — not only Christianity but the commandments of Moses (" Thou shalt not kill ") — and promises to kill all those whom his superior orders him to kill, even his brothers and parents, so long war will not cease; and it will grow more and more cruel, as it is already becoming in our day.

For the disappearance of war there is no need of conferences or peace societies; one thing only is needed, namely, the reëstablishment of the dignity of man. If the smallest part of the energy spent nowadays for articles and fine speeches in the conferences and peace societies were employed in the schools and among the people for destroying false religion and propagating the true, wars would soon become impossible.

THE TURN OF THE CENTURY

Your excellent book has had a great effect in spreading abroad a realization of the horrors of war. It would be well now to show people that they themselves are the ones that bring about all the evils of war by obeying men rather than God. I take the liberty of suggesting that you devote yourself to this task, which is the only means of attaining the end you have in view.

Begging you to excuse me for the liberty which I have taken, I remain   Yours with highest regard   Leo Tolstoi

This year, for the first time, the Nobel prizes were distributed. The date selected was the tenth of December, the anniversary of the testator's death. The peace prize was divided and assigned in equal shares to Frédéric Passy and Henri Dunant. Highly as I regarded and still regard Dunant, persuaded as I was and am of his friendly attitude toward peace, nevertheless his services and his fame rested on a quite different field from that which Nobel had in mind. The granting of the prize to Dunant was once more a concession to that spirit which managed to force its way even into the Hague Conference, and which supports the dogma that the endeavors against war should be discreetly limited to its alleviation.

That Frédéric Passy, the oldest, the most deserving, and the most highly regarded of all pacifists, received the prize was a great satisfaction to all of us — only the whole amount should have gone to him.

I received the following letter from Dunant:

My dear Madam: Heiden, December 10, 1901

I am impelled to offer you my homage on this day, as I have just been informed by an official telegram from Christiania that the Nobel peace prize has been granted to me in conjunction with my honored colleague of many years' standing, Frédéric Passy.

This prize, gracious lady, is your work; for through your instrumentality Herr Nobel became devoted to the peace movement, and at your suggestion he became its promoter.

For more than fifty years I have been a pronounced adherent of the cause of international peace, and a fighter under the white banner. The work of international brotherhood has been my aim ever since my earliest youth. I say this and repeat it to-day more emphatically than ever in my character as founder of the universal institution of the Red Cross and as promoter of the Geneva Convention of August 22, 1864.

When, in the year 1861, I wrote my *Souvenir de Solferino*, my principal aim — be assured of this — was general pacification; I desired as far as I could to awaken horror of war in the readers of my book.

This has been recognized, and I will merely adduce one example. The famous Professor Marc Girardin, of the French Academy, said in an article devoted to my book, " I could wish that this book should be widely read, especially by those who love and glorify war."

And Victor Hugo wrote me: " You furnish mankind with weapons, and you help peace by making war hateful. . . . I applaud your noble desire."

I might say much on this theme, and bring forward a quantity of citations in like spirit from authorities of all kinds and all countries; but I must refrain, and beg you, Baroness, to accept the assurance of my most sincere gratitude and my deepest respect.

Henri Dunant

The yearly meeting of my Union for 1901 took the form of a sort of jubilee; ten years had passed since its establishment.

From among the many letters of greeting that reached me on this occasion I will include a few in these reminiscences, for the reason that they depict

THE TURN OF THE CENTURY

the status of the movement at that time, and also
furnish a résumé of its philosophy.

Gracious Lady and dear Associate: Paris, December 27, 1901

The friend has usually written you; to-day the president of the
French Society for Arbitration among the Nations and — since he cannot hide the title — the first recipient of the Nobel prize sends these
lines to you, though of course the friend is not eliminated. If I am
correctly informed, you are holding the tenth general assembly of the
society of which you are the head. And this is an event which we
cannot permit to pass without notice. It means something for a Union
to have lived ten years, especially for the reason that at its inception
many, even among the well disposed, might reasonably have doubts
of its continuance. You certainly had to meet the prejudice, if not the
opposition, of some; the skepticism and the scruples of others; not to
mention the ridicule of those who could not understand that a woman
might take part in the political questions which, according to their
ideas, are reserved exclusively for masculine intelligence and activity.

But, supported certainly by true and genuine sympathies, you have
put up a good fight, and you have attained your end.

Courage, then, and patience! And may it be permitted me in my
character as dean, and as a veteran of the peace militia, to send to
you, and through you to transmit to your society, the thanks, the congratulations, and the benediction of all those who combine regard for
human life, love for justice, and faith in the future with horror of force
and bloodshed.   Frédéric Passy

Noble and honored Baroness: Budapest, December 21, 1901

The agreeable fact that the Austrian Society of the Friends of
Peace, called into existence by your Excellency, and still conducted
through the indefatigable energy of your Excellency, can now look
back over a ten years' activity, constrains me to congratulate your
Excellency most warmly on this circumstance.

Though there may be many who will be unable to appreciate the
endeavors of the society, I can, as far as I am concerned, assure your
Excellency that I can estimate at their true value all great and noble

ideas, as well as those who labor for the accomplishment of such ideas, and so I follow these endeavors with the warmest interest.

With the highest esteem, I am yours respectfully

Szell, Prime Minister of the Kingdom of Hungary

[Telegram.] On the decennial anniversary of your Union I send you my congratulations, and beg to be enrolled as a life member of the Austrian Peace Society, at the same time calling attention to the ideas expressed in my letter of the tenth of December.

Henri Dunant

Vienna, December 30, 1901

... The friends of peace in various countries have done good service, for it is certain that they have materially contributed to the formation of the Court of Arbitration, and it cannot be doubted that their moral support is necessary to the embryonic undertaking.

I am taking the liberty, my dear Baroness, of most respectfully offering you, who have played so prominent a part in the whole movement, my best wishes for your honored person, as well as for the success of the great work.

With especial respect, yours faithfully

Schönborn, First President of the Imperial Court of Adminstration

Dear Madam and Friend: Paris, December 30, 1901

You are about celebrating the decennial anniversary of the society which you called into life, and which, I hope, as a recompense therefor, will save many human lives. Be undisturbed while those who admire contentions and spectacles make sport of your endeavors; these people are looking out for their own interests, for they feel that they are threatened with ruin; in fighting against peace they are fighting for their own existence. What would become of the so-called patriotic, imperialistic, and nationalistic press in all countries if wars between nations should cease, and if the daily instigations should remain ineffectual? People would then cease buying and reading these papers. And what would become of the great sensation mongers if the continual threat of war should no longer be a burden on each country, and if the peaceful idea of the Court of Arbitration should make its way into the usages of mankind?

The principle of international arbitration has a great portion of the press universal against it, exactly as the same principle in its application to labor and employers of labor has the opposition of certain politicians and agitators.

Nevertheless, this last system has lately made great strides forward, and it seems like the only righteous and reasonable solution of labor difficulties.

It will be so with the international courts of arbitration as soon as the Hague Tribunal shall have begun to exert its activities. That is the real reason why it has met with such obstinate opposition; for if its doors are once opened, it will be difficult to close them again.

So let us, then, beat these doors down. Let us, in common with all true men of all lands, through our united protests compel the governments to renounce their inactivity and their unfriendliness. Let us compel them to comprehend that their duty is in harmony with their interests if they would avoid the social revolution.

After they have had the magnanimous unwisdom to call into existence the Hague Arbitration Tribunal, with the approval of the whole world, they cannot bury it alive now without bringing themselves into condemnation and betraying the fact that they are afraid of justice and are adherents of a system of violence against which public opinion long ago revolted.

In a word, let us demand the opening of the Hague Court of Arbitration! There is our salvation, there is to be found the means for hastening the accomplishment of your hopes and mine.

Most heartily and respectfully yours
D'Estournelles de Constant

Vienna, December 26, 1901

My dear Baroness:

On the occasion of the decennial celebration of the Society of Austrian Friends of Peace I am sending to the Union, and above all to you, — its spiritual head, its soul, — my best congratulations. You can look back with pride and satisfaction over this long period of unceasing activity, which, supported by intrepid faith in your noble cause,

377

rejoices in such splendid success and through the results of the Hague Conference must convert the most obstinate doubter to a belief in its necessity and usefulness.

Accept, Baroness, the assurance of my especial consideration.

Chlumecky, Former Minister

Graz, December 31, 1901

The thought of universal peace can no longer be put out of the world; this is the first result of the League of the Friends of Peace!

We have the same courage — so sorely needed — for peace as the soldier has for war! Salutations, friends, for the New Year!

Peter Rosegger

Aulestad, December 18, 1901

The future of the peace cause always comes to me in the guise of a sunrise. For us Northlanders the sunrise can mean so much more than for the people to the south of us; we expect it only once in a while, and greet it as a miracle. The darkness was so oppressively long, the silence so mysterious, the first glow over the rocky peaks so deceptive! It lasts and lasts and ever grows — but still no sun! Even when the sky is already streaming full of hope — yet still no sun! And it is cold — really colder than before, for fancy has become impatient.

Then suddenly, like a flash of lightning, even while we are gazing, comes the so-long-expected Majesty! So powerful, so compellingly powerful that the eyes cannot endure it. We turn and look at the landscape, which, without our noticing it, has been so long ensouled; at the air which, without our perceiving it, has been so long flooded with light. Everything, everything, even down into the depths, and high up on the summits, is bathed in the sun, clear, complete, filled with warmth, throbbing with music. . . .

So I think it is happening to us. In our yearning we do not take note of what is being accomplished — how near already the great sun of universal peace is. Something is coming, and it seems like a miracle. But it is no miracle; in our impatience we do not see how everything was all in readiness for it.

My greeting to the assembly! Björnstjerne Björnson

378

LXIII

THE LAST YEAR

THE last year of him who was my all.

On New Year's Day, 1902, all sorts of trifling annoyances happened to us.

"You will see," said My Own, more in jest than in earnest, for he was not superstitious, "this is going to be a bad year."

During the first week indeed came bad news, a dispatch from Warsaw, — "Johann von Bloch dead of heart disease." Once more a mighty fellow-combatant gone from us!

The war in the Transvaal still kept on. It was now in its third year. At first the English believed that it was merely a little military promenade; and now these unending sacrifices and losses. I wrote to Philip Stanhope asking him if he could give me some information regarding the situation, and perhaps raise his voice against the continuance of the strife. He wrote back:

3 Carlton Gardens, S.W.
January 25, 1902

Dear Baroness de Suttner:

I am overwhelmed with confusion. I have been since the beginning of December in Italy, and have only recently returned for a short time to find your note of December 14 awaiting me.

I should have been pleased to contribute a few words to the publication of the Austrian Society upon the occasion of its 10th anniversary, though all such words of peace, coming from my country, would be in sad contrast with realities.

However, all great causes have dark moments to traverse, and there will again be a reaction against the militarism and the jingoism of the present age.

I hope to see you in Vienna in the autumn, and to find you in good health.

Please remember me to Baron de Suttner, and believe me

Sincerely yours
Philip Stanhope

This year the Peace Congress was to be held as early as April, and it was to meet at Monaco by invitation of Prince Albert. The neighborhood of Montè Carlo was a circumstance which caused some hesitation among many of our friends, — I did not share it, — and only after a considerable correspondence among the members of the Bern Bureau (in whose hands the organization of the Congress lies) was a majority won for the choice of Monaco. My husband and I were greatly pleased at the prospect of this trip and the visit in this paradisiac corner of the world.

My happy frame of mind was increased by the fact that my book *Marthas Kinder* was on the eve of appearing. The proceeds from it (my publisher, Pierson, had bought the novel with all rights, including those of translation, for an honorarium of 15,000 marks) enabled me to stave off for at least a little while longer the breaking up of our beloved Harmannsdorf, and during this time so much might happen to rescue the estate; so we looked forward with joyous hearts to the coming journey.

Only a few days before the date set for our departure, My Own was attacked by a very sudden indisposition. As he was going to get up one morning, his legs gave way. He was obliged to go back to bed, and he felt pain in his right knee. We hoped it would not amount to anything. Our trunks were already packed, the sleeping-car tickets were already bought, and our rooms in Monaco engaged. Also the lecture which I was going to deliver at a public meeting on the events of the Hague Conference was prepared and announced.

" If by day after to-morrow I am not all right again, you must go," insisted my husband; " it is your duty."

And so it came about. The doctor ordered that the disabled leg should be kept wrapped up and perfectly quiet. This was a great grief to us both; we had counted so much on the journey together, and the separation filled me with tribulation. Up to the last moment he hoped still to be able to go, or at least to follow me a day later, but it was not possible. I had to go to Monaco without him, yet I was not alone; my friend Countess Hedwig Pötting accompanied me. The delight in the visit there was spoiled for me by the separation from him and my anxiety about him. Every day I had a telegram from him, and besides he wrote me three letters. These letters lie in my jewel casket; they are the last which he ever wrote me. They must have a place in these memoirs:

My beloved Löwos: Easter Sunday, 1902

I am afraid this written greeting will be all that you will get from me while you are in Monaco. How happy I should be if this very afternoon I could convince myself that I was going to be able to follow you. When I think that to-morrow you will probably be traveling without me, it makes my heart so terribly heavy! It was not good of Nemo [1] to separate us so cruelly. He might have let us enjoy this little pleasure! But I will not make your heart heavier than it is already. You must keep your head clear and be easy in mind, so as to fulfill the duty which you have no right to shun.

My holiest wishes and my heart's love accompany you on your way, my dear old Löwos, though in these circumstances it is rather a thorny way. But it ought not to be that; you must enter upon it with the joyous feeling that you are rendering a fine service and are going to render fine service yet again. So you must get all the pleasure you can out of the lovely place and the friends who all cling to you with such love and respect.

Enjoy your stay, my dearest, and then you will come back to me with all the more delight and contentment.

[1] A reference to Jules Verne's Captain Nemo, who always helps Captain Grant's children at the right moment, and whom we had jestingly chosen for our guardian saint.

THE LAST YEAR

This is all for this time; and now I take your dear head, my Löwos, between my hands and kiss it a thousand times. Your Own

My dear old heart's Löwos: March 31, 1902

Those were sad hours of loneliness and abandonment after your departure! It enabled me to realize how deep you have grown into my heart, my precious, precious pet. Now I am trying to accustom myself to the unavoidable, but reactions will be sure to return, for I miss you too deeply.

I have followed you in my thoughts on the stages of your journey. Now you are probably through breakfast and waiting for the train at the railway station.

If only days enough had gone by, so that I could say, " Day after to-morrow it will be day after to-morrow, and so on."

I shall not be so well looked after to-day as I am by you. Maria Louise has just been in for a moment; she has taken cold, so is not exactly rosy and merry.

As soon as I have finished writing these lines I must rest awhile. Even writing takes hold of me. I will lie back and think about you. If our nerves were only receptive for telepathy we should certainly be in close contact these days! The doctor is taking his time about his morning visit to-day; but I believe the leg is somewhat better.

Farewell, my dearest, I kiss you many thousand times.
Your Own

My precious Löwos: April 2, 1902

Ten o'clock! There you are perhaps at this very minute standing on the platform and giving your address, which is not very long. So, as far as I can follow it, I am taking part in the Congress. The newspaper reports will not give any very detailed account of it.

Yesterday Chimani[1] was here. He discovered some improvement, but there is still inflammation; therefore strict orders not to get out of bed.

I received your telegram yesterday evening about half past eight. I was beginning to be a trifle uneasy when no word came. My reply,

[1] Richard Chimani, physician to the General Staff, a friend of long standing who owned a place near us.

383

which I intrusted to the messenger, you will not be likely to get until to-day.

It is a beautiful summer's day — and here I am in bed! Have such a longing to get out.

Nothing interesting in the mail. Among other things a crazy letter to you from a crazy photographer in Graz. Then came a letter of twenty quarto pages from Linz and a little book which the author published ten years ago through Schabelitz. Of course I do not send you this stuff.

Thank the Hex [Countess Pötting] for her card and sisterly greeting. Kisses on thy Löwos mouth from

Thy Own

How the poor man would have enjoyed those days at Monaco! The place was all a glory of spring splendor. We had seen the Riviera before, but not at a time of such luxurious profusion of flowers.

A hall in the new building destined for the Oceanographic Museum had been cleared for the proceedings of the Congress. All the speeches and debates had a constant accompaniment of distant hammering. In the immediate neighborhood the work was at a standstill during the hours of session, but not very far away the pounding and sawing and nailing went steadily on. This seemed to disturb some of the orators; yet one of them found in it a welcome occasion for bringing out in a beautiful picture how the work in the name of which we were there assembled was also an edifice, already designed but still unfinished, — an edifice which, like this, would also arise in usefulness and beauty to the honor of the builders and to the advantage of mankind.

After the opening session, which Prince Albert had attended, all the participants stood about in the open space before the entrance to exchange greetings and to enjoy the scenes of recognition which are repeated at every Congress: "Ah, it's you! This is fine!"

This time all addressed me with the question, "And where is the Baron?" I had to tell them about his illness, which elicited general regret. I really believe there was no one in the whole world who had ever known him, even superficially, without being drawn into sympathy with him.

The prince stood not far from me in a group, and was talking with General Türr. I was able to get a good look at him. Of rather more than medium height, of slender and supple figure, he was then at the beginning of the fifties, but not yet turning gray. He wore a closely trimmed, dark beard, and his expression was unusually melancholy. He came up to me and offered me his hand. He was delighted, he said, to see me, for he had long known of my devotion to the cause for the furtherance of which he now desired to work as energetically as he could. He remained some time in conversation with me.

"One thing occurs to me to say to you," he remarked in the course of the conversation; "you see this work going on here," pointing toward the Museum; "this shows the tendency of my aims and endeavors; it is intended as a corrective," — and now he indicated the crags of Monte Carlo visible in the distance and crowned with the Casino, — "a corrective to that inheritance which is so hateful to me."

I especially recollect among the transactions the indignant and pathetic protest of the Frenchman, Pierre Quillard, against the atrocious massacres being perpetrated on the Armenians at that time, and unfortunately still going on. Thus our Congresses definitely assumed the burden of furnishing a forum for the complaints and for the defense of all the persecuted, — a service which the governments, relying on the principle of nonintervention, still refuse to undertake.

In the course of the day we members of the Congress inspected the castle which is the home of the Prince of Monaco, and which rises high above the crags. It is an antiquated edifice with battlements, outside stairways, and porticoes. In the cloistered private garden there is an endless profusion of flowers. Palms as high as a house stand there on rocky ground, to which every atom of soil had to be carried. The state rooms we saw for the first time in the evening, when they were all ablaze with light, at a gala reception given in honor of the Congress; the officials of Nice were also invited. Especially imposing is the throne room, although the throne of such a tiny kingdom is not imposing. My attention was attracted in this room to a kind of tower of flowers reaching to the ceiling. I was told that this was the throne, with its seat, its steps, and its baldachin, all masked by this gigantic screen of flowers.

A second festivity was arranged by the city for our benefit. It was a kind of "Venetian Night." All the ships and boats in the harbor and all the houses along the bay were illuminated, Bengal fires were blazing on the mountains, there were torchlight processions and bands of music. The entire population, strangers visiting the resort, the citizens of Monaco, laboring men, and peasants from the regions round about took part in the gayeties. Tents were pitched on the heights for the Congressists and the prince, and from here there was a fine prospect of the whole region bathed in light. I sat in the prince's tent, between him and his cousin, the Duke of Urach. The latter, an officer in the German army, talked with me on the subject of the Congress. He granted that war would sometime be overcome by civilization, but before that day, he thought, many economic and perhaps also social battles would be fought out with weapons.

" What was discussed in the session this afternoon ? " Prince Albert asked me.

" Propaganda," I replied.

" Look at this picture and listen to this babel of voices; all the people have learned to-day that there is an active peace movement; that is a propaganda," said the prince.

He presided at the final banquet. He sat between Madame Séverine and me. On this occasion he told me much about his labors and his plans. His book, *La carrière d'un navigateur*, had recently been published;

he proposed to send it to me, and told me that I should find in it the whole story of his studies and his — soul!

When it came to the toasts he arose and delivered the first speech:

" It fills me with pride and joy " (these were almost the identical words of his exordium) " to take a place in the peace movement; for the scientific work to which my life is devoted requires for its development the victory of the peace work, the victory over the cruel inheritance of primitive barbarism, the victory over the warlike spirit which poisons the fruits of civilization."

Not in after-dinner speeches alone — which vanish like the foam on the lifted glass — did Prince Albert utter such opinions, but also in the dedication of his book, " A Seaman's Career,"[1] he says:

I dedicate the German version of this book to his Majesty Emperor William II, who is the patron of labor and science, and is thus preparing for the realization of the noblest desire of human consciousness, namely the union of all civilizing forces for the purpose of bringing about the reign of an inviolable peace.

Later I saw the Emperor's manuscript reply, in which, in a page-and-a-half quarto, he thanks his *cher cousin* for the dedication, and in perfect agreement with his ideas repeats the words therein referring to the peace cause.

[1] Authorized German translation, under the title *Seemannslaufbahn*, by A. H. Fried. Berlin, Boll & Pickardt.

THE LAST YEAR

Although the dispatches that I got every day from Harmannsdorf were encouraging, I was feverishly impatient to be at home again. Great was the joy of being reunited. During our twenty-six years of married life this was the first time we had ever been separated for more than a day or two. We had said good-by in tears; in tears I threw my arms again around my dear one's neck. And alas! he had not yet recovered; he was still obliged to lie in bed. His illness, so the doctor said, had been an attack of periostitis, and he was bidden to be very careful for some time to come. When he got up the first time he suffered severely from palpitation of the heart; and this was of frequent recurrence. Under the twelfth of April I find in my diary for the first time the anxious exclamation, " Palpitation again — oh, that is a serious malady. . . . Organic disorder — I am deeply worried."

After some time there was an improvement and my anxieties were allayed.

The Transvaal war showed no sign of coming to an end; to be sure peace negotiations had already been broached, but no armistice was declared at the same time; on the contrary, English reënforcements were shipped anew to Africa. This caused the London *Times* to express great satisfaction. Oh, these war-inciting editorial patriots! The neutral powers were not to be induced to offer mediation. Surely one must not hamper the arm of a fighter! But as far as affording assistance to the fighter by lending money or furnishing horses,—enormous transports of horses were leaving Fiume for the English, — that the neutrals permit themselves to do. *Les affaires sont les affaires !*

Article 27 of the Hague Convention was forgotten. Moreover the Hague Tribunal — the poor new-born infant — seemed condemned to die for lack of sustenance. Then suddenly came a controversy which was submitted to the tribunal — an old quarrel between the United States and Mexico regarding Church property. President Roosevelt brought the matter before the Hague Tribunal.

I knew that our friend D'Estournelles, who had taken upon himself the task of preventing the work at The Hague from dying of asphyxiation, had undertaken a journey to America, where he was making a lecture tour. I suspected that he had not been without influence in bringing about the trial of the Church-property question before the tribunal. And, in fact, this was the case; two documents furnish proof of it. First, the following letter from D'Estournelles in reply to one expressing my conjecture that he had been concerned in the matter. Here is his letter:

Paris, Chamber of Deputies

Dear Friend: September 5, 1902

You have guessed it; my object in going to the United States was in large measure to show President Roosevelt the great part he might play in world politics, now that the liberal spirit in Europe had foregone its chance. I told him the whole story and he understood it.

I said: "You are a danger or a hope for the world, according as you advance toward conquest or arbitration, toward violence or justice.

390

It is believed that you are inclined to the side of violence; prove the contrary."

" How ? "

" By giving life to the Hague Court."

And that is what the President has done. I have waited until the Court assembled before mentioning what I did. It is now in session. That is a great point, and we must praise Roosevelt, first because he deserves it, and secondly that he may find imitators.

The affectionate friend of you both

D'Estournelles

The second document is an extract from a report made by the French embassy at Washington to the Minister of Foreign Affairs in Paris. I received an authentic copy of this extract. It reads:

Washington, Embassy of the French Republic
April 7, 1902

Sir :

We must tell the truth, and render to each what is due. When, nearly two months ago, I presented M. d'Estournelles to President Roosevelt, our fellow-countryman spoke to him with much enthusiasm about the Conference at the Hague ; he held up before his eyes the glory with which Mr. Roosevelt would cover his incumbency if he would open the Arbitral Tribunal for any question, no matter how insignificant, and thus give an example to the world. President Roosevelt was struck with M. d'Estournelles's language, and yesterday I was confidentially informed by him that on the very next day after the latter's visit he charged Mr. Hay to find some matter to submit to the permanent judges of The Hague.

(Signed) Jules Cambon

To the Minister of Foreign Affairs

And thus through the devotion of a single person, supported by the energy of a powerful ally, that machine was set in motion. A proof was given to the world that it could perform its functions. Of course the opponents objected that it was nothing but a quite insignificant case which was submitted — as if insignificant cases had not many times led to war. Not the case but the method is what counts.

My husband had so far recovered that we were able to go to Switzerland together to attend the opening of the Bloch Museum. The preliminary arrangements had been well advanced during the founder's lifetime, but it took his widow's entire energy, her entire capacity for sacrifice, and her extraordinary activity to finish the work. What the six-volume work "War" relates and proves with the printed word, the Lucerne War and Peace Museum reiterates with its weapons, its models, its pictures, and its charts.

The opening festival and the events of the succeeding days took the form of a small Peace Congress; for Madame von Bloch had invited a great number of influential personages belonging to the movement to come to Lucerne as her guests. And thus at this festival the whole company met again, — Frédéric Passy, W. T. Stead, Gaston Moch, General Türr, Madame Séverine, Dr. Richter (the veteran chairman of the German Peace Society), Professor Wilhelm Förster, Moneta, D'Estournelles, and many others.

War is the duel of the nations; the duel is war between two individuals. Now a movement had been started against the primitive custom of dueling so firmly intrenched in the continental countries, though England long ago got rid of it. Prince Löwenstein and

Prince Alfonso de Borbon were at the head of this movement. The latter especially showed a tireless zeal. I wrote him at this time of my intention to bring the objects of the anti-dueling league up for discussion at the next meeting of the Union. The prince replied:

Ebenzweier, August 12, 1902

Madam:

I thank you heartily for your kind letter of July 22 and the prospectus of your Vienna Conference. I hope the Conference may be followed by the best results. You are working, madam, with admirable devotion to your cause. I shall be very glad to see our anti-dueling movement once more approved by your assembly, as it was last year by the one at Glasgow.

With the highest regard, I remain

Yours faithfully
Alfonso de Borbon y Austria-Este

A manager made me an offer to arrange a tour through the United States for readings from my works. I declined; My Own's uncertain state of health would have been a sufficient excuse for refusing the offer. I had no very clear conception of America, but I have a letter from Hodgson Pratt which he wrote after making a flying trip across "the great pond," and in which he says, among other things:

. . . But my visit to the States convinced me that the great treaty would come! I returned quite infatuated with the Yankees, — improved Englishmen I call them, — so bright, so clear in thought and word, so resolute, so animated, so strong! It was almost a new revelation to hear and see those dear younger cousins. They have our British solidity, but with a youthfulness we have lost. I never spent six months of such enthusiasm.

When I first read this letter, dated in 1897, it did not mean much to me. But since I myself have been in America I understand Hodgson Pratt's words, and I subscribe to every one of them. Yes, "clear and strong, resolute and animated," they certainly are; yes, "a revelation,"—so appeared to me, too, that new young world!

In the summer of 1902 we received several interesting visits at Harmannsdorf; I mean visits from abroad, for with our friends of the neighborhood there was always continual going back and forth. The visitors to whom I refer came from St. Petersburg and the Caucasus.

First Emanuel Nobel, my departed friend Alfred Nobel's nephew. I found that Emanuel had many traits of resemblance to Alfred, — the same seriousness, the same depth, the same broad, democratic ideas. In his outward semblance, also, and in his voice the nephew reminded me of the uncle. Emanuel is unmarried. The rumor that he was to marry his friend Minister Witte's sister proved to be false; he lives in absolute devotion to his brother's numerous family. He is at the head of the greatest naphtha business in the world. Fourteen vessels carry its products on the seas. Twice a year he journeys to Baku, where his most productive oil wells flow. When, a few years later, during the Russo-Japanese war, those oil wells were set on fire and blazed up into the skies like pillars of flame, his losses must have been immense.

THE LAST YEAR

The second visit from abroad was from the Princess Tamara of Georgia and her two daughters. They stayed two days at Harmannsdorf, and we indulged in endless reminiscences of the old times in the Caucasus. That beloved, beautiful country, too, was to endure the most atrocious sufferings from that miserable war.

During August of that year my husband and I accepted an invitation from Count Heinrich Taaffe (son of the former Austrian Prime Minister) and his charming wife to visit them at Castle Ellischau in northern Bohemia, where we spent a very delightful week.

A beautiful surprise was sprung upon me there. One evening about nine o'clock, as we sat after dinner on the balcony, from which there is a wide prospect of wooded mountains outlined on the horizon, suddenly on a summit against the dark sky the word " Pax " stood out in giant letters of flame. At the same time, from the distance, little lights, glimmering ever more numerous and ever nearer, approached the castle through the shrubbery. It was a torchlight procession. A throng of people came up, a band of music began to play, and finally the whole procession halted on the open place below the balcony. A man stepped forward — he was the school-teacher — and delivered an address in Bohemian, in which the word " peace " frequently occurred. I had to make a reply, also in Bohemian, my host whispering the words to me, for I do not know my native tongue. To be sure the Kinskys are a Czechish family, but in my childhood the Czechish national consciousness had not awakened, and as I grew older I was no longer receptive to it, having attained the European consciousness. But I was none the less pleased with the schoolmaster's discourse. The village people — those also from neighboring villages — stayed about for a long time; the musicians played a polka and the young people danced. My husband and I were heartily delighted with the clever little festival. Never did a more grateful fireworks audience utter its "ah!" than we at the moment when the lofty "Pax" illumined the evening sky.

Fortunate will be our descendants for whom this word shall gleam on the political horizon, not as a fleeting pyrotechnical display but as an unalterable token.

In September the Interparliamentary Conference was to have been held in Vienna. Baron Pirquet was at the head of the organization committee. The preparations were under way, the programme had been sent out, the opening day was appointed, when, just on the eve of it, a circular was dispatched stating that on account of unforeseen technical difficulties the Conference would have to be given up and postponed until the following year. Baron Pirquet confidentially informed me that the difficulties were not technical but political. This was a hard blow to him.

I also was painfully affected by the circumstance, but at this time I had quite different troubles. While at Ellischau, even while at Lucerne, My Own had often complained of pain, and many of our friends later told me that they had been shocked at his appearance.

A long, long illness began. First — but no. I will not here relate the story of this tragic time — not here. In *Briefe an einen Toten* (" Letters to One Dead ") I have related to the beloved Shade everything, — how he and how I suffered, and how he died.

December 10, 1902, was the day of his death. Up to the ninth I confided to my diary all the phases of my anxiety and my hope, my despondency and my despair. It is astounding how much like a friend such a book becomes to one — how one can tell it all one's thoughts and complaints, how one can shed over it the tears that one must hide from others, particularly from a dear one who is ill. But on the tenth of December I could write no more, and not for a long time afterward.

Much later I came back to this trusty confidant and made a large cross on the last written leaf. On the new page I wrote:

December 29. Here yawns a terrible hiatus in this book. The most awful days of my life, henceforth to be lonely, so inexpressibly lonely. . . .

On the tenth, after an hour of agony, and after he had called me by name, My Own, My very Own, breathed away his precious life!

Maria Louise, Sister Luise, Pauline, the two physicians, and I stood about his deathbed — endlessly sad and tragic hours. . . .

Have lost everything!

Then followed the days and nights of the deathwatch.

So lovely he lay there with his own characteristic smile on his cold, ice-cold lips, which I could not kiss often enough. . . .

397

On the thirteenth solemn service for the dead ; the weeping inmates of the house and the villagers ; the mourning guests. We accompanied the coffin to Eggenburg.

On the fourteenth the journey to Gotha.

On the sixteenth the flaming pyre !

During his lifetime he whom I lost said to me many dear and beautiful words, which are imprinted on my heart; but the loveliest are those which he spoke from beyond the grave, in his last will. After a few last instructions and directions it reads:

And now, My Own, one single word to thee: Thanks ! Thou hast made me happy ; thou hast helped me to win from life its loveliest aspects, to get delight from it. Not a second of discontent has ever come between us, and for this I thank thy great understanding, thy great heart, thy great love ! . . .

Thou knowest that we realized within our hearts the duty of contributing our mite to the betterment of the world, of laboring, of struggling for the right, for the imperishable light of the truth. Though I go home, for you this duty is not extinguished. Thy happy recollection of thy companion must be a support to thee. Thou must work on in our plans, for the sake of the good cause keep up the work until thou also at last shalt reach the end of the brief journey of life. Courage then ! No hesitation ! In what we are trying to do we are at one, and therefore must thou try still to accomplish much !

CONCLUSION

I am going to break off these records of my life at this point; I cannot call that which has filled my days between the tenth of December, 1902, and the present time, life. To be sure, I heeded the injunction which came to me from beyond the grave, and I have worked on; and I have seen in the loom of time much of that red woof to which my thoughts and desires are directed. I shall go on to speak further of that, but not in connection with the other personal things commemorated here. Moreover, the events of the last few years are still too near at hand to furnish a satisfactory perspective.

Since my career, however, does not end with that date of sorrow — since I have not yet reached, as the will says, " the end of the brief journey of life," I shall have much more to communicate concerning the further course of that movement in which I have found my life task.

In the last six years important phases have developed in the battle between the cause of peace and the cause of war: for instance, the Anglo-French *entente*; the series of arbitration treaties following one after another (some among them without the usual limitations); the outbreak and fearful catastrophes of the Russo-Japanese war; the Hull incident, which, through the application of an investigation commission instituted by the Hague Court, was prevented from developing into a world conflagration; Roosevelt's action in restoring peace in eastern Asia; the entrance of the North American group into the Interparliamentary Union; the rising cloud between England and Germany; its dissipation through the exchange of visits of international corporations brought about by the pacifists; the further assignments of the Nobel prizes; the activity and expenditures of Andrew Carnegie for peace purposes; the peaceful separation of Sweden and Norway, the first example of the kind in history; the lessons of the Russian revolution; the recent proposal of the English premier, Sir Henry Campbell-Bannerman, for a union to limit armaments; the calling of the Second Hague Peace Conference; the Interparliamentary Conference at London, at which, for the first time, members of the Russian duma participated, though on account of the dissolution of the duma they were obliged to withdraw (*La douma est morte, vive la douma !*); the labors and congress of the Universal Alliance of Women for Peace and Arbitration under the chairmanship of Lady Aberdeen; the Second Hague Peace Congress, this time including representatives of forty-six countries, with the wedge still further driven in by doubters and opponents determined to change the character of this world parliament so that it shall come to be merely a court to regulate wars; the favorable results, nevertheless, of this Conference resulting from the spirit of the cause and promoted by our adherents who were present; the brilliant début of the South American countries which were represented in it; the determination to continue this international coöperation; the progress of the anti-dueling movement assisted by the King of Spain and the King of Italy; the resolutions passed by the socialist congresses in favor of fighting against war; the increasing number of *ententes*, in which the adherents of the old views, and with them the press of almost the entire world, suspect that they can see aggressive alliances formed against third parties, but which in reality are merely new meshes of the net making for the peaceful organization of the world; the conquest of the air, the most revolutionary event of recent centuries in the development of civilization, but in which the shortsighted see nothing else than a useful means of hurling explosives, although it really involves the abolition of boundaries, fortifications, and customhouses; at the same time the conditions in the miserable Balkan states, where for long years brigandage and manslaughter and atrocities have been raging and the war storm may break at any moment.

I have not held myself aloof from all these things; I have chronicled them in my diaries with notes, documents, and correspondence. During these last six years I have been about the world a good deal and met many interesting people. For four winters in succession I have spent several weeks as the guest of the Prince of Monaco in his crag-seated castle, and have there met prominent personages from princely, scientific, diplomatic, and artistic circles. A journey to America[1] brought me into touch with Roosevelt, and opened before me vistas into that country of unbounded possibilities, or, rather, as it presented itself to me, of impossibilities overcome. I have participated in the meetings of congresses during that time, namely, the Peace Congresses at Boston, Lucerne, Milan, and Munich, and the Woman's Congress at Berlin. I attended

[1] See pp. 405 ff.

as a guest the Interparliamentary Conferences at Vienna and London. I have had frequent meetings with my old colleagues, and I have seen new laborers in the common cause come to the fore: for instance, Richard Bartholdt, founder of the American group; Sir Thomas Barclay, the zealous associate promoter of the Anglo-French *entente;* Lubin, the initiator of the Agricultural Institute at Rome; and Bryan, the candidate for President of the United States. I have been enabled to follow the great services rendered the peace movement in Germany by Pastor Umfrid, by Professor Quidde, and by many others — I cannot name them all. In the year 1905, accompanied by Miss Alice Williams, I made a lecture tour through twenty-eight German cities. In the spring of 1906 I had to go to Christiania to deliver there before King Haakon and the Storthing the lecture required of the recipients of the Nobel prizes. At that time I made a journey through Sweden and Denmark. Finally, in 1907, just as eight years earlier, I was present at The Hague during the time of the Peace Conference, and kept an exact record of all the transactions, personages, and social functions. All these experiences, impressions, letters, and memoranda may sometime come into use for supplementing the reminiscences (so far as they bear upon the historic development of the peace movement) which are here brought to a conclusion; and, should I not myself arrange for their publication, they will be found among my possessions after I am gone.

THE LAST YEAR

What the immediate future will produce in this domain will assuredly surpass in significance the modest and hidden beginnings. Though the contemporary world is quite unconscious of the fact, the movement has spread far beyond the circle of the Unions, of the resolutions, and of the personal activities of single individuals; it has grown into a struggle which involves the very conception of life and all natural laws. It has passed from the hands of the so-called "Apostles" into the hands of the powerful and into the minds of the awaking democracy; within it work a hundred-fold various powers, unconscious that they are thus working. It is a process which is being accomplished by the forces of nature, a slowly growing new organization of the world. The next stage is to be something quite concrete, perfectly attainable, absolved from all theoretical and all ethical universality, — the formation of an alliance of European states.

Whatever the old system may accomplish by its endeavors, however insanely high the supplies of the opposing instruments of destruction may be heaped up, whatever horrors may break out in isolated places in the way of warlike reactions, I have no fear of being discredited in histories written in the future when I here register the prediction, Universal peace is on the way.

And even if to-day many look askance at these prophecies, and turn from the whole cause, — indifferent, yawning, shrugging their shoulders, as if it concerned something impractical, unessential, fanciful, — yet very speedily, if once that which is in preparation, as yet silent and unobserved, comes into sight, there will be awakened the general realization that this cause demands conscious coöperation, that it includes the mightiest task of onward-marching human society, — in a word, that it is "the one important thing."

July, 1908

SUPPLEMENTARY CHAPTER

1904

THREE WEEKS IN AMERICA

FOR the English-American edition of this book I will add a few reminiscences of my visit to the United States as I committed them to paper in October, 1904, while returning to Europe.

Here on board the *Kaiser Wilhelm II* I find time and leisure to set down in my diary some of the multitudinous and vivid impressions whereby the store of my experiences has been increased through my brief, all too brief, sojourn on the other side of the ocean.

The thirteenth World's Peace Congress was opened in Boston on the fourth of September. That was the object of my journey; so I was not induced to cross the ocean by my desire to make acquaintance with the

New World, and yet a wholly and completely new world was revealed to me.

I will begin at the embarkation. My traveling companion and I spent the evening before in the senators' room of the Rathauskeller at Bremen, where the local group of the German Peace Society had arranged a small festivity in our honor.

I saw there the enormous hogshead which holds ever so many gallons, and the one that is filled with such precious old wine that every drop is reckoned as worth so many hundred marks, and the beaker from which Emperor William II is accustomed to drink when he visits the wine cellar, and — what pleased me most — the model of the fountain on which the quaint city musicians of Bremen are portrayed, namely, the ass on which stands the dog which supports the cat on which sits the cock, — possibly very clever, but certainly extremely lean, tone artists.

The next morning, which was bright and clear, we proceeded to Bremerhaven by a special train. This train takes transatlantic passengers only, and stops directly opposite the gangway of the steamship. When we arrived at the dock, gay music was pealing from the deck, and we went on board as if we were embarking for a pleasure sail.

After a brief hour's delay our floating palace, *Kaiser Wilhelm der Grosse*, gets under way. The receding rim of the harbor is filled with people still waving their farewells, and the travelers on the decks are also waving in response. At the same time the ship's orchestra has begun to play again. It is a melancholy moment, although the soul is raised on high with expectation as we sail out over the broad ocean into another portion of the world, into the land of unlimited possibilities, and away from the old home, perhaps never to be seen again. What thoughts fill the emigrant's soul? Experienced globe-trotters, who cross the great pond every year, may be as calm and cool at this moment as we are when we hear the signal for the starting of the train from Mödling Station to Vienna; but I, who was making my first trip across the Atlantic, experienced something of the solemnity of a parting mood, although I left nothing behind save an urn of ashes!

It was a beautiful, smooth passage, with only two or three hours of pitching and discomfort during the whole voyage, which was free from fog and storm. We had a very agreeable captain, — I had the privilege of sitting at his right hand at dinner, — and also very interesting traveling companions. Ah! and this beneficial state of emancipation from the woes and the worries of the day, and no newspaper with descriptions from the theater of war. Fortunately the Marconi system is not sufficiently advanced to give us daily tidings in full detail. That is destined to come about, but it is to be hoped that the news then will contain fewer barbarities. Ultimately the moral improvement of the world must keep step with the technical.

We went through a half hour of anxious excitement on the high seas. We were sitting comfortably on deck, reclining in our steamer chairs, engaged in reading or contemplation of the play of the waves, or lazily thinking of nothing at all, when suddenly a commotion began on board. There was a clamor of voices, and sailors ran hither and thither. The travelers rushed to one place on the quarter-deck.

" It is sinking ! " cries one.

" What is sinking ? " I inquire, with pardonable interest ; " our ship ? "

" No — do you see — yonder — "

Now I, too, hasten to the rail ; I see at some distance a sailing vessel, a three-master, rocking on the waves. It is on fire ; our ship hastens toward her under full steam. Possibly there may be something there to be rescued, — even human beings raising agonized prayers for aid.

That was not the case ; the vessel was a derelict. But if there had been men on board, how we should have trembled, how anxiously we should have followed the work of rescue that our captain would have set on foot with all zeal, and how we should have clamored with jubilation had he succeeded. Even if there had been no more than one man on board the unfortunate craft, and he had been rescued from the extremity of despair, what joy ! But when the next Marconi dispatch brings the news of a bath of blood at Port Arthur or Mukden, — that is merely an interesting piece of news! What an insane contradiction! In regard to this I will only say that such things must cease, for contradictions cannot prevail; they annihilate themselves; that is the law of nature. The time will come when the sacred sea, that binds all nations together, that distributes wealth among them, that has been made serviceable through the powers of man for the aims of happiness, will be no longer desecrated by explosive mines and submarine instruments of destruction.

On the seventh day we entered the harbor of New York; the Statue of Liberty held out her torch to greet us, — a torch so great that a man can take a walk around its handle. But grand and triumphant as the statue is, its ideal falls below it even in America, which in the national hymn arrogates to itself the proud title, "Land of the noble free." If ever there was a dream projected into the future, it is the dream of freedom, up to the present time unfulfilled everywhere, yet ripening toward fulfillment. Perhaps America, the young land unoppressed by ancient traditional fetters, is the land where that torch will first flame forth and then illuminate all the corners of the earth.

I had, by the way, my first taste of its lack of freedom, at the dock, where the vandals of the tariff rummaged in the depths of my trunks and subjected my fur cloak to a searching examination. Heaven be praised, it was not sealskin! And while I was trembling with the excitement of the inspection, three reporters were asking me about the programme of the Peace Congress and about the prospects of the war in eastern Asia.

" Who will win, Russia or Japan ? "

" Both will lose," I replied, opening a trunk — (to the customs officer) " Only old clothes ! " — (to the reporters) " Both will lose, and mankind with them."

We proceeded directly to Boston, and, as night had already come on, the first impression of New York, which we crossed from Hoboken to the Forty-second Street Station, was only one mad whirl of dazzling lights, roaring streets, and houses high as the sky !

Boston has the reputation of being the most European city in the United States, and likewise the capital of intellect. Really I have not much to offer in the way of descriptions and observations; Boston for me was the gathering place of this year's Peace Congress, and as such absorbed all my thoughts and attention. Here I was, then, once more in another quarter of the world, and just as at Rome and Budapest, as in Hamburg and Paris, among good old comrades; once more I was on the international forum, where the ideal of international friendship, with its promise of happiness, is practiced among the participants and is striven for in behalf of contemporary and succeeding generations.

The sessions of the American Peace Congress showed clearly enough what immense strides the peace movement has recently made, in spite of, or perhaps because of, the awful wholesale slaughter in eastern Asia, which arouses universal horror. The conviction that this matter is not only one of the weightiest questions of the time, but is the question of the future, and is the foundation on which a new era of civilization, already dawning, is to be erected, is penetrating into ever wider and wider circles, and is already forming in America a consistent part of public opinion, as was well shown by the course of the thirteenth Peace Congress and the interest taken in it by the people.

Of course there, as everywhere, one finds a chauvinistic tendency, a "yellow press," imperialistic appetites, and the like; but in corroboration of the above-expressed opinion, that the peace question is the predominant one in the public mind, stands the fact that in the presidential campaign now convulsing the whole country the peace sentiment is incorporated into the platform of the Democratic party, and that Roosevelt's opponents are striving to belittle, as an election maneuver, the peace policy which he is now so energetically advocating. The great mass of the people, and especially the more intelligent classes of the country, are strongly opposed to an unlimited increase of the navy, and to the spread of military institutions and of the warlike spirit.

A remarkable land, " Land of Unlimited Possibilities," as it has been called in the well-known book title; verily it might rather be called " Land of Conquered Impossibilities." Indeed, this young world, — in the true sense of the word, this New World, — exuberant in strength, glad in its daring, with peculiar insistency " gets on the nerves " of people of strong conservative feelings. But any one who looks to the future, any one who cherishes a comforting faith in development, will here feel joyously strengthened in his hopes of progress. Certainly all the acquisitions of the New World will redound to the advantage of the Old World, just as all the treasures of culture of the Old have been taken over and will still continue to be taken over by the New. It would be good if Europeans, eager to learn and to know, might be turned to America, in such mighty throngs as America pours into Europe. Yes, the nations have to learn from one another; that is better than for them to blow one another into the air. If one man desires to climb higher than another, he must mount on the other's shoulders, but not throw him down.

The recent period, during which a World's Fair and such numerous congresses — the Interparliamentary Conference and Scientific Congress at St. Louis, the Peace Congress in Boston, and the like — have attracted to America so many Europeans, will do a vast amount toward widening the knowledge and at the same time the appreciation of what we should get from and for America.

But let us return to the peace meetings. This time I was unfortunately unable to attend the Interparliamentary Conference. What a brilliant success it was we shall soon know by report. The members of the

Conference were the guests of the government, and as such were specially honored, not only by the officials but also by the inhabitants of all the cities that they visited; and their two most important resolutions—the calling of a second Hague Conference and the establishment of a permanent International Congress for the discussion of world interests—have been laid before President Roosevelt and by him in a measure put in motion.

Who can doubt that the calling of a new Hague Conference, just as was the case with the first, will meet with much opposition, and that attempts will be made to belittle its significance and render nugatory its results? Nothing great and new is ever accomplished without opposition. But just as the first Conference, in spite of everything, left behind it not only the fact of the tribunal established and the text of the agreements "for the peaceful solution of international conflicts by means of the Court of Arbitration, mediation, and commissions for intervention," but also the solemn declaration that the moral and material welfare of the nations requires a reduction of the burden of armaments, so also the next Conference will certainly bring forth further and fresh results. Granted we have the letter of the law already, all that is required is to breathe into it the spirit of life. "Where there's a will there's a way," says the proverb; but where the way is all open the will must be exerted.

I obtained accurate details concerning the satisfactory proceedings of the Interparliamentary Conference, and the reception of their delegation at the White House, from the lips of several of its members, who, being also members of the Peace Unions, attended the Boston Congress, of which they brought us reports. Among them were William Randal Cremer (the last year's laureate of the Nobel peace prize), Dr. Clark, Houzeau de Lehaye, and H. La Fontaine.

The opening of the Congress in Boston took the form of an imposing festival. Begun with religious exercises, supported by the lively interest of the public and the press, the event was regarded, throughout the country, as the event of the day; and all the more as the first statesman of the United States, John Hay, delivered the address of greeting. In this address, which, by the way, was telegraphed all over the world, there were none of those diplomatic " ifs " and " buts " and " to be sures " and " on the other hands " which are customary on such occasions; it was a frank, unreserved recognition of the justice and attainability of the aim of the Congress, and it contained the declaration that a new diplomacy and a new system of politics henceforth must accept the golden rule (" What ye will not have done unto you, etc.") as a pattern of conduct, — a rule which has been banished from high politics hitherto by so-called practical politicians, on the ground that it was unpractical and idealistic. At this introductory meeting the great hall of Tremont Temple was filled to the last seat, and at least three thousand people tried in vain to obtain entrance.

THREE WEEKS IN AMERICA

About one hundred and twenty delegates came from Europe. That is not a large number; the majority and the most prominent among them came from England. Carnegie, whose attendance had been announced, was prevented from coming, and merely sent a significant letter. There were legions of addresses of approbation from various bodies, religious, scientific, industrial, and the like. One of the most noteworthy addresses, and absolutely unique considering the source from which it came, was subscribed, " Twenty-third Regiment, Massachusetts Infantry."

Besides the regular transactions, which were followed by large, attentive, and receptive audiences, the Congress gave a great series of public meetings at which the peace question was elucidated from different points of view, as, for example, "the peace question and the school," "the peace movement and socialism," "the duties and responsibilities of woman in the peace movement," and the like. The classes concerned thronged to all these meetings, — the women to one, educators to another, and laboring men to the third.

A meeting touching the question of disarmament, and offering as its chief speaker the well-known General Miles, was attended by many military men, — probably by some of that Twenty-third Regiment. If the Twenty-third Regiment has so much intelligence, there is no reason why the Twenty-fourth, and other regiments — and in other states as well as in Massachusetts — should not understand that, though they will do their duty while war exists, nevertheless the "warless time"—as the Prussian Lieutenant Colonel Moritz von Egidy saw it coming—is worth striving for.

The public interest aroused by these addresses was so great that, although several meetings were held simultaneously and in large auditoriums, every place was always filled to overflowing. The speakers were always assured of the greatest applause when they called attention to the fact that America's glory and grandeur consisted in having attained such proportions without a standing army, safe without defense, giving the world an example of peace; likewise when voices were raised against imperialism, which seemed to be gaining ground in many places, or against the threatening increase of the navy and the danger that the poison of militarism might infect the whole land. Since the war with Spain this virus has certainly worked its way into the system; but, judging from what we saw, heard, and read in the papers (with the exception of the "yellow" journals), the American organism is protecting itself vigorously against it and will, it is to be hoped, cast it out altogether.

The scenes that took place at the socialist congress at Amsterdam were repeated on the Boston platform, —a Japanese and a Russian shook hands amid a storm of applause. According to old concepts were not both of them traitors to their native countries? Or is the whole thing somewhat comical? On the contrary, is not this action more attractive than that which was related on the same day in a report from the theater of war. In one grave two dead men were found clutching each other; the hand of the Japanese was clinched on the Russian's throat and the Russian's fingers had penetrated the eye sockets of the Japanese.

A Hindoo, in native costume, from the sacred land of the Lama, was also there. He complained of the desecration that the war had wrought in the monks' places of devotion. "I come from the jungles," so his speech began, "and to the jungles I return."

A tiny Chinese woman, also in national costume, was one of the most popular speakers at the Congress. Her name is Dr. Kim. Educated by English missionaries, she had come to America to study medicine, and now she is going back to China to practice there. She speaks exquisite English, and with the sweetest voice and a smiling mouth she spoke the bitterest truths to the Europeans about the presumption with which they were trying to impose their warlike civilization upon an older and peaceful culture, and their dogmas upon a ripened philosophical view of the world, and, finally, were aiming to treat the Chinese Empire as a country to be looted.

"We can learn much from you, friends" (the word "friends" she spoke with a peculiarly sweet intonation), "that we grant; and if those lusts of conquest prevail, then we shall have to be grateful for learning from you, friends" (spoken tenderly), "the art of defending ourselves successfully against you."

I have had opportunity for but little sight-seeing about Boston, for the days were filled with meetings and labors. But the Public Library I did visit. Oh, those book palaces, those book cathedrals in America! What is not granted there to the people hungry for learning! And in what form it is given! The building is adorned with all the magic of architectural and plastic arts; the frescoes that adorn the palatial stairway — designed by Puvis de Chavannes — are a poem; another great master, Sargent, was intrusted with the decoration of some of the inner rooms. Beauty everywhere!

There is a widespread notion that the American possesses only a business sense and not an æsthetic sense; that the cities with their "cloud-scratchers" and elevated roads and warehouses are ugly. What a mistake! The horn of plenty that has scattered its treasures over this land has not forgotten beauty any more than wealth. Not to speak of natural beauties — Niagara Falls, the Rocky Mountains, and the like — I mean the works of man.· Whoever planted woodbine, ivy, and other vines, to clamber in rich luxuriance up the walls, even to the roofs of houses and churches, knew that he was creating beauty. Here again nature comes to man's aid, for the autumn foliage glows and gleams in colors which are quite unknown in our landscapes. In contrast with the brilliant hues there are soft and tender tones, — such an azure green, such a rosy gray, such a bright golden violet as only the most audacious art secessionist would venture to mix on his palette.

After the close of the Boston Congress public meetings were arranged in many other cities, — New York, Philadelphia, Worcester, Springfield, Northampton, Toronto, Buffalo, Cincinnati, and elsewhere; and in these places the principal men and women who had been speaking at the Peace Congress gave lectures concerning the transactions there and the peace movement in general. Everywhere were the same enthusiastic interest on the part of the public, the same dignified treatment on the part of official circles, and the same detailed and approving reports from the press. Our lectures were desired and applauded in churches, universities, girls' schools, workingmen's homes, concert halls, — everywhere.

On my return to New York I got somewhat acquainted with the city. The word "acquainted," though, seems presumptuous when I had only a few days, or rather a few hours — for the days were filled for the most part with the duties of my calling — to devote to this giant phenomenon, this city of three millions. Nevertheless, even what is seen as quickly as in a lightning flash can leave an abiding impression, especially when it is so surprising and overpowering. If I were to sum up the impression that America made on me, I might say that I was affected somewhat as Bellamy's hero was, who, after sleeping for many years, wakes up in an absolutely changed and improved world. Not as if, as in the case described by Bellamy, several centuries had been passed in sleep, but rather as if two or three decades, filled with discoveries and other advances, had been anticipated; thus seemed everything around me. The woman movement, the anti-alcohol movement, the social movement, technical arts, popular education, democratic spirit, toleration, comfort of living, luxury, physical development, — everything speedily carried forward and upward to a climax. A still deeper impression than the one made by all that was so abundantly flowering there (I grant that there may be also many poisonous plants in the garden) was made upon me by what is planted there, by what is still hidden in the seeds but is full of promise for rich harvests in the future. Education is power, education is freedom, education is ennoblement; and from that treasure, which is indeed imported from the Old World, such mighty systems of culture multiplied and disseminated will be established in the New World that for the coming generations an inestimable raising of the general standard of life is to be expected. I have had the opportunity to see universities, colleges, and libraries, and to hear about the settlements of university extension. " Education," said an American lady to me, " is something which we feel in duty bound to disseminate widely; the whole people must be able to share in it."

All the development of magnificence, all the zeal in conferring donations, which in the Old World has been shown in princely palaces and cathedrals, in the New World — and from far richer sources — flows into places for education. That, indeed, up to the present time, more fundamental knowledge is to be obtained at European universities is indicated by the fact that Americans whose means permit it, and who are particularly ambitious, come to us to study, and that all the professors and scientists there regard it as a privilege to be able to spend a few years as students in our higher institutions; but I am speaking now of the dissemination, especially the coming dissemination, of public instruction, which is still so young in America. Its deepening will come of itself, together with the rejection of much useless educational truck inherited from the olden days and not likely to be any longer useful for the new times.

Unfortunately I did not make the acquaintance of the so-called "smart set," the upper four hundred, whose palaces line Fifth Avenue and who are so constantly regarded as the type of the leading classes in America — though as mistakenly so regarded as a certain Boulevard society is taken for the prototype of French character. It would have been very interesting to study this "smart set." All that I saw was the outside of their palaces, but they certainly presented to the eye no remarkable splendor. Their possessors — the Vanderbilts and Rockefellers and Morgans and Astors and others — at this season of the year were either still at their country estates or away traveling.

· The huge opera house, in which German, French, and Italian operas, each in the original, are performed by the leading artists of the world, was not yet opened. The Italian opera will begin with Puccini's *Bohème*, sung by Caruso and Marcella Sembrich. Madame Schumann-Heink, who is undertaking the rôle of Kundry, is just at present the object of many social attentions and incessant interviews. The performances of *Parsifal*, regarded by Frau Cosima Wagner as desecration, are said to have been of overwhelming beauty.

The Americans are importing all our treasures of refined art and old culture; for us there is only one revenge: we must absorb more and more of their acquisitions, give more attention to the life that is unfolding there, rise above envy and jealousy, above pride and prejudice, — those feelings which in an epoch of international intercourse are no longer suitable, and which in the past have stood in the way of the development of universal comity. For, after all, we are only one world; every treasure, every forward step in whatever corner of the earth, increases the wealth and the potentiality of happiness of the whole human family.

The words "human family" (a family as yet far from united, still living in bitter feud) bring me back to the theme that lay at the basis of my whole transatlantic journey, — the Peace Congress. In New York, among the festivities arranged in honor of the delegates, was a great meeting organized by the Germans living there. It was held in Terrace Garden under the honorary chairmanship of Oscar S. Straus, member of the Permanent Court of Arbitration at The Hague, former Ambassador Dr. Andrew D. White, and the universally respected Carl Schurz. "Why so respected?" This question was once put to Dr. White by Bismarck. "Tell me, on what grounds does the old forty-eighter enjoy such universal and high regard in your country?" "For this reason," replied the American ambassador, "because he was the man who treated the slavery question, which at that time was *the* question, not, as was customary, from the philanthropical or the constitutional, but from the philosophical standpoint, with regard to its significance not for the negroes, but for the country."

Perhaps, I might add, the Americans are so charmed by Carl Schurz because, when he was in a leading position in the public service, he called a halt in the increasing deforestation of the country. And, above all, because he is a personality! I made his acquaintance, and in his house spent one of the most exhilarating hours of my American visit.

I made a pilgrimage to Grant's tomb, on the door of which his exclamation is carved, "Let us have peace!" And I saw the statue of General Sherman, who uttered the famous saying, "War is hell." The hellish reports of the ten days' battle raging in eastern Asia — where, at the very time when we in America were discussing the question of peace, the "field of honor" was covered with incredible numbers of the dead, — brought to us every day a confirmation of that utterance of General Sherman's.

We inspected the famous hotel, the Waldorf-Astoria. It exceeds in size and splendor anything that has thus far been attained in the way of public houses. And yet a new hotel has just been opened in New York, called the St. Regis, which is said to be furnished even more luxuriously, with all sorts of art treasures, old Gobelins, masterpieces of painting, and the like; but it is small — intended only for the upper four hundred; I was told that the lowest price for a room was eight dollars a day.

The ballroom of the Waldorf-Astoria is adorned with a painting proudly proclaimed by the guide as "the biggest canvas in the world." Not the best-painted but the biggest canvas in the world! This naïve boastfulness is rather characteristic of the worship of the gigantic that prevails there. When our shops announce a sale they call it a "great sale"; the American advertisement invites you to a "mammoth sale." The cicerone of the hotel called our attention to the fact that there are three thousand gilded chairs in the ballroom and the adjacent drawing-rooms, each with a different hand-painted scene on its cushion. One of our company immediately sat down on one of these artistically glorified chairs, apparently to test whether or not such delightful artistry aroused special sensations. I had a ride on the underground railway, which was to be opened to the public a few days later, but which had

been " running " regularly for three months so that its
use might be perfected before it was turned over to
the public, — maneuver before the real attack !

I had the opportunity in New York of making the
acquaintance of Mr. Pulitzer, the owner of the most
widely circulated American newspaper, the *World*.
His home (I was invited there to a luncheon) is of
the most exquisite splendor, and two tall, wonderfully beautiful daughters are its life. But with all his
wealth, all his power, the publisher of the *World* is a
poor man. Two of the greatest blessings of life this
otherwise vigorous, young-looking man, not yet sixty,
has lost, — his eyesight and sleep. Nevertheless, he
works incessantly, dictates his leading articles, watches
and regulates the whole course of his great paper, —
a paper which does not belong to yellow journalism,
but, on the contrary, has long advocated the peace
movement. A few years ago, when the relations between the United States and Great Britain were
strained to the danger point, the *World* requested
answers to a series of questions, and among the
responses was one from the then Prince of Wales,
which did much to allay the danger of war.

If I had lunched a day later at the Pulitzer house,
I should have made the acquaintance of Roosevelt's
opponent, Mr. Alton B. Parker. The *World* favors the
Democratic party without yielding to the illusion that
at the present time the election can be won from the
Republicans. Is not that a fortunate country that has

only two political parties? Yet even there not everything is rosy in the political arena. They have their
brazen-faced practice of corruption, economic battles,
— trusts and strikes, — that is to say, capitalism and
labor unions in hostile, threatening opposition (and
various leaders of the latter bodies are said not to be
superior to corruption). Alas! even there, too, there
is need of what all politics, domestic and foreign,
everywhere fails to possess, — the moral perception.

Philadelphia — after New York and Chicago the
largest city of the Union — offered us peace people a
very favorable territory. This city, founded by Puri-
tans, to-day still largely inhabited by Friends, — as the
war-detesting Quakers are called, — dominated by the
statue of William Penn who signed the treaty of peace
with the Indians (the statue crowns the tower of the
city hall), — this city is, so to speak, permeated with the
sap of the peace ideas. Correspondingly cordial, therefore, was the welcome that was accorded the delegates
of the Boston Peace Congress. The speakers at the
public reception were the governor of Pennsylvania,
the mayor of the city, the provost of the university,
and the president of the academy. The governor referred to the widespread diffusion of our idea, which
was daily gaining ground. The time, he said, could not
be far away when collective humanity—the nation, the
state — would be subjected to the same laws which
enjoin upon individuals an appeal to right instead of
violently taking the remedy into their own hands.

THREE WEEKS IN AMERICA

One of the great attractions of Philadelphia is its park, through which we were taken on a drive. It really resembles a landscape rather than a park, so enormous, so extensive are all its dimensions. Where we have only a clump of trees, there they have a grove; where we have a grassplot, they have a prairie. At the same time it is carefully tended and richly adorned with flower beds, fountains, and statues, like a prince's beautiful castle garden.

Washington was not included in the schedule of cities where lectures were to be given; but I ran over there for two days in order to get some idea of the capital city, and especially to meet the President.

Washington has a character very different from that of the other cities of the Union. It is not a city exuberant with trade and business; it has no skyscrapers, no elevated or subterranean railways, no bank or trade palaces, — only very quiet, very broad streets, planted with trees and bordered by villa-like houses. Even the embassies and legations are not housed in palaces but in similar elegant villas. On the other hand, that part of the city where the Capitol, the Congressional Library, and the obelisk rise from amidst wide-stretching grassplots, is of overpowering magnificence. You might think yourself transported to an antique world. But no — it is the new world, the world of the future.

The Public Library is unquestionably one of the most splendid edifices in the world. The private citizen who goes thither to read after his day's work is accomplished can give himself up to the feelings that are quickened by an environment of harmonious splendor. You seem to be in fairyland, and the paintings and marble columns and stairways have an especially imposing effect when the lofty dome of the central hall is illuminated with electric lights.

On the seventeenth of September I had the honor of being received by the President of the United States, and of having a private talk with him about the cause which is so dear to my heart. Friendly, sincere, evidently thoroughly impressed with the seriousness and the importance of the matter discussed, — so seemed Theodore Roosevelt to me. Gallant *Soldatentum* — even more, adventure-loving *Roughridertum* — is in his blood, but he has a far-seeing social good will in his spirit; and this last makes him the pioneer of a new era. He was the first to put into action the tribunal of The Hague; he is now going to call a new Hague Conference.

" Universal peace is coming," he said to me; "it is certainly coming — step by step."

It would be unbecoming in me to repeat what was said in an unconstrained conversation; only the following I might be permitted to state here. I had mentioned the Anglo-American Arbitration Treaty that came so near being concluded in 1897, and suggested that the present would be an appropriate moment for taking it up again.

" I have the intention," replied the President, " of inaugurating treaties, not with England alone, but with all nations, — with France, Germany — "

" Do not forget my Austria," I interrupted.

He smiled. " And Austria and Italy, and England of course. But England should not be the sole and only one, else the treaty might be misunderstood as an alliance of the English-speaking races. It is America's duty to make treaties simultaneously with all civilized nations. And I contemplate one other thing, namely, that these treaties shall be more far-reaching in their scope, and with fewer limitations, than those already concluded in Europe."

The President said among other things that he especially admired Austria's acquisition of power in Bosnia; he called this "a feat."

I went from Washington directly to Cincinnati. Cincinnati is a manufacturing city, therefore somewhat gray and smoky, but nevertheless it is surrounded by a girdle of smiling villas and is provided with a public garden which, not without justification, is called Eden Park. The lectures of the peace delegates were delivered in a concert hall which holds four thousand people, and which on that evening was filled to overflowing. The heads of the official departments, among them a bishop, delivered the introductory addresses, and I was given the flattering surprise of seeing, over the platform, the title of my book gleaming in electric letters, " Lay Down Your Arms."

On our way back we stopped at Buffalo, and from there made an excursion to Niagara Falls. One thing with which I might reproach this splendid spectacle of nature — and yet it is not its fault — is the circumstance that around the raging waters, on the steep, wooded banks, there stand, in place of Indian wigwams, modern villas and hotels, and — worse yet — on a plateau mirrored in the rolling flood a billboard, twenty meters long, calls the attention of pilgrims to Niagara to a certain species of biscuit! On the other hand, it is bewitching when from various positions brilliantly colored rainbows, accompanied by others of paler hues, appear and vanish and hover over the rising mists like veils.

I brought my visit to America to a close with a visit of several days in Ithaca at the house of the former ambassador, Dr. Andrew D. White. Ithaca and its famous university is a little world in itself.

Thus these three weeks in America have flown like a dream, and I am again on board, homeward bound — richer in magnificent impressions, with my mental horizon enlarged more than I had ever dreamed possible. I have looked through a new window — hastily, I must confess, and through only a narrow opening — into the universe.

INDEX

INDEX

433

INDEX

RECORDS OF AN EVENTFUL LIFE

INDEX

438

INDEX

439

INDEX

RECORDS OF AN EVENTFUL LIFE

INDEX

Wormser, I, 97, 99

Wrangel, Marshal von, I, 60

Wratislav, Count, I, 86

Wrede, Prince Alfred, I, 342, 445; II, 139

Yang-Yü, Ambassador, II, 253, 261, 275, 360, 362; his wife, II, 253, 261, 271

Zanini, Count, II, 237

Zeretelli, General, I, 221

Zichy, Count Eugen, II, 115, 121, 124, 161, 249

Zola, Émile, I, 414; II, 34, 172, 174, 180, 343

Zorn, Professor, II, 293, 295, 298, 299, 301, 309, 323

Zychy, I, 253

Lightning Source UK Ltd.
Milton Keynes UK
12 August 2010

158312UK000